A History of the Tajiks

A History of the Tajiks

Iranians of the East

Richard Foltz

I.B.TAURIS

LONDON • NEW YORK • OXFORD • NEW DELHI • SYDNEY

I.B. TAURIS
Bloomsbury Publishing Plc
50 Bedford Square, London, WC1B 3DP, UK
1385 Broadway, New York, NY 10018, USA
29 Earlsfort Terrace, Dublin 2, Ireland

BLOOMSBURY, I.B. TAURIS and the I.B. Tauris logo are trademarks of Bloomsbury Publishing Plc

First published in Great Britain 2023

Cover image: Dushanbe, Tadjikistan, Chaikhana 'Rakhat', 1960s. (© Mark Redkin/FotoSoyuz/Getty Images)

A catalogue record for this book is available from the British Library.

ISBN: HB: 978-0-7556-4964-8
PB: 978-0-7556-4965-5
ePDF: 978-0-7556-4966-2
eBook: 978-0-7556-4967-9

Typeset by RefineCatch Limited, Bungay, Suffolk
Printed and bound in Great Britain

In Memoriam

Richard Nelson Frye

1920–2014

Contents

List of Illustrations

Figures

All photos are by the author, except where noted.

Maps

Plates

All photos are by the author.

1 6th century Sogdian wall painting from Panjikent, Tajikistan.
2 6th century Sogdian wall painting from Afrasiab, Samarkand.
3 Poi kalon complex, 12th to 16th centuries, Bukhara.
4 Tomb of 14th century Naqshbandi Sufi master Baha al-din Naqshband, Bukhara.
5 Shrine of 15th century Naqshbandi Sufi master Khwaja Ubaidullah Ahrar, Samarkand.
6 Registan, 15th to 17th centuries, Samarkand.
7 Rudaki Avenue, Dushanbe.
8 Persian literature class, Istaravshan.
9 Kamol Khujandi monument, Khujand.
10 Farm workers, southern Tajikistan.
11 Khorugh, Gorno-Badakhshan, Tajikistan.

Preface to the Second Edition

It came as a welcome surprise when my editor at Bloomsbury, Rory Gormley, invited me to prepare a revised and expanded second edition of this book a mere three years after its initial publication. To be sure, much has happened since 2019 that deserves to be addressed. The global COVID-19 pandemic which began in the fall of that year, the Taliban takeover of Afghanistan in August 2021, and Russia's invasion of Ukraine in February 2022 are just a few of the recent events that have had a major, and in some cases transformative impact on the lives of Tajiks.

Preparing this revision has also provided me with the opportunity to address some shortcomings in the first edition. Readers have pointed out a few details that called for correction or clarification, and this has been done where possible (within the limits of the publisher's typesetting budget). More importantly, it has given me a second chance to add material I felt was lacking in the original draft concerning Tajiks living outside the borders of the Republic of Tajikistan. My initial treatment of Tajiks in Uzbekistan, a country that occupies most of what they consider their historical homeland and where the Tajik population remains higher than in their nominal republic, was limited by the fact that I had not physically been there since 1995 and that very little had been said about them since I published two short articles the following year.[1] A much overdue return trip to Uzbekistan in April and May of 2022 enabled me to write a whole new and up-to-date chapter on the Tajiks living in that country.

Unexpectedly for me, the most enthusiastic response to the book has come from the Tajiks of Afghanistan. In hindsight this makes perfect sense – they are, after all, the largest contingent of Tajiks on the planet, and that by a considerable margin. In my Excursus, 'Afghanistan at a Stone's Throw,' I expressed my discomfort at writing what was meant to be a comprehensive treatment of Tajiks given my own lack of knowledge and experience of the country where they are most numerous, and my frustration at being unable to go there. Yet it was an organization of Afghan Tajiks who fêted the book by organizing a launch at London's School of Oriental and African Studies in May 2019, where they presented me with lavish gifts and an official invitation to travel to Afghanistan with all expenses paid. A few months later a Darī Persian translation of the book by 'Abd al-Khaliq La'lzad was published by the Afghanistan Institute for Strategic Studies (AISS) in Kabul, after which I was invited to participate in a live online discussion of it on Afghan television. Unfortunately, due to the pandemic I was unable to follow up on my invitation to travel to Afghanistan, and with the Taliban's return to power in 2021 that opportunity is now closed and the short-lived Darī edition of the book is no longer available. (AISS has relocated to Sussex University in the UK, without access to its warehouse in Kabul.) On a more positive note, the Darī text has been transcribed into Cyrillic by colleagues in Dushanbe, with the aim of publishing a Tojikī edition in the near future.

La Malbaie, Québec
30 June 2022

Preface to the First Edition

This book was inspired to a large extent by the work and vision of the late Harvard Iranologist Richard Nelson Frye. He was arguably the greatest scholar of Iranian languages and culture that North America has produced – not that there have been many. Most of the important experts in this field have been Europeans or Iranians. One should of course give credit to A.V. Williams-Jackson (1862–1937), a native New Yorker and specialist in the Zoroastrian sacred text, the Avesta, who laid the foundations for Iranian Studies at Columbia University following his appointment there as head of the newly created Department of Indo-Iranian Languages and Literatures in 1895. But it was Frye's efforts at Harvard during the 1950s that firmly established Iranian Studies as a field of study in North America. Numerous scholars before and since have surpassed Frye's depth in particular areas of their own specialization, but none has equalled the sheer breadth of his erudition in all matters pertaining to Iran, or his immense contribution to enhancing Westerners' appreciation of Iranian culture. I do not know if he was the first to coin the term 'Greater Iran' – a welcome reminder that the influence of Iranian civilization extends far beyond the modern borders of the Islamic Republic – but certainly nothing better evokes the concept than his own long and illustrious career.

Although Frye studied both Persian and Turkish as a graduate student, it was the Tajiks, and not Central Asia's Turkic-speaking peoples, that would occupy most of his attention. For his doctoral research he chose to prepare an English edition of the tenth-century Samanid historian Abū Bakr Muḥammad b. Jaʿfar Nars͟hak͟hī's *History of Bukhara* (*Tārīk͟h-i Buk͟hārā*), a project that Frye initiated in 1941 but was interrupted when he was enlisted by the US government's Office of Strategic Services – forerunner to the CIA – to serve in Afghanistan during the Second World War. Sadly, some seven decades later this wartime service was taken up by a small group of ignorant fanatics in Iran as a pretext for denying Frye the burial in Esfahan that had been his dream, despite its having been authorized by two successive Iranian presidents.

Narshakhī's *History of Bukhara* can be considered as one of the principal surviving examples of Iranian reawakening during the Samanid period in tenth-century Central Asia. Although like most scholarly works of the time it was originally composed in Arabic, the lingua franca of educated Muslims everywhere, it no doubt served the Samanids' aims by associating the former Sogdian lands (and, by extension, the Samanids themselves) with the much-admired pre-Islamic Persian culture of the Sasanians.

Less than two centuries later, in 1128, another local scholar, Abū Naṣr Qubavī, translated Narshakhī's *History of Bukhara* into Persian, making the comment in his introduction that 'most people do not show a desire to read an Arabic book'.[1] The fact that no copy of Narshakhī's Arabic original survives would seem to support such an assertion – Frye's English translation was made from Qubavī's heavily modified Persian edition, the Arabic version being unavailable. For Qubavī's Persian rendition, meanwhile, Frye had access to no less than six different manuscripts, out of a total of thirty-eight that are currently known to exist.

Were it possible to compare the lost original version of the *History of Bukhara* with the Persian adaptation left to us by Qubavī, we might well perceive the two works as being so different as to hardly constitute the same book. Qubavī did not limit himself to the role of translator, but assumed those of editor and author as well. He deleted many passages from Narshakhī's text that he found uninteresting, while adding copious information of his own filling in the two centuries between his time and Narshakhī's, to such an extent that the Persian *History of Bukhara* as we now have it could rightly be considered a co-authored work. Qubavī was not exceptional in this regard. For example, Elton Daniel has noted that the Samanid-era Persian version of Ṭabarī's encyclopaedic *History of the Prophets and the Kings* was 'neither a translation nor an abridgment but a work in its own right with much material not found in Ṭabarī at all'.[2] It is curious that Frye doesn't say more about the implications of Qubavī's highly active role in giving the book its extant form.

Since its overriding theme is the Islamization of Bukhara during the early to mid-eighth century, Narshakhī's *History* can be considered on one level as marking the emergence of the Tajiks as a people – representing a kind of Islamicized rebirth of the Sogdians – and in this sense Frye can be said to have begun his academic career as an historian of the Tajiks. He would bring this connection full circle in the 1990s by writing a history of Central Asia which, as he explains in the introduction to that work, he first conceived while living in Tajikistan 'as an attempt to give an ancient and medieval history of that land'.[3]

Frye's choice of the word 'land' is telling, since in fact Tajikistan did not become a political entity until 1924, achieving the status of independent state only as recently as 1991. Hence Frye's work necessarily focused not on Tajikistan as such, but rather on the parts of Central Asia where Persian-speakers – the Tajiks – were numerically or culturally dominant during the region's history. In that sense these two books – one produced at the beginning of Frye's career and the other at the end of it – can really be considered as ethnic histories of the Tajik people and their principal ancestors, the Sogdians.

Frye had travelled to Tajikistan upon retiring from his position at Harvard in 1990 and taught Tajik history to university students in Dushanbe for several terms. It was during this time that he was inspired to write his 'history of Tajikistan', but confronted with the conundrum that most of what could pass for Tajik history had in fact occurred outside the borders of the present-day republic, he elected instead to produce a work far broader in scope.

I never had the chance to study under Frye personally, since his retirement from Harvard in 1990 coincided with my arrival there to pursue my PhD. I did see him frequently, however, since he remained active on campus where he retained his office and participated in seminars and other activities. Having known Professor Frye in this informal capacity I looked forward with great enthusiasm to reading the fruits of his time in Tajikistan, but when *The Heritage of Central Asia*was finally published in 1996 I realized that a book devoted specifically to the history of the Tajiks was yet to appear, at least in English. Since the present work is in some sense an attempt to pick up where Professor Frye left off, it seems only appropriate to dedicate it to his memory.

Montréal, 15 September 2018

Acknowledgements

My thanks go first and foremost to my new family: my wife, Fatima, her parents Svetlana and Vitaly who were so supportive through difficult times, and our two delightful children Roger Alan and Sophia Dzerassa. I am also grateful to my good friend and colleague Professor Touraj Daryaee, whose kind invitation for us to deliver the inaugural Semnani Family Foundation Richard N. Frye Memorial Lectures at the University of California-Irvine in February 2016 served as the catalyst to start writing this book. Kamol Abdullaev, Masood Farivar, John Heathershaw, Pavel Lurje and Luke Treadwell each provided valuable suggestions on individual chapters of the text, and Rustam Shukurov, Iradj Bagherzade and two anonymous reviewers on the book as a whole; here again, I assume full responsibility for any errors or misinterpretations.

I have learned much from many Central Asian (and Central Asianist) friends, colleagues and acquaintances over the years, and benefitted from the kind help of many more. I am deeply indebted to them all. I hope that this book may serve as a tribute to their rich history and diverse cultures, focusing as it does on the particular aspect – Iranianness – with which I am most familiar; this is not to diminish in any way those many other related areas where my own personal knowledge is weak.

I was particularly fortunate to enjoy the unrivalled hospitality of the University of Central Asia during stays at their campus in Naryn, Kyrgyzstan in 2017 and in Khorog, Tajikistan in 2018. My special thanks go to Diana Pauna, Dean of Arts and Sciences, for authorizing and organizing these visits, and to Dr. Sultonbek Aksakolov for skilfully and gracefully managing the logistics while I was there. In Samarkand we were exceptionally well cared for by Professor Juma Hamroh, Chair of the Department of Tajik Philology at Samarkand State University, whose colleagues rightfully describe him as 'the most hospitable man in all of Uzbekistan.'

Historical Timeline

c. 2300–1700 BCE	Oxus Civilization (The Bactria–Margiana Archaeological Complex); settled non-Aryan society in present-day southern Central Asia; connections with Mesopotamia
c. 2200–1800 BCE	Sintashta Culture: proto-Indo-Iranian speakers around southern Ural Mountains; invention of spoke-wheeled chariot
c. 1800–1000 BCE	Andronovo Culture: Indo-Iranian pastoralists expand across Eurasian steppe
c. 1300 BCE	pre-Zoroastrian petroglyphs in Seven Rivers region of present-day southern Central Asia
c. 1200 BCE	Life of Zarathustra, founder of Zoroastrianism, possibly in Seven Rivers region
546–539 BCE	Persian Emperor Cyrus II conquers Sogdiana, founds Cyropolis in Ferghana Valley near present-day Khujand
529 BCE	Cyrus killed in battle against Scythian Massagetae led by Queen Tomyris
327 BCE	Alexander III of Macedon conquers Sogdiana
312–63 BCE	Hellenistic Seleucid Empire, blending of Greek and Iranian cultures in Central Asia
129 BCE	Chinese emissary Zhang Qian reaches Ferghana Valley in search of 'heavenly horses'
247 BCE–224 CE	Arsacid (Parthian) Empire rules the Iranian world from Mesopotamia to the Oxus and Indus Rivers

30 BCE–410 CE	Indus Valley–based Kushan Empire; spread of Buddhism throughout Bactria
1st BCE to 8th CE	Sogdian merchant communities dominate Silk Road trade networks; protected by nomadic Turkic tribes from sixth century
712–22	Muslim conquests of Central Asia
755–83	Revolt of Sogdian prophetic figure Muqanna'
819–999	New Persian Renaissance under Bukhara-based Samanid Empire
858–941	Life of New Persian poet Ja'far b. Muḥammad al-Rūdakī in Samanid Bukhara
940–1020	Life of Iranian national poet Abū'l-Qāsim Firdawsī in Samanid Khurasan
999–1211	Southern Central Asia under rule of Turkic Qarakhanids from Eastern Central Asia and Western China
879–1215	Tajik Ghurid Dynasty rules from Afghanistan
1218–22	Mongol armies devastate Central Asia, utterly destroying Silk Road cities of Marv, Balkh and Nishapur
1366–1507	Samarkand-based Timurid Empire; era of cultural flourishing
1507–1740	Uzbek dynasties rule from Bukhara
1740–7	Brief reintegration of Central Asia into Iranian Afsharid Empire of Nader Shah
1747–1920	Uzbek Manghit dynasties rule from Bukhara and Kokand

1864–85	Russia gains control of Tashkent and Samarkand, vassalizes truncated khanates of Bukhara and Kokand
1878–1954	Life of Tajik intellectual Sadriddin Ainī
1918–31	Basmachi ('bandit') movement resists Russian rule
1920–4	Bukharan People's Soviet Republic established by Bolshevik revolutionaries
1924	Tajik Autonomous Soviet Socialist Republic created within newly established Uzbek SSR
1929	Tajik SSR given full Union Republic status within USSR
1929	Ḥabībullah Kalakānī briefly serves as first (and only) Tajik King of Afghanistan
1908–77	Life of Tajik academician Bobojon <u>Gh</u>afurov
1991	Fall of USSR; Tajikistan becomes independent republic
1992–7	Tajik Civil War; almost complete disintegration of Tajik society, industry and infrastructure
1994–present	Emomali Rahmon(ov) is President of Tajikistan
2001	Afghan Tajik resistance fighter Aḥmad <u>Sh</u>āh Mas'ūd assassinated by Tunisian suicide bomber
2018	Improved relations between Uzbekistan and Tajikistan suggests easing of pressures on Uzbekistan's Tajik population
2020	Pushtun-led Taliban return to power in Afghanistan
2022	Major uprisings among ethnic Pamiris are brutally suppressed by the Tajik government

A Note on Transliteration

Given that this book covers a long period, wide-ranging geographical settings, and draws on sources from a number of different languages, attempting to force all the many non-English words and phrases into any overarching transliteration system hardly seems appropriate and has not been attempted here. This is true even for the so-called 'New Persian' language ('new' only in the context of the eighth century where it first appears), since there are now established conventions for writing it in both the Arabic and Cyrillic alphabets, each based on different dialectal pronunciations. Unfortunately, most of the standard transliteration systems in use today tend to privilege the phonetics of only one language for any given alphabet – for example Arabic or Russian – leading to often considerable departures from those of other languages that use the same alphabet. For that reason, no such standard system is used in this book.

Since the subject of the book is Tajiks it seems only fair to privilege modern 'Tojikī' forms when transliterating contemporary sources from Cyrillic; let us recall, though, that Tajiks in Afghanistan still use the Perso-Arabic alphabet, and those in Uzbekistan now use the Latin. For the pre-modern period and for materials written the Perso-Arabic alphabet, I have not strayed far from the system of the *International Journal for Middle Eastern Studies* (IJMES), as representing a more historically conservative pronunciation – closer to modern Tojikī – than does the phonologically innovative modern spoken Persian of Tehran; my transcriptions nevertheless reflect the latter form when referring to contexts associated with the Persian-speakers of contemporary Iran.

Where a familiar English version of a name or term exists, I have used that. English translations are mine unless otherwise noted.

Introduction: Who Are the Tajiks?

This is the first book devoted specifically to the long history of the Tajiks to be written in any Western language.[1] The Tajiks, a Central Asian people who number anywhere from 18 to 25 million and are spread out principally among the contemporary nations of Afghanistan, Tajikistan and Uzbekistan, can be considered historically as the eastern branch of Persian-speaking Iranians, whose definitive political separation from Iran dates back only to the mid-eighteenth century. In the most general sense, Tajiks can be defined as 'Iranians of the East'. The Samarkand-centred Sogdians of ancient times, who are their main ancestors, were the principal agents of Silk Road trade and cultural exchange during more than five centuries preceding the Arab conquests from 712 to 722 CE, and it was the first identifiably Tajik state, that of the Samanids during the tenth century of the Common Era, that brought about the revival of Persian culture in its new Islamic form.

As a political notion, however, 'Tajikistan' has existed for less than a century, first as an 'autonomous republic' carved out from within the newly established Uzbek Soviet Socialist Republic in 1924 and elevated to the status of full republic in 1929, then as an independent nation after the fall of the Soviet Union in 1991. This book, therefore, is not a history of Tajikistan but rather of the Tajik people, a large majority of whom live outside the borders of the contemporary Republic of Tajikistan.

Moreover, for the Tajiks themselves, a sense of national pride rests largely on political and cultural achievements dating back more than a thousand years, to the time of the Samanids and to the Sogdians before them. This glorious history contrasts painfully with the realities according to which almost all Tajiks live today, whether in Tajikistan which is the poorest and most underdeveloped of all the former Soviet republics, in Uzbekistan where they are a persecuted minority or in war-torn Afghanistan where they chafe under Pashtun dominance and face daily threats of violence.

The term 'Tajik' bears some discussion and clarification, especially in its relationship to the better-known designation of 'Persian'. One might object to using it at all, since in a broad sense Tajiks and Persians can be considered as a single people and Tajikistan merely one of the eastern territories of Greater Iran. Persians today consider the totality of Tajik history to be merely a part of their own, the Tajik lands being in their minds part of an imagined region they refer to as 'Greater Khurasan'. Tajiks, for their part, having been conditioned through seventy years of Soviet propaganda, conversely see the entirety of Iranian history as 'Tajik' history, to the extent that even the medieval Shirazi poets Saʿdī and Ḥāfiẓ are classified as 'Tajiks'. Without necessarily taking sides in this matter, it should be acknowledged that in any case historical events have created divides and distinctions between Persians and Tajiks that are very real, and to ignore these, as some nevertheless attempt to do, would seem overly romantic.

Even so, it is interesting to note that in some ways the words 'Tajik' and 'Persian' have at many times in history functioned as virtual synonyms. The term 'Tajik', from a late Middle Persian form 'Tazig', derives from the name of an Arab tribe, the Tayy, and was originally applied by the non-Muslim Iranians to the Arab Muslim invaders during the seventh century. As native Iranians gradually succumbed to Arab dominance and began joining the growing Muslim community, 'Tajik' lost its specific ethnic sense and came to refer to Muslims in general, especially in eastern Iran where Muslim armies were often engaged in fighting with pagan Turks. By the time the Arab-led Muslims were finally able to subdue the Sogdian lands of Transoxiana during the first half of the eighth century, most of the actual soldiers and those who followed in their wake were ethnic Iranians, so 'Tajik' came to mean 'Iranians who have converted to Islam'.

Since the Arabs who settled in Central Asia were vastly outnumbered by Iranians, the principal transmitters of Islam to the region were Persian-speakers from Iran. As the local population became Islamicized over the following century they began to give up their original language (Sogdian) in favour of Persian, just as the Aramaic- and Coptic-speakers of the Near East and Egypt abandoned their native idioms for Arabic. By the mid-tenth century this transformation had progressed to the point where a scholar commissioned by the ruler of the Bukhara-based Samanid government to translate the works of Ṭabarī from Arabic into Persian could proclaim, 'Here, in this region, the language is Persian (*pārsī*), and the kings of this realm are Persian kings (*mulūk-i 'ajam*).'[2] This assertion may have been more a reflection of the Samanids' desire to insert themselves into the Sasanian royal tradition than of actual linguistic reality on the ground at the time, when much of the population likely still spoke Sogdian.

It is possible that some of Bukhara's elites, perhaps those associated with the court and perhaps some priests, may have been Persianizers even in pre-Islamic times due to their connections with the Sasanian world. The common term for Persian in the East, *darī*, literally means 'the language of the court', but we cannot trace its origins or early development with any clarity. Ibn al-Muqaffa' and other writers of the early Islamic period refer to *darī* as having been spoken in late Sasanian times, presumably alongside Pahlavi Middle Persian, and Shafi'ī-Kadkanī makes the point that 'The very eloquence of poets like Rūdakī and authors like Bal'amī bespeaks the status of *darī* as a language that had been in use for quite some time',[3] though he wonders why no Sasanian-era verses in *darī* were included in later anthologies.[4]

Narshakhī's tenth-century *History of Bukhara* tells us that when the Arab conquerors first imposed Islam during the early eighth century a group of several hundred local converts had to recite their Qur'anic prayers in *darī* because they couldn't speak or understand Arabic.[5] Why would ordinary people in Bukhara be speaking 'the language of the court' instead of their own native vernacular which was Sogdian? Did *darī* mean something else at that time? Was Narshakhī referring to Muslim settlers from Persia?

In the commentary accompanying his English translation of Narshakhī's *History* Richard Frye acknowledges this problem and offers the second of these two possible explanations, namely that the passage refers to Persianized urban-dwellers,[6] but one wonders how Sasanian influence could already have replaced Sogdian to such an extent in Bukhara when just a short distance away the contemporaneous Mt. Mugh documents left by the last Sogdian ruler, Devashtich, are in Sogdian.[7] More than a century later, at his trial in 840 the rebellious Afshin of Ustrushana stated that his subjects wrote to him in 'their own language',[8] which was presumably a form of Sogdian as well.

The Iranian geographer Ibrahīm Iṣṭakhrī, who was a contemporary of Narshakhī, wrote that even in their time (i.e. two centuries after the Arab conquest of Central Asia) the language of Bukhara was the same as Sogdiana 'except for some alterations'.[9] Another tenth-century writer, Ibn Ḥawqal, likewise states in his revision of Iṣṭakhrī that 'The language of Bukhara is that of Sogdiana with some small differences; the people *also* use the Persian language' [emphasis mine].[10] These observations would seem to contradict Frye's contention that already by the time of Ismā'īl Sāmānī several decades earlier 'Persian was the common spoken language of the townspeople'.[11] Frye considered that *darī* 'was really a simple style of New Persian free from Arabic words, whereas the term *fārsī* [more often *pārsī*, in the sources of the time – RF] in this period was a designation of the style of the New Persian language which was greatly mixed with Arabic words and was ornate rather than simple'.[12]

However, according to the eighth-century Iranian scholar Rōzbeh pūr-i Dādōē – known in Arabic as Ibn al-Muqaffa' – the term *darī* originally referred to the language of the Sasanian court at Ctesiphon in Mesopotamia, as opposed to *pārsī* which was the language of Fars (Pars) province and also the Mazdaean clergy.[13] It is somewhat easier to believe that at the time of the Arab conquests in the early eighth century Bukhara's courtly elite might have spoken a late Middle Persian form of *darī* imported from the Sasanian West, than to accept Frye's contention that *darī* was the spoken idiom of Bukhara's urban population in general, but the mosque-goers in Narshakhī's passage mentioned above are said to have converted in order to avoid paying the *jizya* (a protection tax levied on non-Muslims), suggesting they were more likely to have been merchants or common folk. Perhaps Narshakhī's use of the term *darī* in this context is anachronistic, or simply imprecise; his intention may have been merely to signal that they knew only their own local, unspecified Iranian language (which would presumably have been a dialect of Sogdian). Or – which is in our view more likely – the word may have been introduced by Narshakhī's twelfth-century Persian translator, Aḥmad Qubavī, reflecting the usage of that later period (the Arabic original not having survived).

The passage in Narshakhī's account of *darī* prayers being recited in Bukhara includes an important clue which strongly suggests that whatever word he may have used to describe it in his original Arabic text, the language of the Bukharan converts in question was Sogdian, and not Persian. Noting that in any case these worshippers had been ordered by Qutayba b. Muslim to attend the congregational Friday prayers, along with promises of a two-dirham sweetener for anyone who showed up, Narshakhī states that their prostrations were directed by someone standing behind them shouting *bknītā nkīnt*! ('bow!') and *nkūnīā nkūnī*! ('prostrate!') in the local Sogdian dialect.[14]

One supposes in any case that by Qubavī's time Persian had displaced Sogdian almost entirely, although a modern version of the latter tongue persists today in tiny pockets of the Fon mountains of Tajikistan, where it is known as Yaghnobī. Returning to our discussion of the semantic transformations of the term 'Tajik', we may note that by the period of Turkic rule under the Ghaznavids and Seljuks in the eleventh and twelfth centuries – that is, in Qubavī's time – the designation 'Tajik' was applied by Turks to *all* Iranians, most of whom were now Muslim.[15]

By the eleventh century the term had begun to acquire a more broadly sociological meaning, of which being a Persian-speaker was merely one component. The expanded sense was that of a civilized person, an urban-dweller or agriculturalist, as opposed to a 'Turk', which referred not just to the fact of speaking Turkish but more generally to a rustic, nomadic lifestyle. 'Turk and Tajik' became an established dichotomy: as Safar Abdullo has pointed out, 'In the historical sources if anyone said "Tajik," it was in conjunction with "Turk."'[16]

In the classical Persian literary tradition – the entire vocabulary of which consists of stock phrases and images – 'Turk' and 'Tajik' are stand-in terms for easily recognizable social stereotypes: one simple but violent; the other wily but civilized. Rūmī turns this on its head, however, in the following couplet: 'Attack upon attack came the darkness of night/Be strong like a Turk, not soft like a Tajik' (*Yek hamleh va yek hamleh, āmad shab va tārīkī/chostī kon va 'Torkī' kon, na narmī va 'Tājīkī'*). Often 'Turk' was also used to refer to the poet's beautiful young (unattainable) beloved, as in the following lines from Sa'dī: 'Maybe they'll tell the King/"Your Turk (i.e., your Beloved) has spilled Tajik blood"' (*Shāyad ke be pādshah begūyand/Tork-e tō berīkht khūn-e Tājīk*), or elsewhere, 'Show your Tajik face, not Abyssinian black/That the Heavens may obliterate the face of the Turks' (*Rū-ye Tājīkāna-t benmā, tā dāgh-e habash/Āsmān chehre-ye Torkān yaghmā'ī keshad*).

Contemporary Tajik historian Kamoludin Abdullaev defines Tajikness as being constituted of 'Iranianism' – an attachment to the Persian literary tradition – plus sedentarism, with identity being more tied to one's village than to a tribe as is the case with nomads.[17] From the eleventh century onwards successive Central Asian governments assigned bureaucratic duties to Tajiks while leaving military matters in the hands of Turks, a system formalized by the establishment of a 'Ministry of Tajiks' (*Dīvān-i Tājikān*) and a 'Ministry of Commanders' (*Dīvān-i Amīrān*) during the time of the Timurid dynasty (1370–1507).[18] The Turk–Tajik dichotomy, at times hostile and at others symbiotic, persisted into the twentieth century when Soviet identity engineering completely restructured the linguistic and cultural landscape of Central Asia.

Up to the fifteenth century at least, the term 'Tajik' was used in a way quite similar to how we now use 'Persian' or even 'Iranian'. Tajiks were settled Persian-speakers who lived from Iraq in the west all the way to the Hindu Kush Mountains in the east, conceived in opposition to other kinds of people who lived throughout the same areas, usually warlike Turkic-speaking nomads, who were seen as being less culturally refined.

This fact can perhaps shed light on what appears at first glance to be an outrageous Soviet-era distortion of historical reality by Tajik writers, according to which all the great figures of medieval Perso-Islamic civilization – from poets and artists to scientists and statesmen – were classified as 'Tajiks'. Iranians, and indeed most amateurs of Persian poetry today, generally balk at the identification of such figures as Firdawsī, Sa'dī, Ḥāfiẓ and Jāmī as 'Tajiks', seeing them rather as 'Persian' or 'Iranian' writers.

From a contemporary nationalistic point of view Tajik claims to the Samanid poet Abū 'Abdullah Ja'far b. Muḥammad Rūdakī could seem less problematic, given that he was born and buried within the territory of modern-day Tajikistan. The great medieval polymath Avicenna too is perhaps not too much of a stretch, since his native region of Bukhara is still predominantly Tojikī-speaking despite being located in Uzbekistan. The hugely popular mystic poet Jalāl al-dīn 'Rūmī', also known as Mawlānā, 'our Master' – who is usually said to be a native of Balkh – was in fact born in the village of Vakhsh in what is now southern Tajikistan, then educated in Samarkand before the imminent onslaught of the Mongols caused his father to flee with him to Anatolia ('Rūm', at that time lately part of Byzantine 'Rome'), where he spent the rest of his life. Strangely, modern Tajiks have expended rather little effort in asserting Rūmī as one of their own, as compared with other luminous personalities of medieval Persian literature.

Herat and Balkh in contemporary Afghanistan produced many of the great figures of Iranian civilization, and the Persian-speaking inhabitants of these regions are referred to today as Tajiks; their efforts to project present-day national identities onto the past should not surprise us too much. Still, the contemporary Tajik tendency to refer to the Persian poets Ḥāfiẓ and Saʿdī, who were both natives of Shiraz far to the West, as well as Firdawsī and many others, as 'Tajiks', tends to elicit the scorn, if not the ire, of modern Persians living in Iran. The point to bear in mind is that in current usage these words carry nation-state implications, whereas this was not the case in the past. In fact many classical poets did occasionally employ the term 'Tajik' in reference to themselves, usually as a literary convention contrasting with its binary opposite which was 'Turk'.

The designation 'Tajik' can be deceptively fluid even now. It is applied by the Chinese government to a recognized nationality consisting of Pamiri-speaking Ismāʿīlī Shīʿites living in Tashkurgan county south of Kashgar. On the other hand, I was surprised during a visit to Alamut castle north of Qazvin in the spring of 2015 when I asked locals if the mysterious inhabitants of three closed villages in the region – where Ehsan Yarshater and others have suspected that the Mazdakite religion may still be secretly practised – spoke a language of their own distinct from Persian: Yes, I was told, their language is called 'Tājīkī'.

In contrast to the prevailing historical norm, where the label 'Tajik' is first and foremost an indication that the person in question speaks Persian, here we have two cases, at opposite ends of the Iranian world, where the word refers to people who are *not* Persian-speakers. Rather, the sense is of differentiating them from the surrounding majority – this, in fact, recalls the original use of the term at the beginning of the Islamic period. The issue becomes less problematic if one accepts that identity can as easily be a 'both/and' proposition as 'either/or': Identities are layered constructions, with the various strata always in constant flux with regard to each other depending on the situation.

Prior to the Soviet-period Central Asians – and, following them, Russians – most often used the term 'Tajik' to refer to mountain-dwellers, many of whom, such as the Pamiris, spoke Iranian languages other than Persian. This may help explain the apparent irony whereby the most active defender of the Bolshevik-determined 'Tajik' nation was an ethnic Pamiri, Shirinsho Shotemur. Pamiri filmmaker and sometime politician Davlat Khudonazarov, a native of Khorugh at the western edge of the Pamirs, relates that as a six-year-old child in 1950 he would return home from school and ask his grandmother, 'Who are we?' 'We are Tajiks,' this Shughnī-speaking lady would reply. 'Then what is the language we are learning in school?' '*Pārsī*,' she would say. 'Then who are those people who live on the other side of the river (in Afghanistan)?' 'They are Badakhshanis.' 'So what about the people in Dushanbe, who are they?' 'They are *shahrī* (city-dwellers).'[19] Clearly, even as recently as seven decades ago, identity labels circulating within the broader Tajik society were highly fluid, and did not necessarily correspond in all cases with their general usage today.

If we choose to adopt the most wide-ranging definition of the word, non-Persian-speakers of other Iranian languages (such as the various Pamiri tongues) can be considered as 'Tajiks' in relation to non-Iranian-speakers, while with respect to Persian-/Darī-speakers they might instead prefer to foreground their own distinct differences in language, religion and customs. In recent years some Pashtun-speaking tribes in Pakistan have begun to profess a 'Tajik' identity, sometimes even undertaking to learn Persian as their 'original' native language. Another confusing case is that of the Central Asian Jews, whose primary spoken language since at least as early as the ninth century has been Persian. They have at times been categorized as 'Tajiks', and at others as constituting their own ethnic group.[20] Central Asia's gypsies, known as Lūlīs, also typically speak Persian.

Out of this admittedly complex discussion emerges one general observation which is highly significant but rarely made: throughout the long history of the word 'Tajik', until a century ago it was not, in the overwhelming majority of cases, an endonym. It was applied by *others* to the people in question, and not by the 'Tajiks' to themselves. From the tenth century onwards and up to the Soviet period, the term was most commonly used by Turkic-speakers whose intention was to distinguish the settled, 'soft' Iranians from their own nobler, braver selves. Central Asia's Persophones, meanwhile, who became increasingly bilingual in Fārsī/Darī and Turkī over time, identified themselves primarily by other, non-linguistic criteria, such as religion, family, profession or place of origin. While urban merchants, bureaucrats and religious scholars wrote in Persian and can be assumed in most cases to have had Persian as their mother tongue, their ability to function just as comfortably in Turkī when circumstances called for it meant that language alone could not be their primary marker of identity. Most of Central Asia's Persian-speakers at the dawn of the Soviet Union do not appear to have had in their minds such a thing as a 'Tajik national identity'; this was constructed for them by others.

This fact is essential to understanding how national identity formation worked so devastatingly against the Tajiks at the beginning of the Soviet period. The literate urbanites who succeeded in transforming themselves into the new Central Asian ruling elite in the wake of the Bolshevik Revolution would appear in hindsight to have been mostly 'Tajiks' (at least *potential* Tajiks, since we are talking about invented identities) in terms of their social class and education. Yet in the event, many of these same emerging political and intellectual leaders instead made the choice to identify themselves as 'Uzbeks' – once a derogatory term, now rehabilitated by Bolshevik ideologues to designate a newly imagined 'nation' – and to promote the development of 'Uzbek' identity and national interests, with catastrophic consequences for those who accepted to be labelled as 'Tajiks'. Why did they do this?

The national delimitation strategy of the Soviets, first envisioned prior to the Revolution by a young-ish Joseph Stalin, has been extensively studied and need not be detailed here.[21] What we will note is the effect that this policy had on determining the future of Central Asia's Persian-speakers, who were initially denied a republic of their own. The Persian-speaking cities of Bukhara and Samarkand, rightly considered by today's Tajiks as the constituting the historical centres of Tajik civilization, were allotted to the newly created Uzbek Soviet Socialist Republic, with Samarkand as its capital.[22] (The capital was moved to Tashkent in 1930.) The Tajiks were accorded merely an 'autonomous republic' within the Uzbek SSR consisting of sparsely inhabited mountainous areas in what had been the southeastern part of the Bukhara khanate, without a single significant urban centre. A new 'capital city' was founded for them on the site of a weekly market: 'Dushanbe' means 'Monday' in Persian. This event remains as distressing to the Tajiks now as it was nine decades ago; many consider it to have been an act of 'deliberate decapitation of Tajik culture' perpetrated by the Soviet authorities.[23] The elevation of the Tajik ASSR to full republic status in 1929, along with the attachment of the geographically separate western Ferghana Valley and the economically important city of Khujand, did little to assuage Tajik resentment.

Contemporary Tajik scholars – such as the notoriously combative historian Rahim Masov (1939–2018) – have labelled the early Soviet Central Asian ideologues and activists as 'Tajik traitors' who sold out their nation to the Uzbeks. The reality is perhaps more nuanced. Being bilingual in Fārsī (soon to be rechristened as 'Tojikī') and Turkī (reconfigured as 'Özbekcha'), these individuals were free to choose their national identity, since the very notion itself was still in the process of being defined – in fact, they themselves were the very people who were in the process of defining it. There are several reasons why as a whole – though with some exceptions, notably the writer Sadriddin Ainī – the new indigenous class of Soviet leaders chose a Turkic identity over an Iranian one.

One reason is that Central Asian intellectuals had been deeply influenced by the modernist ideas of the Jadidist movement, which had been led by Turkic-speaking reformers such as the Tatar activist Ismail Gasprinskii, as well as by those of the Young Turks in the Ottoman Empire. Turkish was, in the early decades of the twentieth century, the principal language of modernist reform in the Muslim world. Persian, by contrast, being the language of the religious classes and the bureaucracy of the displaced despots, was associated with the very backwardness Central Asia's new idealists hoped to overcome. Another factor was that by that point the Russians had been in close relations with Turkic-speakers since their conquests of the Kazan and Astrakhan khanates during the sixteenth century, and were therefore habituated to communicating with their Muslim subjects in Turkic.[24]

Thus, while with the eventual establishment of a national republic and the validation of its associated language and culture the Tajiks were able to salvage to some extent their status as a recognized nation, they have nevertheless spent the past century chafing under the shadow of their Uzbek neighbours. This is all the more true for those living in the Uzbek republic (who are probably at least as numerous as in Tajikistan, possibly even more so), where for many decades identifying as a Tajik was actively discouraged or even subject to outright repression. Following the breakup of the Soviet Union in 1991 the Uzbek regime, under the Stalinesque leadership of President Islom Karimov

(1938–2016) – who was, ironically enough, himself of Tajik background – sought to downplay and suppress the Tajik presence in Uzbekistan. Officially Tajiks were said to constitute less than 5 per cent of the population, the true proportion being probably at least triple that and possibly much more.[25] It is impossible to know for sure, since most Tojikī-speakers in Uzbekistan are registered as Uzbeks on their identity cards, and only after one has gained their confidence by speaking to them in their own language will they sometimes discreetly re-identify themselves as Tajiks.

Even so, one has merely to spend a few moments on the streets of Samarkand or Bukhara – the country's second and third largest cities – to realize that most passers-by are speaking amongst themselves in Tojikī, not Uzbek. Nor is the language restricted to these urban areas. During my fieldwork in Uzbekistan as a graduate student in the mid-1990s, my former wife and I had the occasion to venture out of the heavily Russified capital, Tashkent (illegally, since our visas were for Tashkent alone), into some of the surrounding mountain villages to the east, where Tojikī was the only language we heard. Travel in those days was slow and difficult even over short distances, and I can recall spending an entire day hitching rides to get up into the hills which we finally reached only at nightfall. Realizing there was no way to get back to the city at that point and overhearing the conversation of some locals standing around in a dusty village lane lined with cypress trees, I asked them in Persian if there was a *mehmānkhāneh* (guesthouse) in the vicinity. They looked at each other in puzzlement, then turned to me arms outstretched and exclaimed, with their easily understood Tojikī pronunciation, *Injo har khona mehmonkhonast*! ('Here every house is a guesthouse!'), at which point they all launched into a debate over who would receive the honour of hosting the foreign couple for the night.

The historical importance for Iranian civilization of the two principal Tajik cities now in Uzbekistan, Samarkand and Bukhara, can hardly be overstated. In his 1965 monograph entitled *Bukhara: The Medieval Achievement*, Richard Frye reminds us that 'Bukhara, at the end of the 9th and in the 10th century, became the capital of the eastern Iranian cultural area, and thereby became the heir of a centuries-old tradition, independent of western Iran'.[26] It was here in Central Asia, Frye notes, that one may locate the 'New Persian Renaissance' which, after two centuries of Arab political domination, successfully blended

Iran's ancient culture and traditions with those emerging in Islam. The Tajiks, in this sense, were the principal agents of the tenth-century Persian cultural revival, encompassing not just literature but perhaps even more importantly a valorization of Iranian identity as symbolized by the pre-Islamic past, which then spread back to western Iran.

Given the many different contexts in which the term 'Tajik' has been applied throughout history, any attempt to circumscribe its use is necessarily somewhat arbitrary. For purposes of this book, the focus will be on the Tojikī-Darī-speakers living to the east of present-day Iran in Tajikistan, Uzbekistan and Afghanistan and their ancestors who occupied these regions; that is to say, Transoxiana, Herat and Balkh. Of the history of 'Iran proper' we have written elsewhere.[27]

1

The Prehistory of the Tajiks

The first of the good lands and countries which I, Ahura Mazda, created, was Airyana Vaejah.

Avesta, Vidēvdāt 1.2

Language is one of the basic markers of cultural identity, and in that sense the Tajiks are most immediately recognizable as Iranian-speakers. They are, as noted in the Introduction, today's Iranians of the East. Identities, however, are complex and sometimes fluid phenomena. They are constructed of layers, among which language is often – but not always – merely the most visible. Few of the world's ethnicities are 'pure' in any meaningful sense; most are the result of thousands of years of mixing among culturally diverse groups.

In the case of the Tajiks it is possible to single out two distinct prehistoric societies – very different in their socio-economic makeup – as being especially significant in contributing foundational strata to the eventual formation of Tajik identity, although others surely played a part as well. The linguistic layer, along with other important components such as religion and mythology, was provided by a conglomeration of warlike pastoral-nomadic tribes of west Siberian origin calling themselves *Aryo*, or 'Aryans', from which the term 'Iranian' derives. These tribes migrated southwards into Central Asia, and thence onto the vast mountainous plateau south of the Caspian Sea, in successive waves throughout the centuries of the second millennium BCE, filling up the space from Mesopotamia in the west all the way to the Indus Valley in the east and imposing their rule over the diverse peoples who already inhabited these widely spread regions.

Another layer, less apparent but no less significant, came from a more advanced agricultural and urban society that had settled along the Central Asian oases that later came to constitute the Silk Road. Overwhelmed by waves of Aryan invaders, this oasis society left almost no linguistic traces. They did bequeath considerable archaeological remains, however. These are collectively referred to by specialists as the Bactria-Margiana Archaeological Complex, or BMAC, recalling the Greek names of two important Central Asian provinces in ancient times. A more popular term is 'the Oxus Civilization', after the river that divided these two regions.

The ancient Aryans

The modern language known as 'Tojikī', which is the official language of the Republic of Tajikistan, is an eastern variant of Persian (*fārsī*[1]), which is spoken in Iran and also in Afghanistan where it is called *darī*. All three dialects are mutually comprehensible, and should therefore not be treated as separate languages as is sometimes done, usually for political reasons. The ethnonym 'Tajik' is most often used today to refer to the Persian-speakers living in the eastern part of the Iranian world, beyond the borders of modern-day Iran in Tajikistan, Afghanistan and Uzbekistan.

Persian is a member of the Iranian branch of the Indo-European language family, a large and widespread grouping of genetically related tongues that also includes the Germanic, Romance, Indic and other branches. All descend from an ancient, unattested proto-language that was spoken in the west Eurasian steppe region north of the Caucasus mountains by bands of bellicose pastoral nomads some 5,000 years ago.[2]

One of these Indo-European-speaking groups had settled around the southeastern edge of the Ural mountain range (in what is now Russia) by around 4,000 years BP ('Before Present'). They are known today as the Sintashta people, after a small river – a tributary to the Tobol – beside which significant finds related to them have been discovered. Because the archaeological record they left connects them with the religions and cultures found later in Iran and India, it is generally supposed that they spoke an Indo-European language that later diverged into the Iranian and Indic written idioms attested in sacred texts such as the Zoroastrian Avesta and the Hindu Vedas. For purposes of convenience, linguists therefore label this prehistoric stage of the language – only hypothetically reconstructable – as 'proto-Indo-Iranian'. By extension, the tribes assumed to have spoken this conjectural language are usually referred to as 'Indo-Iranians'.[3]

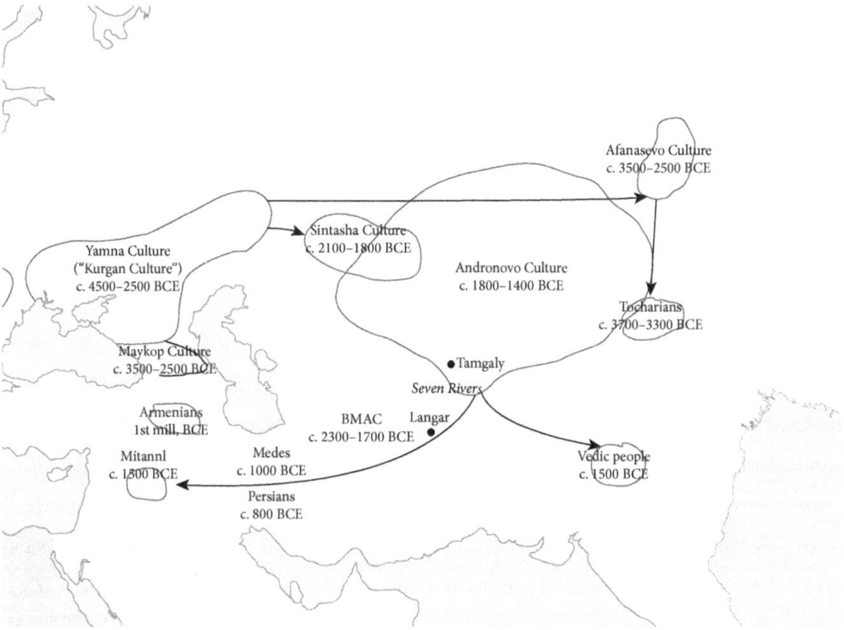

Map 1 Indo-Iranian migrations (the Sintashta and Andronovo peoples) during the second millennium BCE.

The people in question appear to have had a name for themselves, however, which was *Aryo* or 'Aryan', meaning '(We), the Noble (Ones)'. They called their west Siberian homeland *Airyanəm Vaējah*, 'Land of the Noble Ones', a designation they carried with them as they migrated southwards throughout the second millennium BCE towards the arid, mountainous plateau south of the Caspian Sea. In historical times the pronunciation of *Airyanəm Vaējah* became simplified to *Ērān-wej*, and eventually *Īrān*.

The Afghan national airline, Ariana, is another modern reflection of the ancient name. More infamously, beginning in the nineteenth century German racists (mis)appropriated the term 'Aryan', along with one of that ancient culture's most sacred symbols, the swastika, which was originally a sign of auspiciousness and remains so for Hindus in India where it is still commonly seen. Needless to say, Iranians and Indians today bear no responsibility for the atrocities perpetrated by the Nazis, and have every right to use their ancient terms and symbols without being automatically associated with racism or genocide.

At the same time, what we can glean of the ancient Aryan culture through their religious myths, which boast of forcibly 'liberating' livestock and women from inferior tribes that don't deserve them, does suggest they held strong notions of their own superiority vis-à-vis their neighbours. Moreover, the extraordinary sweep of Indo-European-speaking peoples across the globe – Indo-European being by far the most widespread of all the language families, stretching from Ireland in the west all the way to China's Tarim Basin in the east, and in modern times to the Americas as well – was due to violent conquests that spanned across several millennia.

These conquests, which often entailed the subjugation of societies that were in many ways more advanced, were made possible by two major advantages held by the Aryans. One was their possession of the horse, which was domesticated somewhere in Central Eurasia no later than about 3500 BCE,[4] complemented by the development of the spoke-wheeled war chariot about fifteen centuries later.[5] The other was their skill in metallurgy – they were a quintessential Bronze Age people – which enabled them to forge superior weapons by which to vanquish their enemies. Their access to rich copper deposits in the Ural Mountains facilitated their use of this technology.

In respect to these considerable advantages in both mobility and weaponry, the Sintashta archaeological sites offer our first clear picture of the Aryan culture that had taken shape by around 2000 BCE. (The Aryans' ancestors had arrived several centuries earlier from farther West, imposing themselves on the existing inhabitants who may have spoken early forms of the Uralic languages one still finds in the region today. It has been suggested that the Aryan migrations were motivated by climate change, a decrease in rainfall which moved the forests northward and expanded the range of the steppe lands amenable to pasturing livestock.[6]) All of the houses excavated from this pivotal period contain forges, indicating that their inhabitants were engaged in making weapons. Many traces of these have been found, including arrowheads, spears, daggers and battle axes. The large quantities of such items occurring at the various Sintashta excavations – far more than are found in earlier sites – attest to a significant increase in warfare.

The same archaeological strata contain elaborate burials of sacrificed horses, along with the earliest surviving traces of war chariots. The arrangement of objects accompanying these interments correlates in many ways with the instructions provided in the oldest Sanskrit text, the Rig Veda, for the *asvamedha*, or horse sacrifice. Although the Rig Veda itself was first written down in India sometime during the first millennium BCE, it was transmitted orally for centuries before that, and parts of it may trace back to the time of the Sintashta people or even earlier.

The horse sacrifice in later, Vedic times in India was restricted to the royal elite – horses being both prohibitively expensive and far more valuable alive than dead – so its performance at Sintashta suggests a society that was already stratified into distinct social classes. The religio-mythical system of the Aryans, which can be reconstructed through a comparison of later forms found in the Avesta and the Vedas, appears to have given rise to the caste system which the Aryans later imposed on India.

Within the Aryans' pyramidal social structure, a small elite of priestly chieftains ruled the tribe. One presumes they asserted their authority by means of their privileged knowledge of secret rituals (including shamanistic ones using psychotropic drugs), which were believed to ensure the group's survival through effective communication with unseen forces. The next, larger social category was made up of warriors, merciless bands of cattle-raiders whose heroic exploits were celebrated by talented poets. The Aryan tradition of epic poetry, later echoed by Greece's Homer and Iran's Firdawsī among many others, ensured the heroes' immortality by providing them with 'everlasting fame'.[7] Finally, the base stratum of Aryan society was composed of 'producers' such as farmers or herders. Arriving in the heavily populated Indian subcontinent some centuries later, the Aryans conceived a fourth caste which they applied to the far more numerous pre-existing inhabitants who joined them, the *sudra*s, as well as a fifth category they saw as the dregs of society, that of *dasa*s or 'natural born slaves'.[8]

The Sintashta Aryans lived in small villages of fifty or so sunken dwellings made of logs. These villages were generally situated beside rivers, which provided both a water source and a means of transportation. Since proto-Indo-European times rivers had been seen as vital lifelines by these pastoralists, and the goddess associated with them was their most important female deity. In the historical period Iranians called her Anahita, but she had other names throughout the Indo-European world.[9]

The Aryan economy was based on the rearing of livestock, especially cattle, along with some small-scale farming of barley and millet, as well as the export of smelted metalwork to locations further to the south. Given the extreme west

Siberian climate, with its long winters and unpredictable rainfall, these domestic activities were highly vulnerable, and the survival of the community could be ensured only by successful raiding of neighbouring tribes. In such circumstances it is not hard to see how and why the Aryan warriors, charged with bringing home booty and slaves, would be revered as heroes and celebrated in epic song.

Because violent skirmishes with neighbours were a fact of Indo-Iranian life, the principal Sintashta villages were organized according to a rectangular, oval or circular plan and surrounded by double-wall fortifications. To date twenty-one such fortified towns have been excavated, covering as much as 35,000 square metres, across a region extending over some 30,000 square kilometres. Many more unfortified villages have been detected as well; presumably their residents would have fled to the protected sites when under attack. The larger settlements may have had a thousand or more inhabitants each. Due to frequently muddy conditions the walkways were paved with logs, as remained the case in Russia up to early modern times. Individual homes, unusually for the period, were served by covered drains.

Burial sites were similar in structure to houses, sunken into the ground and with walls made of timber. Earthen mounds were built up over the roof to create barrows known as *kurgans*. This technique survived across Eurasia for many centuries, and *kurgans* are still visible in many areas today from the Balkans to Mongolia. Based on the types of items found in the graves – mainly weapons and sacrificed animals in the case of men, and jewellery in that of women – it would appear that only those belonging to the warrior caste were entitled to be buried in formal tombs. Women, who comprise about 20 per cent of those found at these burial sites, were typically dressed in warrior clothing. All in all only about 30 per cent of the total estimated population had the privilege of such lavish burials, suggesting that warriors made up about one third of Sintashta's Aryan society.

After only a few centuries, by about 1700 BCE the Aryans were on the move again, most likely due to climate change. Many continued eastwards across Siberia, presumably seeking out better pasturelands for their livestock, and eventually settled in the area between the Ob and the Yenisei rivers. Archaeologists refer to this second-millennium steppe society as the Andronovo culture, after a village near modern Krasnoyarsk, where its remains were first discovered.

The Aryan cultural continuum stretched over an immense territory of several thousand kilometres, from the Volga River in the west to the Yenisei in the east, from the taiga forests in the north to the Tien Shan Mountains in the south. The Andronovo Aryans seem to have dominated – but probably also mixed with – the prior inhabitants of this vast, sparsely populated landscape. These included the pastoral nomadic Afanasevo peoples, with whom the Aryans shared many cultural traits as well as a common Indo-European origin. The Afanasevo tribes likely spoke an early form of Tokharian, the easternmost Indo-European language group which survived in the Tarim Basin of western China up to the twelfth century CE. Their material culture suggests that Afanasevo society was less stratified and less martial than that of the Andronovo Aryans who overwhelmed them.

The organization and architecture of the Andronovo peoples was similar to that of Sintashta. Some of the houses were large, with a number of rooms, and were likely inhabited by extended families as has remained a preference for Iranians up to modern times. In addition to horses and cattle they raised sheep and goats. As their migratory society reached the Altai Mountains which separate the west Siberian steppe from Mongolia, new sources of copper were discovered, enabling the Aryans to export their metalwork not just to the oasis towns to the south but back towards the west as well.

The survival of primarily Indo-Iranian place names across northern Central Asia suggests that the Aryan language was the lingua franca within Andronovo society and even beyond, although the presence of loanwords from Uralic languages provides evidence of contact with non-Indo-European forest-dwellers to the north. Turkic-speakers from northeast Asia probably did not begin moving into the area until sometime after 1500 BCE, since the human skeletons from prior to that time are of Europoid, rather than Mongoloid, type.[10]

During this same period most of the Aryan bands seem to have begun moving south. Some of the western tribes settled in Khwarazm where the two great Central Asian rivers the Oxus and the Jaxartes emptied into the Aral Sea. (These rivers, now called the Amu Darya and the Syr Darya, have since the Soviet period been siphoned off for irrigation and no longer reach the Aral, once the world's fourth-largest lake, which has all but dried up over the past thirty years causing massive ecological disaster.) An important archaeological site at Gonur-Tepe north of Marv in eastern Turkmenistan may have been inhabited by proto-Iranians, in the view of Greek-Soviet archaeologist Viktor Sarianidi who led the excavations.[11] Temples found there include the kind of fire altars later associated with Zoroastrianism, though fire worship was widespread in ancient societies and cannot be taken in and of itself as evidence for any particular religion.

Other Aryan groups, including the ancestors of the Medes and Persians who would become the first Iranians to appear in historical sources, kept on heading south and eventually spread out across the lands south of the Caspian Sea, reaching the Zagros Mountains on the fringes of Mesopotamia by around 1100 BCE. These territories were already inhabited, but as elsewhere, over the following centuries Iranian language became dominant across the plateau. Further east, Indo-Iranian tribes more directly related to today's Tajiks took up residence to the north of the Tien Shan Mountains.

Just as later textual evidence from sources such as the Avesta and the Rig Veda can be taken to shed light on the myths and rituals of the early Indo-Iranians, a rich collection of petroglyphs dating to the second half of the second millennium BCE provides evidence of the Aryans' arrival in the Seven Rivers region (Kaz. Zhetisu; Rus. Semirech'ye; Pers. Haftrud) of what is now southern Kazakhstan. In one location alone, the overdramatically named Tamgaly 'Gorge' (really more of a gully) between the modern city of Almaty and Lake Balkhash, no less than 5,000 Bronze Age petroglyphs have been found, at what has now been classified as a UNESCO World Heritage site.[12]

The subjects artistically rendered in these archaic rock wall engravings provide an important source for re-imagining many aspects of Aryan society, including their animal-based economy, their social organization and their religious beliefs and rituals. Similar collections have been found elsewhere in southern Kazakhstan at Kuljabasi, Aqqainar and other locations, as well as in Kyrgyzstan on the northern shore of Issyk Lake near Cholpan-Ata, in Uzbekistan at Sarmish-say northeast of the city of Navoi and in Tajikistan both along the Zarafshon Valley and at a number of sites in the Pamirs, most notably Akjilda and Langar.

Among the most striking of these rock-carved illustrations are solar symbols, including a number of bizarre polka-dot and sun-headed figures that

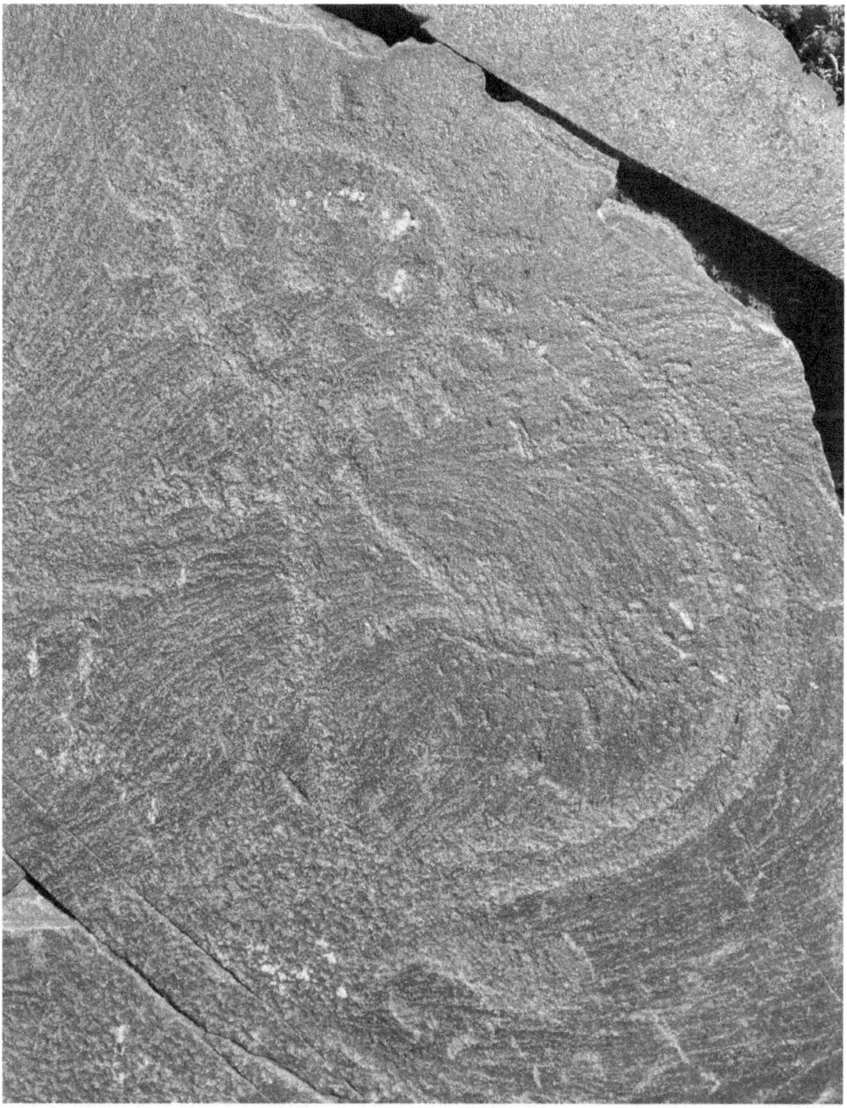

Figure 1.1 Bronze Age petroglyph figure possibly representing the 'thousand-eyed' Aryan god of contracts, Mithra. Around thirteenth century BCE. Tamgaly, Kazakhstan.

may possibly be representations of Mithra, the all-seeing (thousand-eyed) god of contracts, associated with the sun, who was likely the principal deity for the Aryan warrior class (see Figure 1.1). Juxtapositions of solar symbols with bulls provide further evidence connecting the makers of these petroglyphs with the ancient Mithraic bull-cult, which is attested from Iran to northwestern

Europe (traces of which perhaps survive in the Spanish *corrida*). Depictions of wheeled chariots, one of the defining elements connected with the martial caste, also commonly appear. Other images portray women giving birth, and in a number of locations one can see paired human figures engaging in front-to-back sex.

There are also many images of zoomorphic beings, perhaps representing the shamanistic priests who would often dress in animal skins when performing their rituals. Animals too are frequently shown, reflecting their importance to the Aryan economy as well as the fact that they were sacrificed for religious purposes (see Figure 1.2). Human figures with their arms stretched out towards the sun may symbolize priests engaged in prayer. (The fact that they have large erections calls for additional interpretation. Are they praying for fertility? Excited by the prospect of battle? One can only speculate.) The Tamgaly petroglyphs are grouped around a semi-enclosed area that appears to have served as an open-air temple where sacrifices, dances and other religious ceremonies would have been carried out.

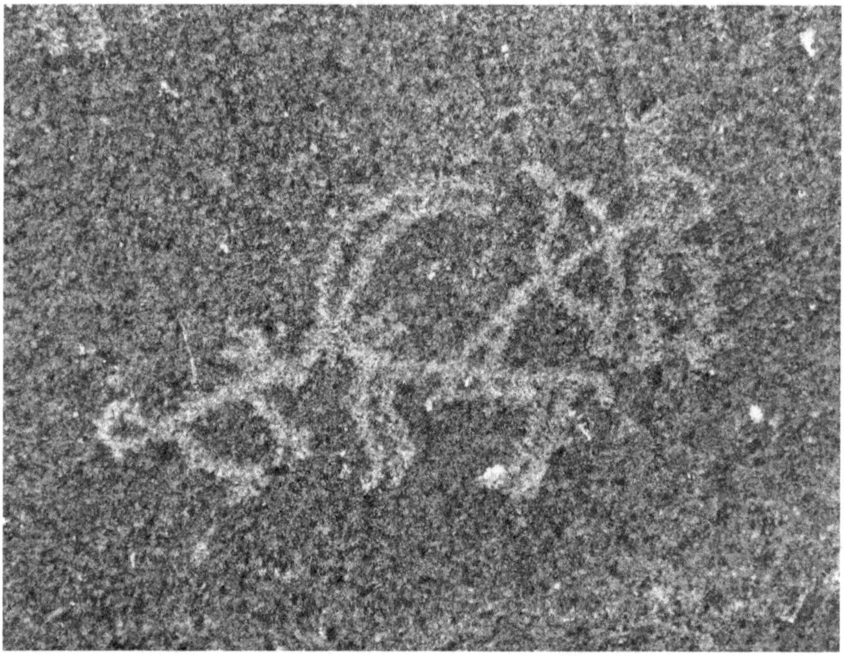

Figure 1.2 Hunting scene (ibex with hunter on right and dog on left). Bronze Age petroglyph. Langar, Tajikistan.

The Seven Rivers region was at the eastern edge of the urbanized Oxus Civilization with which the Aryans of Sintashta had been trading since at least 2000 BCE. From the middle of the millennium onwards, the southward migration of the Aryan tribes brought them into more permanent contact with the settled cultures of the Central Asian oases, leading to a cultural synthesis that would prove transformative for both sides.

The Oxus Civilization

The Bactria-Margiana Archaeological Complex (BMAC), or Oxus Civilization, refers to an ensemble of Bronze Age sites, dating to the late third and early second millennium BCE, situated east and west of the Oxus River from the Köpet Mountains between Turkmenistan and Iran to the Pamir Mountains of modern Tajikistan. These sites, which reveal the existence of an advanced urban society in the heart of ancient Central Asia, were discovered and excavated only beginning in the last quarter of the twentieth century. Thus, the description and interpretation of this remarkable civilization, from which no written texts have yet come to light, remains very much a work in progress. Little is known for certain about its origins, and even less what language its people spoke, but material remains give a fairly good picture of the kind of society it was.

In contrast to the nomadic Aryans of the Eurasian steppe, the roots of BMAC culture appear to derive from the Near East, particularly Elam, and can be traced back at least 8,000 years. Farmers lived in mud brick houses and raised goats (which were first domesticated in the Zagros Mountains, adjacent to Elam) and sheep, rather than primarily cattle as was the case with the Aryans. They did not use horses, but they may have been the first to domesticate the Bactrian camel, which would become essential to the development of Silk Road commerce later on.

The Oxus people also cultivated wheat and barley, both of which had been imported from the Fertile Crescent along with their associated irrigation technologies which were necessary for agriculture to flourish in the arid Central Asian climate. The iconography of their artistic tradition – as evidenced through their jewellery, sculpture and rock engravings – suggests that BMAC religion was centred on a goddess who was responsible for the fertility of livestock and vegetation. (Her later Sogdian incarnation was the goddess Nanai, presumably a local variant of the Mesopotamian Inanna, who comes to be conflated in some cases with the Iranian Anahita.) A bird-headed hero is also frequently shown in combat with a dragon, although in contrast to the Indo-European mythical tradition, the dragon is never killed.[13]

Urbanization, as evidenced by the sites at Namazga and Altin-Tepe in southern Turkmenistan and at Sarazm in western Tajikistan, was underway in the region by the early third millennium BCE.[14] This included the construction of monumental palaces, temples, forts and, at Altin-Tepe, a twelve-metre-high ziggurat – that is, a terrace-stepped pyramid of the type found throughout Mesopotamia. A wide range of wheel-thrown ceramics were produced, along with sophisticated jewellery and other decorative or ritual objects made from gold, turquoise, lapis lazuli, carnelian, ivory and agate. The cultivation of grapes suggests that the BMAC people drank wine. (In historic times Samarkand was famed for its vineyards.) Copper smelting was done in 'industrial zones' away from residential areas.

BMAC cities, such as the one excavated at Altin-Tepe, were divided into three types of neighbourhoods in accordance with social class. The poorest quarters were inhabited by craftsmen such as potters and other workers, while large houses in other districts suggest a wealthy class of managers and businesspeople. A smaller sector contained the mansions of the ruling elite.

The BMAC trade networks incorporated Elam, Mesopotamia and Anatolia to the west, Sintashta to the north, Jiroft to the south and, to the southeast, the Indus Valley civilization with whom they may have been culturally and linguistically connected. Many items of Harappan origin have been found at Oxus sites, including divination tools, decorative beads and seals (most often used to identify transported goods), including one that may contain as yet undeciphered writing. The Oxus region, meanwhile, was the major source of tin for the Near East.[15] Distinctive BMAC seals have been found in all these locations, further evidence of the Oxus peoples' participation in extensive trade networks.

By the turn of the second millennium BCE there appears to have been an eastward migration of BMAC peoples towards the Marv oasis and then southwards across the Oxus River into Bactria. By this time they may already have begun assimilating with Aryan tribes moving down from the north, a process which would result in the Aryanization of Margiana and Bactria and thereby lay the foundations for what would much later become the culture of the Tajiks.

The religion of Zarathushtra

The Aryan tribes preserved much of the mythical and ritual system they inherited from their steppe-dwelling proto-Indo-European ancestors, showing many discernible similarities with those of their Greek, Roman, Germanic and Slavic cousins. Indeed, it is through comparison of these various later systems that one can back-project a reconstruction of what the older common religion must have been like. The proto-Indo-European pantheon held numerous deities associated either with natural phenomena such as wind, rain, thunder or fire, or with abstract qualities like wisdom, dominion or keeping one's word. The male sky god reigned supreme within this deeply patriarchal culture, while the divine, life-giving earth was seen as feminine.

Deities were propitiated through rituals that included the recitation of sacred formulas – a 'trade secret' of the priests, passed on from one generation to the next among priestly families – and usually culminated in the sacrifice of an animal, which was consumed as part of a shared feast among humans and the divine. Cattle, being the basis of the pastoralists' economy, figured prominently in both myth and ritual, and horses had an important role as well. For the Aryan priests, a plant-based hallucinogenic beverage – called *haoma* in Iranian and *soma* in Sanskrit – was a major 'sacrificial' substance which, following careful preparation, enabled them to soar with the gods.

The Indo-Iranians also worshipped fire and water, elements that were paired together in their rituals and mythology. An early attestation of this can be seen in the temple excavated at Jarkutan in southern Uzbekistan, dating to around 1500 BCE at a time when the in-migrating Aryans had begun to integrate with the native Oxus culture.[16] Both the Indic Vedas and the Iranian Avesta preserve myths of a fire deity emerging from the water, a phenomenon sometimes observable in nature, as has been the case at the Caspian oilfields near Baku, Azerbaijan since ancient times. Pre-Islamic sanctuaries across the Iranian world from Mesopotamia to Central Asia often associate the two elements, and all over Europe Roman temples to the Iranian god Mithra, called by the Latin epithet *sol invictus* or 'the invincible Sun', are paired with sacred sites dedicated to water goddesses.[17]

Priests, as mentioned earlier, constituted the elite caste of Aryan society; the profession was hereditary. Moreover, there were several distinct categories of priests, each specializing in a particular kind of ritual. Sometime during the second half of the second millennium, one Aryan priest by the name of Zarathushtra (probably meaning 'owner of many camels' – priests tended to be well recompensed for their services) radically reimagined the traditional religion. Zarathushtra, more often known in the West as Zoroaster, expressed his ideas through the composition of hymns, the *Gāthās* (literally, 'songs'), which became the basis for a religious practice we now call Zoroastrianism.

Few, if any, religions in history have had a more lasting, if rarely recognized, influence than Zoroastrianism,[18] but it is probably safe to say that none is plagued by as many unresolved historical questions. Even very basic points such as when, where or if Zarathushtra lived remain the focus of heated debate. More vexingly still, the texts attributed to him – the Gathas and sometimes also a long liturgy known as the *Yasna Haptaŋhāiti* (Seven-Part Sacrifice) – are in a language that is not attested through any other sources and is poorly understood even by the most diligent and accomplished scholars. Called Old Avestan, after the Zoroastrian holy book of which they comprise the most archaic parts, its closest linguistic relative is Vedic Sanskrit. Despite their many similarities, however, the two languages are different enough that a comparison between them raises as many questions of interpretation as it answers.

Nevertheless, these two sacred tongues are close enough in structure and vocabulary that their oldest forms, which were preserved orally for many centuries before being written down, must date to a time shortly after some of the Aryan tribes broke off and continued their migration southeastwards through what is now Afghanistan. The Indo-Aryans, as this latter branch are known, traversed a difficult mountain range known as the Hindu Kush (a much later Persian term meaning 'Indian killers'), then moved into the Indus Valley region of the northwestern Indian subcontinent in successive waves during the middle of the second millennium BCE. There, their form of the

Aryan religion began a long process of interactions with the many indigenous traditions found throughout the subcontinent, the variegated results of which are now called by the catch-all term of 'Hinduism'.

Old Avestan and Old Vedic are the two most archaic forms of Indo-Iranian language to be preserved in any kind of substantial written records, which in both of these cases are liturgical texts used by priests while performing rituals. (Some terminological traces of common Indo-Iranian are found in documents from the Mitanni kingdom of northern Mesopotamia dating to around 1400 BCE. This has been taken to show that a small group of Aryan warriors had travelled there and imposed themselves as the ruling elite, but they were fairly quickly assimilated into the local Hurrian population.) As sacred – and secret – oral formulas that had to be memorized by successive generations of priests without any alteration, the Avestan and Vedic texts became fossilized and increasingly archaic, while the spoken dialects of the Indo-Iranian peoples evolved and changed over time. Thus, it is likely that within a few centuries of their composition the priests responsible for remembering and passing on these ancient liturgies no longer fully understood their meanings.

For this reason, the 'teachings' of Zarathushtra are far from clear, since translations of the Gathas and other Avestan texts are highly speculative and their interpretation continues to be hotly contested among scholars and practitioners alike. Frustratingly for scholars, modern Zoroastrians' understandings of the Avesta (and indeed of their religion as a whole) have been heavily shaped by the interactions between the Parsi Zoroastrians and European scholars and missionaries in India during the nineteenth century, such that Zoroastrianism came to be entirely reframed according to modern Christian notions. Zoroastrians today, for example, will proudly claim that theirs was the 'first monotheistic religion', whereas the Avestan texts are decidedly polytheistic. Similarly, Zarathushtra is claimed to be a 'prophet' (sometimes even 'the *first* prophet'), despite the fact that he was not a mouthpiece for the Divine – which is what the term usually implies – and his hymns were not originally understood as 'Divine Revelation'.[19] Rather, the Old Avestan texts constitute a recitative liturgy used by priests to accompany the performance of rituals. They are communications *to* the Divine, rather than *from* it, in which Zarathushtra, not Ahura Mazda, is usually the narrator.

Modern Zoroastrian claims of monotheism take as their basis one of the central themes of the Gathic hymns, which is that one deity, Ahura Mazda, is supreme and most deserving of sacrificial rites. Since even here the gist is one of elevating a particular deity above all others, the Gathic message would perhaps more accurately described as 'henotheistic' than monotheistic. (The same can be said for biblical Judaism: 'Thou shalt have no other gods *before* me', a tacit admission that rival gods exist. Passing aside the problem of the Christian Trinity, one can say that true monotheism appears only with the Islamic *shahāda*: 'There is no god but Allah'.)

Moreover, the texts of the so-called 'Young Avesta', which seem to have been compiled several centuries later than the Gathas, consist of hymns and sacrifices directed to gods and goddesses *other* than Mazda. These include the god of contracts, Mithra, the water goddess Anahita, the rain god Tishtrya and the goddess of feminine obedience, Ashi, to name only a few. Indeed the Young Avestan texts, which appear to have taken their final shape somewhere to the south of Zarathushtra's native territory, can be seen as preserving an archaic and highly complex Iranian religious system that is not in its origins or essence 'Zoroastrian' but was rather at some point 'Zoroastrianized', and not altogether coherently at that.[20]

Since the various categories of priests each specialized in the performance of their own types of rites, the confusion can perhaps best be explained through a model of professional competition. Zarathushtra laid the foundation for a priestly specialization in the cult of Mazda, the god of wisdom, making the argument that devotees should patronize his cult and not any other. In this respect Zarathushtra's mission was not a success. Indeed, the texts themselves tell us that he was disregarded by his own people and had to seek the patronage of a far-off 'king' (more likely some kind of minor chieftain), Vishtaspa. Most of the Aryan tribes happily carried on sacrificing to a wide range of ancient gods and goddesses, as the Young Avestan texts show, although the surviving forms of these deities and their associated rituals have been heavily edited by later generations of Mazdaean priests so as to subjugate them to Mazda.

Herein lies the problem with understanding Zoroastrianism's historical spread and development: Given the extraordinary difficulties in deciphering Old Avestan, the earliest Zoroastrian texts have been filtered through centuries of evolving interpretations, the many layers of which are now difficult to unpack. Some of these interpretations are demonstrably wrong. For example, priests of the Sasanian period (224–651 CE) when Zoroastrianism enjoyed the status of state religion in Iran, claimed that Zarathushtra lived in Media '258 years before Alexander (the Great)'. The linguistic character of Old Avestan as well as the socio-ecological environment it evokes makes both the geographical and temporal aspects of this claim vanishingly unlikely, but the Median priests (the Magi) had been custodians of the Zoroastrian rite for centuries, and it made sense for them to try to tie Zarathushtra to their own region as well as to the historical era when they first began to achieve strong royal patronage.

Another example is that, contrary to the received Zoroastrian narrative, an analysis of both the language and content of Old Avestan would tend to situate Zarathushtra in the Iranian east, perhaps around 1200 BCE. This was a time of significant social change within Aryan society, when some tribes were in the process of beginning to assimilate the trappings of settled civilization while others still held to nomadic warrior ways. Zarathushtra is critical of the latter, especially the seizing of cattle through violence and the religious systems of myths and often orgiastic rituals that supported such activities.

The question remains of how the Zoroastrian rite came to be transmitted to western Iran, since it clearly originated far to the east. Perhaps the lands ruled by Vishtaspa, where Zarathushtra found his success, lay to the west of the reformer's original homeland? The Medes had been moving in this direction, eventually settling in the northwest Iranian territory that came to bear their name (Media) – this was accomplished by perhaps a century or two after Zarathushtra lived.

Ancient Greek writers identify 'Zoroastres' as a Median, and later as a 'Persian sage'. But there is no internal (i.e. Iranian) evidence that Zoroastrianism held any official status within the Median confederation that overthrew the neo-Assyrian Empire in 612 BCE, nor amongst the Persians during the time of Cyrus the Great (r. 559–30). It is not until the reign of Darius I (r. 522–486) that one sees the first mention of Mazda in any Iranian written sources, and even then, and for centuries thereafter all the way up to the Sasanian period, the partisans of Mazda had to compete with the many rival cults that existed throughout the various and widely dispersed Iranian-speaking societies of Central and Western Asia.

After independence in 1991 it became popular among Tajik nationalist intellectuals to claim Zarathushtra as a 'Tajik prophet' and Zoroastrianism as their original national religion. Such notions, however – just as with the traditional accounts of practicing Parsi or Irani Zoroastrians – should be approached with caution. Referring to Zarathushtra as a 'Tajik' is anachronistic to say the least, even if his native society was likely a part of the cultural composite that much later came to comprise today's Tajiks. The most probable candidate for his homeland is southern Kazakhstan, not Tajikistan. More importantly, the historical development of the Zoroastrian rite took place in western Iran, and therefore most properly belongs to the history of the Persians.

By contrast, the lands now inhabited by the Tajiks were at times home to numerous other faiths, including Judaism, Christianity and Buddhism, alongside various local cults such as that of Siyāvash in Bukhara and the river god Vakhsh around the upper Oxus basin. The evidence for Central Asian Zoroastrianism is scant, and, where discernible at all, it shows signs of being a late and somewhat superficial import from the west towards the end of the Sasanian period. Hence, although most contemporary scholars of Zoroastrianism seem to take for granted that it was the principal religion of pre-Islamic Central Asia, such unexamined assumptions should be treated with scepticism until more concrete proofs come to light.

The Aryan-Oxus synthesis

The southward movement of Aryan tribes throughout the second millennium BCE brought them into more direct and lasting contact with the remnants of the Oxus Civilization, which had been in many ways more economically and technologically advanced than their own. Yet by historical times the Oxus peoples had given up their original language in favour of Sogdian, an east Iranian dialect imposed on them by the nomadic Aryans.

Still, the cultural influence of southern Central Asia's settled peoples over the Aryan immigrants was considerable. Those Indo-Iranian tribes that decided to put down roots in the region became urbanized, learned more productive forms of agriculture and acquired industrial skills hitherto unknown to them.

The extent of this influence can be seen in changes to the Aryan vocabulary. Although the BMAC language remains a mystery, it appears to have provided a number of loanwords to late Indo-Iranian, including the terms for 'camel', 'donkey', 'brick', 'wheat' and 'irrigation channel'.[21] Since loanwords usually indicate the introduction of something new and foreign, it may be assumed that the Aryans first learned the use of these vital resources and technologies through their interactions with the Oxus peoples.

In the realm of religion, the Indo-Iranians adopted many elements of BMAC myth and ritual, some of which likely originated in the Near East. Here one may cite two prominent examples. The first is the conflation of the Indo-Iranian river goddess, who came to be known as Anahita, with the extraordinarily popular Central Asian deity Nanai who was a local form of the Sumerian Inanna, associated in turn with the Babylonian Ishtar. The prevalence of a winged goddess depicted on BMAC artefacts may be an early reflex of this transmission. She was apparently the chief deity in the BMAC pantheon,[22] and it is interesting that centuries later, the Greek historian Herodotus says of the nomadic Scythians who lived just north of this region, that – uncharacteristically for the patriarchal Aryans – their principal deity was a goddess, Tabiti.[23]

Another example of cultural transmission from the Near East to Central Asia is the martyr figure of Siyāvash, who appears prominently in Iranian literature, including the Zoroastrian Avesta and, later, Firdawsī's *Book of Kings*, and who became the central figure of the most important religious cult in pre-Islamic Bukhara. In many respects, the myths, features and even mourning rituals associated with the Iranian Siyāvash can be shown to have derived from the Mesopotamian story of Tammuzi: a beautiful young man, unjustly killed, whose sacrificial blood nourishes the soil at the onset of winter so that plant life may again flourish in the spring. Here we have two illustrative cases of Mesopotamian culture being conveyed via well-travelled trade routes to the Oxus people of Central Asia, who then passed these elements on to the proto-Iranians.

Another interesting consideration is that the Oxus peoples may have used locally occurring psychotropic plants in their religious ceremonies, which were then taken up by the Indo-Iranians – for example the *haoma* or *soma* rituals known from the Avesta and the Rig Veda. The evidence for this is twofold.

First, the varieties of hemp and ephedra found in the Pamir and Tien Shan mountain regions at the eastern edge of the BMAC territory are especially potent hallucinogens. Second, the Indo-Iranian terms for these plants appear to be BMAC loanwords.[24]

Clearly, within a millennium of their integration into BMAC society Iranian-speakers had evolved a new hybrid identity. The result of this emerging synthesis was the Sogdians, direct ancestors to many of today's Tajiks and famous in history as the masters of the trans-Eurasian trade networks known collectively as the Silk Road. While the Sogdians are identifiably Iranian in terms of both their language – an east-Iranian dialect closely related to Avestan as well as Old Persian – and many aspects of their culture, including religion, the BMAC imprint was nevertheless hugely significant. This included the legacy of a settled urban civilization fed by a sophisticated system of agriculture, and, perhaps even more importantly, an established place at the centre of international trade.

2

Sogdians and Bactrians

[The Sogdians] excel in commerce and love gain; once a man reaches the age of twenty, he goes off to the neighbouring realms; wherever there are profits to be made, they go.

Xin Tang Shu 221: 6233

The people [of Bactria] are poor in the use of arms and afraid of battle, but they are clever at commerce.

Sima Qian, Shiji, 123

Due to a lack of written sources, reconstructing the historical development and differentiation of the various Iranian dialects must remain speculative, as must the migrations of the Iranian tribes that spoke them, and many puzzles remain. The most important Iranian language of Central Asia to appear in historical times was Sogdian, which, along with Bactrian which developed further south, is classified by linguists as belonging to the 'East Iranian' branch. Such 'geographic' labels are often anatopic, however, since some tribes criss-crossed during the course of their historical migrations. Thus, the 'East-Iranian'-speaking Ossetes, descendants of the nomadic Sarmatians and Alans, are located today in the middle Caucasus, while the 'West-Iranian' Baluch are spread out across the southern parts of eastern Iran, southern Afghanistan and western Pakistan.

The Pontic Greek geographer Strabo, writing around the beginning of the Common Era, leads us to understand that the various eastern Aryan dialects were at that time still mutually comprehensible: 'The name also of Ariana is extended so as to include some part of Persia, Media, and the north of Bactria and Sogdiana; for these nations speak nearly the same language.'[1]

The earliest written trace of Sogdian – a series of bricks from Kultobe near Shymkent in southern Kazakhstan – dates back only as far as the second century CE,[2] but Sogdiana (Suguda) is listed as an Achaemenid province in the Bisotun inscription of the Persian king Darius I seven centuries earlier, so a Sogdian identity distinct from that of neighbouring Iranian tribes must have taken shape sometime prior to that. The Sogdians are also mentioned in the Young Avestan text known as the *Vidēvdāt*, parts of which may pre-date the Achaemenids: 'The second of the good lands and countries which I, Ahura Mazda, created, was the plain (?) which the Sughdhas inhabit.'[3]

Cyrus II ('the Great') conquered Sogdiana in 540 BCE and founded a city he then named after himself, Cyropolis, probably at Kurkat (Sog. **Kuru(š)-kanθā-* 'Cyrus' city', Gk. *Kyra Eschata*)[4] near modern Khujand. Returning to Central Asia ten years later in an attempt to consolidate his conquests there, Cyrus was killed in battle fighting the Massagetae, a Saka tribe led by Queen Tahmirish, known to the Greeks as Tomyris. Herodotus writes that Tomyris had Cyrus decapitated and his head brought to her in a blood-filled wineskin,[5] recalling a widely attested steppe tradition where a defeated ruler's skull would be used as a wine cup.

Interestingly, contemporary Tajik nation-building ideology has been able to accommodate both Cyrus and Tomyris as 'Tajik' national heroes. The legacy of the Achaemenids is commemorated in monuments throughout Tajikistan and in school textbooks, notably in Khujand at the Hall of Aryan Culture in the Sughd Museum and in a modern mosaic going up the steps of Somonī Park across the Syr Darya. Situated halfway between these two, however, on the south bank of the river a row of statues honouring great historical 'Tajik' figures begins to the left with a fearsome-looking bust of Tomyris. (It ends with one of the Soviet academician Bobojon Ghafurov on the right.)

Sogdiana represented the northeastern limits of the Achaemenid Empire and has formed the edge of the Iranian world ever since, a transition zone between the settled urban oases of southern Central Asia and the nomadic steppe societies to the north. Its importance to the Achaemenids was marginal, however. For them it was a buffer zone against the nomads, and a place to resettle exiled populations from the heart of the empire. This may have included Jews from Babylonia, who have a long history of presence in Bukhara, Samarkand and throughout the region. The 'Bukharan Jews', as they were historically known, became culturally Iranicized, speaking Persian up to the present day, and they were an important community across southern Central Asia up to modern times (though most have now migrated to Israel or the United States). By the late Achaemenid period Sogdiana was governed from the satrapy of Bactria, which lay south of the Oxus in what is now Afghanistan.

The settled inhabitants of southern Central Asia had long been trading with the northern nomads – mostly Iranian-speakers ancestral to the Sakas/Scythians – but gemstones such as lapis lazuli and garnet were exported to western Iran, as had been the case since the BMAC period. The oldest surviving example of a knotted pile carpet, found at Pazyryk in the Altai Mountains and dated to around the fourth century BCE, was apparently produced in an urban workshop in either Sogdiana or Bactria, but using dyes obtained from the Saka nomads.[6]

Samarkand, at the centre of the Zarafshan River valley that constituted the Sogdian heartland, was already a walled city by the time Cyrus brought the region under nominal Achaemenid control. Other urban sites of the period have been identified at Kök-Tepe some 30 kilometres to the north and near Shahr-i Sabz to the south, as well as east of Sogdiana in the Ferghana valley.

Alexander in Central Asia

By the late Achaemenid period imperial rule weighed lightly on the eastern part of the Iranian world. The Persian army defeated by Alexander of Macedon at Gaugamela (near modern Duhok in Iraqi Kurdistan) in 331 BCE included a division led by the satrap of Bactria and Sogdiana, Bessos, who had been ruling the eastern provinces virtually as a private fiefdom. Following Alexander's victory, Bessos, together with the satrap of neighbouring Arachosia, Barsaentes, arrested and executed the defeated Achaemenid emperor, Darius III.[7] This set off an impressive series of betrayals, which ultimately resulted in the Macedonians establishing their rule over Central Asia.

Upon executing Darius, Bessos had himself crowned as the new emperor and moved the imperial administration east to Bactria away from the advancing Macedonian armies. The Central Asian Achaemenid rump state proved short-lived, however. Alexander conquered Bactria in the spring of 329, and Bessos fled to Sogdiana. There, his Sogdian deputy Spitamenes turned on Bessos and handed him over to the Macedonians for execution.

Alexander demonstrated his intention of bringing Central Asia fully into the Hellenistic fold by building Greek-style cities – all of which he named after himself – in which to settle his garrisons. Remains from these Hellenistic towns have revealed a rich trove of relics attesting to the blending of Greek and Iranian cultures in the region during the centuries following Alexander's conquests.

It was while founding another of these settlements, Alexandria Eschata ('Alexandria the Furthest') in the Ferghana Valley – likely at Khujand near the site of the town established earlier by Cyrus the Great – that Alexander received word that Spitamenes had raised a rebellion in Sogdiana and had put the Macedonian garrison at Samarkand under siege. The army he sent to confront the Sogdians was roundly defeated. Moreover, the Sogdians then began to march on Bactria, which was defended by the former Persian satrap Artabazus, who now ruled there on behalf of Alexander. The Sogdians and the pro-Macedonian Bactrians held each other to a standoff until late 328 when Spitamenes was treacherously murdered by his own wife, who then sent his head to Alexander as a peace offering. Modern Tajiks, ever in search of patriotic national heroes, have recently renamed an administrative district near Khujand in Spitamenes' honour.

Notwithstanding the mariticide of their leader, a group of Sogdians continued to defy the Macedonian invasion, taking refuge in a fortress known as the Sogdian Rock. When Alexander finally succeeded in penetrating this stronghold in early 327 his gaze fell upon Roxana, the sixteen-year-old daughter of a Sogdian-Bactrian nobleman, Oxyartes, who had joined the anti-Macedonian resistance. Impressed by Alexander's gentlemanly treatment of his captives Oxyartes switched his loyalties to the Macedonians, and was eventually rewarded with a governorship in India. Alexander married Roxana later that year.

Roxana accompanied her husband on his successful India campaign but then went to live in Susa, the former Achaemenid capital in southwestern Iran. Following Alexander's unexpected death in 323 she became embroiled in the subsequent succession struggles on behalf of her unborn son, who was crowned at birth as Alexander IV. The great conqueror's direct descendant and first successor was half-Sogdian! It was not to last, however. After years of civil war which lasted throughout his childhood, in 309 the fourteen-year-old Alexander and his mother were both assassinated on the orders of the usurper Cassander.

The Seleucid Empire

In the event Cassander was not the most successful among the so-called *Diadokhoi* ('the Successors') who sought to claim the legacy of Alexander the Great. He did manage to maintain control over peninsular Greece in the west, but the territories from Babylonia all the way across Iran and Central Asia to India were consolidated by 312 under the rule of another Macedonian general, Seleucus I Nicator. Seleucus had followed Alexander's bridging-of-cultures example by marrying the executed Sogdian commander Spitamenes' daughter Apama in 324.

Seleucus ruled for some thirty years, establishing such important cities as Antioch on the Mediterranean coast (modern Antakya in southern Turkey) and Seleucia-on-the-Tigris in Mesopotamia. Both became cosmopolitan centres, where East and West would meet and mix. Seleucus was succeeded by his son, Antiochus I Soter (r. 281–261), who, through his mother Apama, was half-Sogdian. Over a cumulative reign of half a century, father and son laid the foundations for a Hellenistic–Iranian hybrid empire that would unite the diverse peoples inhabiting lands from the Mediterranean to India, creating a cultural melting pot the likes of which the world had never before seen. Greek migrants spread their language, along with their architectural, theatrical and philosophical traditions, all across the Middle East, Central Asia and northern India, even as they assimilated many aspects of local culture wherever they settled.

Bactria became a region of central importance under the Seleucids, whereas Sogdiana remained on the imperial periphery to the north, ever a buffer against nomadic raids. The Greeks did carry out a number of building renovations in Samarkand, however, and Greek coins were the first to be used there in what had previously been a barter economy. Indeed, these coins continued to circulate throughout Central Asia even after the Seleucids and their

Greco-Bactrian successors were overrun by waves of nomadic invasions from the steppes during the mid-second century BCE.

The archaeological site at Ay Khanum in northern Bactria, which has been identified as the Hellenistic town of Alexandria-on-the-Oxus, revealed a fertile synthesis of Greek and local Iranian cultures during the Seleucid period. One can see a vivid example of this in the conflation of their respective deities, which were sometimes even worshipped within the same physical structure. A shrine in honour of the city's founder, Kineas, contains a Greek inscription from Delphi inscribed by a visitor who may have been the philosopher Klearchos of Soloi, a student of Aristotle:

> Παῖς ὢν κόσμιος γίνου,
> ἡβῶν ἐγκρατής,
> μέσος δίκαιος,
> πρεσβύτης εὔβουλος,
> τελευτῶν ἄλυπος.
>
> As a child, be well behaved;
> As a young man, self- controlled;
> In middle age, be just;
> As an elder, be of good counsel;
> And when you come to the end, be without grief.[8]

The overall urban plan of Ay Khanum is decidedly Greek, featuring monumental buildings with Corinthian, Doric, and Ionian columns, a gymnasium, an agora (market) and a theatre able to seat 6,000 people. On the other hand, the three religious temples found there are all Iranian in design. The mansions of the wealthy were also built in the regional style, suggesting that local elites continued to do well under Hellenistic rule. In the realm of household items, both Greek and local Iranian pottery techniques were used.[9] The remains of other, smaller Hellenistic cities in the region have been identified at Saksanokhur and Kalai Mir in southern Tajikistan, at Dalverzin Tepe in southern Uzbekistan and at Dilbergine Tepe northwest of Mazar-i Sharif in northern Afghanistan. (Bactria at that time included the regions both north and south of the Oxus River.)

Another site on the Tajikistan side of the river, where the Vakhsh joins the Panj to form the Oxus, is the complex at Ta<u>kh</u>t-i Sangīn, which has also been dated to the Seleucid period.[10] The most significant building at the site is the so-called 'Oxus temple', which was devoted to the local river god, known to the Iranians as Vakhsh (or Wakhshu) and to the Greeks as Oxes. An altar at the temple contained a bronze statue with the donor's dedication in Greek: 'Atrosok devoted to Oxes according to promise.' The temple may have been the source of the so-called 'Oxus treasure', a rich hoard of gold and silver objects including sculptures, coins, jewellery, votive plaques and drinking vessels that were discovered around 1880. Most of these precious items are now housed in the British Museum in London.

Bactria's economic importance under the Seleucids continued to overshadow that of Sogdiana, just as it had in Achaemenid times. Rich in irrigated agriculture, the region also supplied soldiers and elephants (from India) for the imperial army, and – as had been the case for several thousand years at least – it served as a transit point for lapis lazuli mined in nearby Badakhshan. The administrative apparatus of the Achaemenids was maintained, but Greek replaced Aramaic as the language of the bureaucracy. The secretarial class appears to have been mainly Persian rather than local, a holdover from the time of Achaemenid rule.[11]

Nomadic invasions

From the mid-second century BCE onwards the eastern Iranian world fell under the sway of warlike nomadic groups migrating southwards from the steppes. The written records of these events are mostly Chinese, so the point of view they represent is somewhat removed from the Central Asian context. It would appear that the political balance amongst the various bands of nomads living to the north of China was shifting, causing some tribes to migrate towards the southwest, where they took over control of Sogdiana and Bactria.

Steppe politics were always determined by ever-shifting alliances among tribes that were often culturally and even linguistically diverse, sometimes to a high degree. This makes it difficult in any given historical context to determine accurately the ethnic makeup of any particular tribal confederation. Throughout the second and first millennia BCE the Eurasian plains were dominated by nomadic populations who spoke old Indo-European dialects, including both Indo-Iranian and Tokharian, but by around 500 BCE various Altaic peoples – speakers of proto-Turkic and proto-Mongolian – were also moving into the region from the East, adding their languages and DNA to the fluid cultures of the steppes.

Connecting with China

The Chinese sources indicate that during the first half of the second century BCE a people they call the Yuezhi (月氏) – whom Western scholars have identified as most likely having been an ethnically mixed group under the leadership of Indo-European-speaking Tokharians[12] – were driven out of their homeland in Gansu province by a rival nomadic group they call the Xiongnu (匈奴), possibly ancestors to the historical Huns. The Yuezhi, made up of five major tribal groups, moved west and mixed with Iranian-speaking Saka tribes. Together, they progressively asserted their control of the eastern part of the Seleucid Empire, establishing suzerainty over the settled peoples of Sogdiana and Bactria.

In 138 BCE the Chinese Han emperor Wu, feeling hemmed in economically by the growing power of the Xiongnu to the northwest, sent a military delegation headed by an official named Zhang Qian to seek an alliance with the Yuezhi against their common enemy. Unfortunately for Zhang Qian he was captured by the Xiongnu along the way and imprisoned for the next ten years. Eventually, however, he was able to escape and cross the Tian Shan mountains into the Ferghana Valley (called Dayuan –大宛 – by the Chinese).

Zhang Qian was impressed by what he saw there, including the production of wine and, more importantly, high-quality horses such as were not bred in China. (He stated that these horses 'sweated blood', but this appearance may have been due to skin parasites.) From Ferghana he continued westward into Sogdiana proper (Ch. Kangju, 康居), then south to Bactria (Ch. Daxia, 大夏) where he witnessed the hybrid Greco-Iranian culture into which the Tokharian-Saka Yuezhi nomadic elite had recently begun to integrate themselves. Heading back towards China after a year-long stay amongst the Yuezhi, the hapless Zhang Qian was captured a second time by the Xiongnu. Once again he escaped, this time after only two years. He reached the imperial capital at Chang'an (modern Xian) in 125 BCE, thirteen years after he had originally set out.

Zhang Qian's remarkable adventures and rich reports of Central Asia are celebrated in the official chronicles written by the Han historian Sima Qian (d. 86 BCE), who says of the Sogdians that 'The men all have deep set eyes and profuse beards and whiskers. They are skilful at commerce and will haggle over a fraction of a cent.'[13] This depiction would lay the foundation for Chinese stereotypes of the Sogdians that would endure for nearly a millennium.

An informal consensus among modern Western scholars has credited Zhang Qian with 'opening the Silk Road', though this is a somewhat questionable attribution for a number of reasons. First, while the Chinese traveller was indeed able to provide the imperial court for the first time with detailed information about Central Asia, in practice due to the presence of the Xiongnu the Chinese were not able to act on it so as to establish regular trade with the region. Second, the steppe nomads had already been serving as conduits for goods and technologies between China and the West for a millennium or longer (it was presumably they who introduced wheeled chariots and forged weapons to the Chinese by around 1200 BCE), so it seems somewhat arbitrary – not to say wholly inaccurate – to single out Zhang Qian's experience for special attention.

And last, but certainly not least, it should be pointed out that the very concept of a 'Silk Road' is a modern construction. The term was first coined by a German geographer-spy, Ferdinand von Richthofen, only as recently as the 1880s, against the backdrop of his country's desire to compete with Britain and Russia in Europe's imperialist 'Great Game' for control of Central Asia. In the final analysis, however distantly in the past we can speak of trans-Eurasian overland trade, and whether we date it to the second century BCE or to a millennium or even two before that, the fact is that none of the actors involved had any notion they were participating in anything so discrete or identifiable as the term 'Silk Road' implies.

In any case, it is during Han times that the Sogdians first enter the documented historical record via Chinese sources. A set of official records from Xuanquan, near Dunhuang, mentions Sogdian delegations visiting China as early as 52 BCE. The same group of documents registers the complaint of another party of Sogdian merchants thirteen years later, who felt they had been cheated by their

Chinese hosts; not surprisingly, the local court found in favour of the Chinese. Valerie Hansen suggests that the latter may have deliberately mistreated the Sogdians as punishment for cooperating with the Xiongnu.[14]

Further to the west, the nomadic newcomers called 'Tocharoi' by Greek writers – apparently identical with the Yuezhi of the Chinese sources whom the Xiongnu had pushed out of the Gansu corridor – established themselves as successors to the local Greco-Bactrian kings. (A northern province of Afghanistan retains the name 'Takhar' to this day.) They maintained many of the existing local institutions, such as the minting of coins in Greek. By the second half of the first century they had also adopted Bactrian – an east Iranian dialect close to Sogdian – as their official language, and they used the Greek alphabet for writing it. Within a few decades one of the five original Yuezhi tribes, the Kushanas, took control of the confederation. Over the next two centuries they expanded their state towards the East, incorporating much of northern India even as far as Benares, to create what came to be known as the Kushan Empire.

The Kushan civilization is poorly documented by written records, such that establishing its history has proved highly vexing. It left a rich artistic legacy, however, particularly in the realm of Buddhism. Buddhist art – first associated with the region of Gandhara in what is now north-central Pakistan – developed as a result of Greek influence, and flourished throughout the early centuries of the Common Era when depictions of the Buddha through sculpture and, later, painting became common. Much of the population in Gandhara and Bactria became Buddhist during this period, perhaps thanks to the more inclusive approach favoured by practitioners of the newly emerging populist Mahayana movement as compared to the daunting rigorousness of the earlier Nikaya schools, of which only the Theravada survives today. Bactria, including southern Transoxiana, remained a Buddhist stronghold up to the time of the Muslim conquests of the seventh and eighth centuries.

The Kushan elites were generally supportive of Buddhism, but ruling over a highly cosmopolitan society they were pragmatic enough to support Iranian and Greek cults as well and even in some cases Indian ones such as that of Shiva. Often the various ethnic deities were conflated, for example the Greek Zeus with the Zoroastrian Ahura Mazda or the Indian Shiva with the Avestan wind god Vayu. Such syncretism is abundantly attested through Kushan gold coins, which bear an impressive range of identifiable iconographies.

Jewish communities had existed in the region since the eighth century BCE, as attested in II Kings 18:11: 'And the king of Assyria carried Israel away unto Assyria, and put them in Halah, and in Habor, on the river of Gozan, and in the cities of the Medes.' Later on, Christianity, thanks to the religious tolerance of the Parthians and the Kushans, became firmly established in the eastern Iranian lands during the second century CE. Amongst the Bactrian general population, however, the most important deities appear to have been the youthful Iranian solar deity Mithra (identified with the Greek Apollo or Helios), the east-Iranian fertility goddess Ardokhsho (who appears in the Avesta as Ashi) and the god of the Oxus River, Vakhshu. Cults devoted to other Iranian deities such as Atsho (Av. Atar, 'fire') and Farro (Av. Khvarnah, 'divine glory'), as well as the Greek hero Herakles (or his unknown Iranian counterpart) were also widespread.

There is little or no evidence, however, for the presence of a specifically Zoroastrian rite – as distinct from pan-Iranian polytheism – in Bactria prior to the Sasanian incursions which followed the Kushan period.[15] The early Sasanians, following the directives of the Zoroastrian high priest Kardir in the late third century CE, destroyed all manner of religious sites during their campaigns in an effort to stamp out competing cults. This included Buddhist stupas throughout Bactria, as well as sanctuaries devoted to Iranian and other deities such as the 'Victory Temple' of Kanishka at Surkh Kotal where Mithraic, Hellenistic and Indian elements have been found.[16]

In 84 CE, the Kushans crossed the Tian Shan Mountains to assist the Han Chinese in suppressing a rebellion in Kashgar that was supported by the Sogdians. By 116 the Kushans had taken Kashgar, Yarkand and Khotan from the Chinese. This territorial expansion placed the Kushans at the nexus of commercial activity between India, China and even as far as the Roman Empire in the west. The resulting stabilization of trade routes – what we now call the Silk Road – facilitated the transmission of Buddhism, and later Christianity, Manichaeism and Islam, from Central Asia into China.[17] The oasis of Khotan on the southern rim of the Takla Makan desert became a major centre of Buddhist activity under the Kushans.

Most of the Sogdian lands – those referred to as 'Kangju' by Zhang Qian – remained outside the Kushans' northern borders. (The region south of the Hisor Mountains in modern Tajikistan was historically part of Bactria.) Sogdiana was under the nominal suzerainty of a succession of nomadic confederations, such as the Hunnic Chionites and Kidarites, the ethnically mixed Hephtalites, and, finally, the Turks. In practice, local authority was exercised by petty rulers based in towns such as Kish (modern Shahr-i Sabz), Chach (Tashkent), Samarkand, Paykand (southwest of Bukhara) and Nakhshab (today's Qarshi).

Archaeological remains suggest that Samarkand had undergone a considerable decline in population and economic activity since Seleucid times,[18] a trend that was exacerbated by its invasion and subsequent looting and destruction by the Sasanian army under Shapur I around 260 CE. During the following century, the Sogdians fared better as vassals of the nomadic Chionites and Kidarites with whom their economic relationship was symbiotic, rather than competitive as it was with the more urbanized Sasanians. (It is unclear whether the Chionites were Iranian-speaking nomads or, as is sometimes argued, proto-Turks. Their Middle Persian name, Khyon, may have been transferred at some point to an unrelated group known to Europeans as the Huns.) While the Sogdians' relationship with the peoples of the steppe was not always free of conflict, in general terms they were more inclined to ally themselves with their nomadic Central Asian neighbours than with the comparatively distant imperial power of Iran, notwithstanding their closer ethnic affinity with the latter.

Despite the increasing role of Sogdian merchants in trans-Asian trade, agriculture remained the mainstay of the Sogdian economy, especially throughout the Zarafshan River basin. Even as late as the seventh century when Sogdian trade was at its peak, a Chinese account states that half of the population of the Sogdian colony at Suyab were farmers and the other half traders.[19] Reflecting the ancient Indo-European model the Sogdians had a class-based society comprised of landowning aristocrats, called *azarkar* (Pers. *dihqān*), tradesmen and labourers – urban craftsmen and rural peasants – in addition to substantial numbers of slaves. The latter category included prisoners of war, hostages and individuals who willingly enslaved themselves for protection. *Azarkar*s had at their disposal private armies of armed subjects, called *chakir*s. The highest ranking among the *azarkar*s was called the Ikhshid. In written documents this term was represented by the Aramaic ideogram *MLK*', meaning 'king', but in reality he was more like a local chieftain.

Sogdian trade

Sogdiana would never come to be a strong unified state, yet Sogdian traders dramatically increased their participation in the expanding Central Asian trade under the Kushans, thereby laying the foundations for a network they would soon come to dominate. Chinese records show that Sogdian trading families lived in both China and India by the second century CE.[20] Earlier Indian sources such as the Mahabharata and the Puranas mention the Sogdians (Skt. Cūlīka), though not specifically in connection with trading activities. However, Indic loanwords in Sogdian – including the words for 'caravan' (*sārtha*) and 'price' (*mūlya*) – attest to the antiquity as well as to the importance of commercial interactions between Sogdians and Indians.[21]

The so-called 'Sogdian Ancient Letters' found at Dunhuang, which include detailed information about business transactions among Sogdian traders, provide evidence that Sogdian merchant communities were well established in China by the early fourth century, and that they constituted an organized, widely spread trading network.[22] Closer to India, a proliferation of Sogdian graffiti found in the 1980s during the construction of the Karakorum Highway in the Upper Indus Valley – more than 650 of them – offer an indication that Sogdian merchants were beginning to displace their Bactrian competitors by around the same time.[23] Sogdians served as middlemen for the Parthians to the west, who supplied Rome with Chinese silk. It is remarkable that within the space of a few centuries the Sogdians would be able to achieve such a primary status in the trans-Eurasian economy, in the absence of any strong state support at home.

Sogdian traders and translators played a central role in the transmission of Buddhism, Manichaeism and Christianity to China. Strangely, however – and even though Samarkand became an important administrative centre for both the Manichaean and Nestorian Christian churches – none of these religions ever seems to have been practised by more than a small proportion of the population of Sogdiana itself, where local varieties of ancient Iranian cults predominated up to the time of the Muslim conquests.

Even Zoroastrianism (or, more correctly, Mazdaism) is rather weakly attested there, at least in the form it has come down to us which took shape in Sasanian Iran during the third to sixth centuries. Sogdiana was nominally incorporated as a Sasanian province in the year 260, but as with previous empires its distant location ensured that imperial rule rested lightly if at all. Although many scholars interpret the presence of fire temples to mean that the Sogdians were Zoroastrian, the use of fire in religious rituals is not distinctive of Zoroastrianism, and, as previously noted, there is little in the way of textual or archaeological evidence for a specifically Mazdaean rite in Central Asia. Well to the contrary, most surviving traces of pre-Islamic religious practice there suggest rather different uses and interpretations of ancient Iranian symbols and rituals than what is found in western Iran, despite their often similar appearance.

The native Sogdian pantheon was regionally diverse, with the cult of the youthful martyr god Siyāvash being particularly strong in Bukhara, for example. Siyāvash's death was commemorated every year with laments known as *kīn-i Siyāvuš*,[24] likely a survival of mourning rituals for the youthful god Tammuzi imported from Mesopotamia during the BMAC period. On the occasion of the vernal equinox every Bukharan was meant to sacrifice a cock in his honour before dawn to mark the New Year.[25] The mourning songs and dances known as *tanbars*, which are often depicted on Sogdian ossuaries, have been connected with Siyāvash's cult, and traditional forms still practised by Tajiks today may derive from them.[26]

The Mesopotamian fertility goddess Nanai was the deity enjoying the most widespread following among the Sogdians, as had apparently already been the case among the Oxus/BMAC peoples two millennia previously (Figure 2.1). Numerous altars have been found that were dedicated to her, and Sogdian texts mention many individuals whose names – such as 'Nanaivandak' (servant of Nanai), 'Nanaidhat' (gift of Nanai), 'Nanaifarn' (Nanai-given Fortune) and others – reflect the popularity of her cult. The extraordinary persistence of this goddess-worshipping tradition is likely due to the centrality of agriculture to the region's economy. Material culture, including coins and household objects, shows that from late Kushan times Nanai gradually became assimilated to the Iranian water goddess Anahita and was eventually subsumed by her, probably due to Sasanian influence; this transformation began in Bactria and then moved further north.

Against this backdrop, where the majority followed local versions of various Iranian cults, the attachment of some Sogdians to foreign religions

Figure 2.1 Sogdian wall painting depicting the goddess Nanai or Anahita. Seventh or eighth century CE. Museum of National Antiquities, Dushanbe.

was likely due to the fact that Buddhism, Manichaeism and Christianity were all missionary faiths that developed extensive networks of monasteries along the trade routes. This created a reciprocal relationship whereby traders on business trips could reliably find lodging in the local establishments associated with their chosen faith, which they would support in turn through financial donations. Monasteries also served as warehouses for merchants' goods, and would lend them money at interest rates as high as 10 per cent per month.[27]

Most surviving Sogdian texts are religious in nature, but a majority of these come from China, where they were left by Sogdian expatriates. Sogdian translators living in exile – travelling merchants being of necessity multilingual – rendered a wide range of Buddhist, Manichaean and Christian holy scriptures from their original languages into Sogdian, Chinese or other languages. At the same time, large numbers of Sogdians who settled in China continued to observe their native Iranian cults, as attested by the temples and funerary monuments they built in the Sogdian quarters of Chinese cities. Although the Sogdian religion shared many ancient Iranian divinities and mythological elements (such as the souls of the deceased passing over the Chinvat bridge) in common with the Zoroastrianism of the Sasanians in Persia, in China the bureaucracy considered the two to be distinct religious systems and treated them as such.

By the fifth century Sogdians were the principal agents of trade between China and the West, with permanent colonies all along the northern and southern routes around the Takla Makan desert, at Dunhuang near the edge of the Gansu corridor, and in Chinese cities such as Chang'an and Luoyang. The Chinese government incorporated the leaders of Sogdian communities into their administration, according them the title *sabao* (from Sogdian *sartapao*) which meant 'caravan leader'. Trading mainly in luxury goods such as silk, these communities thrived in China and many Sogdian merchants became extremely wealthy, as attested by the lavishly decorated stone tombs they built for themselves. Sogdians became recognized figures in Chinese popular culture, stereotyped as being genetically programmed for commerce. As one Chinese writer put it, the Sogdians are 'mostly avaricious and take account of money matters even between father and son'. The same writer notes, however, that 'Rich men are honoured and esteemed, and there is no distinction between the well-born and the low-born. A millionaire … may lead a simple and coarse life.'[28]

Sogdians had also been trading with the northern nomads since prehistoric times. With the gradual encroachment of Turkic tribes into the steppe world from the fifth century onwards, Sogdian traders served as intermediaries between the Turks and the Chinese. (Sasanian Iran, which had never managed to exercise real control beyond the Oxus, formally ceded Sogdiana to the nomadic steppe-based Turks in 560.) As such – since without a strong state of their own they were not seen as a political threat by either side – Sogdians served to link the nomads with the civilized world, transmitting to them religion and literacy, among other cultural commodities, while enjoying the Turks' political protection in return. During the seventh century the Sogdians extended their agricultural colonies northeastwards as far as the Seven Rivers region: The Sogdian towns of Talas, Navakat (near today's Bishkek) and Suyab (modern Tokmak), all situated in what is now Kyrgyzstan, grew and thrived through their interactions with powerful tribal confederations such as the Göktürks.

As the Turks' political power increased across the Eurasian steppe, so rose the fortunes of the Sogdian merchants under their protection. Sogdians served as the Turks' ambassadors to the great imperial states: China in the East, and Sasanian Iran and the Byzantine Empire to the West. On the other hand, the efforts of Sogdian merchants to gain direct access to Iran were thwarted by the Sasanian government, since they were seen as competing with the Persians as intermediaries between Eastern and Western markets.[29] To circumvent this, in 568 an embassy led by the Sogdian merchant Maniakh succeeded in opening up trade with the Byzantine Empire by bypassing Iran via the steppe routes north of the Caspian Sea, enabling the Sogdians to sell the Byzantines silk received by the Turks as payoff from the Chinese. A trading post called Sogdaia was established in Khazar territory on the Crimean Peninsula along the northern coast of the Black Sea, presumably an indication of Sogdian presence there.[30] The Sogdians traded not just in silk but also in slaves, silver and other precious metals, brass, amber, musk, turmeric and sugar.

The Tang period was marked by an uncharacteristic Chinese fascination for foreign cultural products as well. Sogdian musicians, singers and dancers accompanied the China-bound caravans; their performances were highly appreciated by the Chinese elites, and they also found ready employment in the oasis towns of the Silk Road. Sogdian dances – the most famous of which was the so-called 'Whirlwind Dance' – were immortalized in paintings and on decorative plates and other vessels. The celebrated ninth-century Tang poet Bo Juyi writes evocatively of a performance by dancers from the city of Chach (modern Tashkent):

> Matched pair spread flat – the brocaded mats unroll;
> Linked beats of triple sounds – the painted drums drive on.
> Red wax candles are taken away, peach petals rise;
> Purple net shirts are set in motion – the Chach (dancers) come!
> Girdles droop from gilded thighs, flowered waists are heavy,
> Hats revolve with golden bells, snowy faces turn.
> I watch – too soon the tune is done, they will not be detained;
> Whirling in clouds, escorted by rain, they are off to the Terrace of the Sun.[31]

Sogdian merchants established colonies in all the major Chinese cities and became the principal agents of Chinese commerce with the West. They lived in their own neighbourhoods, constituting communities that were officially recognized by the Chinese government. Sogdians in China left many traces, including material culture, religious temples and funerary architecture, some of which have survived up to the present day. Their close relationship with the steppe nomads – who were a constant threat from the Chinese point of view – is summed up in a Tang dynasty official's report to the Emperor which stated that 'The Turks [Ch. Tujue, 突厥] are essentially artless and uncomplicated, and one may promote discord among them; unfortunately there live among them many Sogdians who are cunning and shrewd and who instruct and direct them'.[32]

Sogdian art

Wealthy elites have always been the principal patrons of art, and the Sogdians were no exception. The success of Sogdian businessmen in trans-Eurasian trade from the fourth through the eighth centuries created a social class with sufficient disposable income to spend on building lavish homes, which in many cases were decorated with spectacular wall paintings. The best preserved of these have been found at Afrasiyab in the northeastern part of Samarkand, at Panjakent across the border of Tajikistan some sixty kilometres to the east, and at Varakhsha near Bukhara. Further examples have been uncovered in the region of Ustrushana (Istaravshon) southwest of Khujand, and at Erkurgan in Qashqadaryo.

The mural paintings from Sogdian houses display a wide range of iconographies. Some depict deities or religious themes, while others show scenes from heroic tales of popular literature. Still others elicit the lives of the Sogdian elites themselves, such as banquet scenes. The murals are in many cases quite large, up to four metres in height and eleven metres wide.

Perhaps the best known of these wall paintings are those found in the so-called Hall of Ambassadors at Afrasiyab, dating to the mid-seventh century. One wall seems to portray a New Year ceremony (Nawrūz), although some have argued that it depicts a religious rite. Another wall is related to India, and includes images of Krishna fighting demons – or, as has alternatively been proposed, perhaps it is meant as an illustration of the Vedic horse sacrifice (*asvamedha*). A third wall is replete with Chinese motifs, including possibly the Chinese New Year celebration. It includes a ritual hunting scene, and also a pond with a woman in a boat feeding a fish. Taken together, such murals may have been a way for well-to-do Sogdians to flatter visiting business partners from India and China by connecting local cultural ceremonies with their own.[33]

At Panjakent about one-third of the houses excavated to date had mural paintings in at least one of their rooms, representing a considerable expense for their owners.[34] These have been dated to the 740s, well into the period of Muslim incursions into the region. The homes of the wealthiest typically had religious paintings facing the entrance hall, depicting the owner's favoured deity or deities. Illustrations on the surrounding walls were of hunting expeditions and lavish banquets evoking the elites' lifestyle, or else of popular stories associated with Rustam or other Iranian legendary heroes. Again reflecting the Sogdian merchants' international connections, one also finds images from works of Indian literature such as the Mahabharata and the Panchatantra (the basis for the Kalila and Dimna animal stories that would become so popular in later Islamic times) as well as Aesop's fables from Greece such as 'The Goose Who Laid the Golden Eggs', and even in one case a depiction of Rome's legendary founders Romulus and Remus as babies being suckled by a wolf.

Further west at Varakhsha, the eighth-century palace of the local Bukharan ruler Tughshada provides additional examples of Sogdian wall painting, dating to around 730. Tughshada spent several decades trying to fend off the invading Muslims through armed resistance, and when that didn't work, by feigned submission, which he would then recant whenever he thought he could get away with it. A mural in the Eastern Hall of his palace shows him, together with his wife, performing devotions to the Sogdian god of war, Vashagn (the Avestan Verethragna), clear evidence that his periodic professions of 'submission' (Ar. *islām*) to the Muslim imperialists were purely opportunistic.

Central Asian Buddhism

Buddhism established strong roots in Bactria during the Kushan period, and it appears to have thrived there until the time of the Muslim conquests. The colossal Buddhas of the Bamiyan valley of central Afghanistan – tragically destroyed by the fanatical Taliban regime in 2001 – were the best-known relics of this legacy, but in fact Buddhist objects have been found all over Bactria, including what is now southern Tajikistan. Thanks to the material support of

Buddhist merchants who dominated the trade networks linking India and the West with China, many Buddhist monasteries became fabulously rich. This led to frequent attacks by nomadic raiders seeking to plunder their treasures. In Tajikistan today, remains of such institutions can be found throughout the southern province of Khatlon (at Kofir-kala, Kofarnihon, Khuttal and Ushtur-mullo), as well as in the Wakhan corridor at Vrang on the upper reaches of the Panj River which forms the border with Afghanistan. Survivals of Buddhist influence can be seen today in traditional Tajik jewellery – for example, in wedding diadems and filigree brooches from around Kulob.

The celebrated Chinese traveller Xuanzang, a monk who travelled overland to India in search of authentic Buddhist manuscripts during the mid-seventh century, left a detailed account of his journey. He portrays Bactria as a major Buddhist centre with over one hundred monasteries spread throughout the region, inhabited by more than 3,000 monks. Describing the Nava Vihara (New Monastery) on the outskirts of Balkh Xuanzang mentions a statue of the Buddha 'adorned with famous jewels' as well as 'halls decorated with rare precious substances'. He notes that 'For this reason, the rulers of various countries attacked the monastery, in order to capture its valuables'.[35] Xuanzang visited Sogdiana as well but found little trace of Buddhism being practised there. He visited two abandoned monasteries at Samarkand, where Buddhist pilgrims[36] seeking a place to spend the night would be chased away by 'fire-worshipping priests', defenders of the local Iranian religion.

Buddhist presence is more evident in southern Tajikistan, where a former Buddhist monastery at Ajina-Tepe functioned for about one hundred years until it was destroyed by Muslim invaders in the mid-eighth century. A twelve-metre reclining Buddha statue from this site, now in the Museum of National Antiquities in Dushanbe, is the largest surviving relic of Buddhist art in all of Central Asia (see Figure 2.2).

Muslim invasions

The political, social and economic upheavals to Western Asia brought about by the eruption of a highly motivated and effective Muslim army out of Arabia beginning in the 630s were slow to reach Central Asia. While the Arabs were

Figure 2.2 Reclining Buddha. Seventh century. Ajina-Tepe, Tajikistan. Now in the Museum of National Antiquities, Dushanbe.

certainly inspired by the sense of unity and religious superiority the recently revealed Qur'an had provided them, the primary impulse for their campaigns was arguably economic. Raiding had always been central to the Arab economy, and with all the Arab tribes now being united under one leadership they could no longer raid each other and had to turn elsewhere. It is no accident that the Arab campaigns aimed at bringing the major commercial centres and trade routes under their control, and that with each new victory their first action was to take over the administration of the marketplace.

With the fairly rapid collapse of the Sasanian Empire the Persian mercantile and landowning classes soon submitted to Arab rule. The Arabic word *islām* literally means 'submission', and the evidence suggests that many early 'converts' understood this as submission to the Arabs *themselves* in the first instance and only secondarily to their new religion, which had not yet assumed its full shape and would take another two to three centuries to do so. Moreover, the Arabs absorbed much of the defeated Persian soldiery into their army so that by the time the Muslims reached the Sogdian and Bactrian lands a significant proportion of them were ethnic Persians. Given the existing political, economic and cultural connections between the Sasanians and Sogdiana it was only natural that Persian converts should serve as the major vectors for transmitting Islam to the Sogdians, to a much greater extent than the Arabs who would have seemed far more foreign to them.

The Muslims early on established a garrison at Marv, from which they launched raids on Khwarazm and Sogdiana (which they referred to as *Mā warā' al-nahr*, 'That Which [Lies] Beyond the [Oxus] River', a calque on the older Greek name 'Transoxiana'), as well as Bactria, but these initial incursions had limited success. In 674 the Arabs besieged Bukhara but left the city in peace after securing a promise of tribute. They managed to capture Samarkand two years later. The Muslim advance was halted, however, by the outbreak of anti-Umayyad revolts – the so-called 'Second Fitna' – in the Islamic heartlands of the Middle East. This intra-Muslim conflict, which provided a welcome reprieve for the Sogdians, lasted until 692.

It is interesting that the Sogdian merchant community at Marv appear to have been the principal financial backers of Arab raids in Central Asia, suggesting that their loyalties lay more with profit than with the welfare of their original homeland. As de la Vaissière comments, 'They financed the [Arabs] and expected to be reimbursed with plunder.'[37] A passage in Ṭabarī's *History* mentions an Arab personality by the name of Attāb al-Ghudanī who borrowed money from Sogdian creditors in order to participate in the Bukhara campaign, and when he didn't go, they had him thrown into debtor's prison.[38] It is highly telling that they had the standing to do so.

Following the stabilization of intra-Muslim politics under the caliph Walīd I, a sustained attack on Central Asia was finally launched by the Arab general Qutayba b. Muslim beginning in 705. Balkh capitulated fairly quickly, and some regional chieftains, including the Tarkhan-Nizak of Badghis and Tish, the Khuda of Chaghanian, joined forces with the Muslims. Strengthened by this influx of local fighters, Qutayba turned his attention to Sogdiana.

Bukhara, being embroiled in a domestic power struggle at this time, seemed an attractive target, and in 706 the Muslim army was able to capture the nearby city of Paykand after a two-month siege. No sooner had they moved on, however, than the inhabitants rebelled. The Muslims returned and laid waste to the city, executing the men and enslaving the women and children. This brutal reprisal caused the Bukharans to put aside their differences and make common cause with the principalities of Kish and Nasaf against the invaders. The Muslim campaigns of 707 and 708 were rebuffed, but following the death of Bukhara's ruler, the Bukhar-khuda, they finally succeeded in forcing the submission of that city in 709.

On hearing of Bukhara's fall, the ruler of Samarkand, (the?) Tarkhun,[39] sent envoys to Qutayba acknowledging his submission. The local nobility opposed this, however, and conspired to have Tarkhun replaced by a more independence-minded ruler by the name of Gurak. Tarkhun was thrown into prison, where he committed suicide soon after, whereas Gurak, by skilfully playing off the Muslims against the Turks, managed to hold onto power for another twenty-five years. In Bactria, meanwhile, the Tarkhan-Nizak of Badghis raised a rebellion which the Muslims were unable to suppress until the following year along with several other uprisings in the region.

In 712 Qutayba returned to Bukhara and installed the Sogdian prince Tughshada as his vassal. Qutayba forced Bukharans to give over half of their living spaces to Arab soldiers so that the latter 'might be informed of their sentiments' – a spy in every home! – and he 'made (the practice of their local religion) difficult for them in every way'. The Arab conqueror converted Bukhara's renowned Makh temple into a congregational mosque, and simultaneously bribed and ordered the people to attend it. Nevertheless, Narshakhī admits that the Bukharans 'accepted Islam in appearance but in secret worshipped idols'.[40]

The ability of the Sogdians to fend off the Muslim onslaught was hampered by the decentralized nature of their regional power, which, as had always been the case in the past, remained dispersed among often-bickering local rulers. Nevertheless, Sogdian revolts – characterized as 'apostasy' by later Muslim historians who projected a religious interpretation onto the Sogdians' periodic submissions to Arab rule – went on for decades, assisted at times by the Turks and/or the Chinese.

One of the best documented cases of Sogdian resistance is that of Devashtich, the ruler of Panjakent, who withdrew to nearby Mt. Mugh in 722, where his administration left a trove of written records, mostly legal and economic archives. Like his contemporary Tughshada in Bukhara Devashtich had nominally submitted to the Muslims, but he later fled to his mountain hideout when he feared they would replace him as local governor. After a short time the Muslims (the Sogdian texts use the differentiated terms *Tāc̲h̲īk* and *Pārsīk*, meaning Arabs and Persians[41]) were able to penetrate the Mt. Mugh castle, which they burned along with its temple and a number of private houses; they imprisoned Devashtich along many of his followers. Remains from the site reveal that all the way up to the bitter end Devashtich had considered himself the legitimate 'king of Sogdiana', and that he had continued to practice his original religion in which the goddess Nanai was paramount.

Just as the successive 'submissions' of Sogdian political figures were demonstrably opportunistic in nature, the Islamization of the mercantile class was likely driven in many cases by a desire to secure one's survival within the trade networks that had come under Muslim control. Of course, even a nominal conversion in the first instance would generally lead to the next generation receiving an Islamic upbringing, so the process of cultural transformation could be accomplished fairly quickly thereafter.

As Islam established itself across the eastern Iranian world during the first half of the eighth century it did so primarily in Persian, not Arabic.[42] The Iranian character of Islam's development in the east was greatly accelerated by the Khurasan-based Abbasid revolution from 749 to 751, after which the Caliphate's centre of gravity was shifted from Syria to Iraq at the western edge of the Iranian world. The so-called 'Abbasid' movement was led by a Khurasani general, Vihzādān Pūr-i Vandād Hurmuz, known in the Arabic sources as Abū Muslim, who was married to a Sogdian noblewoman from Samarkand. His troops comprised not only what one might refer to as 's̲h̲ī'izing' Iranian Muslim converts (though they were not 'S̲h̲ī'ite' properly speaking)[43] and Iranicized Arab settlers, but also many Khurasani Zoroastrians and Bactrian Buddhists from among the local population.

The eighth Abbasid caliph, al-Mu'taṣim (r. 833–42), was the son of the legendary ruler Hārūn al-Rashīd. His mother was a Sogdian concubine named Marida, who seems to have imparted a measure of Sogdian identity to the future head of the Islamic Empire. Mu'taṣim's reign saw the incorporation of significant Sogdian influences into the caliphal administration, most notably an increasing reliance on a Sogdian-style private guard corps of *c̲h̲akirs*. This established the groundwork by which later generations of slave soldiers, mostly of Turkic origin, would eventually rise up to take control of the empire from within.

In Sogdiana, non-Muslims continued to speak Sogdian, but as Islamization progressed, first in the cities and only later in the countryside, the language went into a slow decline. It would seem that by Samanid times many people were bilingual in Sogdian and Persian, using the former in the personal sphere and Persian professionally. By the twelfth century evidence for native Sogdian speakers becomes exceedingly scarce, although a related dialect survives in Tajikistan's Yaghnob River valley even up to the present day.[44]

Still, since the merchant classes were among the first to embrace the new Perso-Islamic culture, the emerging 'Tajik' identity should properly be seen as having evolved out of the Sogdian and Bactrian – through a mixing of the latter with Persian-speaking Muslims and gradually adopting their religious and linguistic culture – rather than simply having 'replaced' them. The masters of the Silk Road during the first Islamic centuries were the Tajiks, who to a large extent simply reappropriated the role previously held by their own Sogdian ancestors.

Sogdians and Uighurs

The Muslim advance towards China was definitively halted after the Battle of Talas (in what is now northwestern Kyrgyzstan) in 751. Fresh from their victory over the Umayyad dynasty in Syria the year before the Abbasids defeated the Tang army, a triumph probably made possible by the defection of a Turkic contingent from the Chinese to the Muslim side. But the Muslims could not progress further due to overextended supply lines, so for the time being the Tien Shan mountain range became the de facto dividing line separating Muslim and Chinese imperial ambitions. Muslim control over Sogdiana was henceforth assured, however. A significant side note to this event is that in the wake of the Muslims' victory they apparently learned the art of paper-making from their Chinese captives: Samarkand went on to become famous throughout the world for the quality of its paper.

The Sogdian mercantile presence remained firmly established beyond Abbasid borders, both among the Turks of the steppes and within the lands held by the Chinese. The Tang emperor had entrusted the western frontier to a general of mixed Sogdian-Turkish parentage, Rokhshan ('Radiant-face'), known in Chinese as An Lushan (安祿山). In 755 he launched a rebellion and succeeded in taking the two most important Tang cities, Luoyang and Chang'an, driving the Emperor into exile. An Lushan was murdered on orders of his own son the following year and the steppe-led rebellion eventually petered out, but the reputation of Sogdians living in China became henceforth suspect.

To quell the rebellion the Tang Emperor Suzong had enlisted the help of an emerging Turkic tribal confederation to the north known as the Uighurs. Probably as a means of securing the cooperation of Sogdian merchants who had converted to Manichaeism, the Uighur ruler Tengri Bögü nominally accepted that faith and made it the official religion of the Uighur state beginning in 762. Since it can hardly have been the central Manichaean teachings of world renunciation, non-violence and vegetarianism that made the religion so attractive to this ruthless warrior chieftain, one assumes that his aim in promoting Manichaeism was most likely to counterbalance the influence of Buddhists who were present at the Tang court, particularly Buddhist merchants with their wide-ranging trade links. It is surely relevant to consider that the Sogdian metropolis of Samarkand, one of the key nodes of trans-Eurasian trade, had by this time become the administrative centre of Manichaeism due to the re-settlement there of refugees fleeing persecution from the Abbasids in Mesopotamia. Manichaean commercial networks were therefore a viable alternative to Buddhist-controlled ones at that time.

The Uighur Empire was short-lived, however, and already by the last decade of the eighth century it began to break up following invasions from Tibet to the south and rival Turkic tribes to the north. Two much-reduced Uighur states survived: one in the Turfan Basin city of Qocho and the other in Gansu to the east. Manichaean manuscripts in a number of languages, including Sogdian, Parthian and Uighur Turkish, were sealed away in hidden libraries and thereby preserved thanks to the exceedingly arid Turfan climate, to be re-discovered by Western archaeologists during the early twentieth century. Paintings from Manichaeism's brief Uighur heyday – both book illustrations and wall murals – provide the principal legacy of the religion's rich artistic tradition, which heavily influenced those of Christianity, Buddhism and Islam.

The Revolt of Muqanna'

Anti-Muslim resistance in eastern Iran, which continued well into the ninth century, most often took the form of religious movements rallying behind a charismatic prophet figure. The most successful of these was Hāshim b. Ḥakīm, called Muqanna' ('the Veiled One'), a preacher and skilled magician of Sogdian or Bactrian origin who led a rebellion against Abbasid authority beginning in Bukhara around 773. Muqanna' and his followers, called 'the White Garmented Ones' (*Sapīd-jāmagān*), soon seized control of Samarkand, where he began to strike coins, a standard way of declaring independence.

Muslim writers state that Muqanna' preached the religion of Mazdak, a para-Zoroastrian reformer of late sixth-century Sasanian Iran who is sometimes described as a 'proto-communist'. (He apparently taught that wealth and women should be re-distributed from among the rich to members of all social classes.) Muqanna''s followers seem to have been mainly Sogdian peasants along with some Turkic tribesmen – peoples who had not yet been Islamicized and were seeking to reassert a local form of religion and social organization. Narshakhī states that 'In Sughd most of the villages accepted the faith of Muqanna', [and m]any of the villages of Bukhara ... They attacked caravans, pillaged villages, and caused much devastation.'[45]

According to Narshakhī, when reports of the uprising reached Baghdad the Caliph Mahdī was so concerned that he sent out 'many troops' in order to quell it. The Caliph eventually travelled out to Nishapur himself to oversee this effort, since 'He feared that there was a danger that Islam would be lost and that the religion of Muqanna' would spread throughout the entire world.' Aided by the arrival of Turks attracted by the promise of booty, Muqanna''s movement held out for several years, but after repeated attempts the Abbasid army finally managed to suppress it once and for all around 783, roughly a decade after the rebellion had first started.

The end of Sogdian autonomy

By the second half of the eighth century it appears to have at last become clear to the Sogdian nobility that further resistance against Muslim rule was futile.

Nevertheless, their gradual acceptance of Muslim power seems to have been more political than religious since apart from a few eighth-century mosques one does not begin to see any large-scale spread of Islamic institutions until sometime later.

The last Sogdian holdout against the Abbasids was the region of Ustrushana (modern Istaravshon in northern Tajikistan), whose ruler, the Afshin Kharākhana, submitted only after the Caliph Hārūn al-Rashīd sent out an army against him in 794. The Muslim force was headed by Faḍl b. Yahyā, scion of the highly influential Barmak family of Bactria that had been custodians of a major Buddhist shrine in Balkh until their conversion to Islam. However, Kharākhana's son and successor, Kāvūs, repudiated his father's alliance with the Muslims; he accepted Islam himself only years later, after fleeing to Baghdad following a family struggle in 822. Kāvūs's son Ḥaydar succeeded him as Afshin of Ustrushana, and was sent by the Caliph Mu'taṣim to suppress Iran's last major anti-Muslim nativist rebellion, that of the neo-Mazdakite Bābak in Azerbaijan, which Ḥaydar finally crushed in 837.

Despite his service to the Caliphate, Ḥaydar was plagued throughout his career by accusations that despite being a nominal Muslim he had in fact persisted in following his original faith. Cited as evidence for this was the fact that he punished some Muslim religious leaders in Ustrushana for converting a local shrine into a mosque on the basis that the locals had been promised freedom by the Muslims to continue practicing their own religion. This would suggest that as late as the mid-ninth century – after more than 120 years of Muslim overlordship – much of the population of Ustrushana had still not embraced Islam, and that even certain local rulers held sympathies towards the traditional religion.

Ḥaydar was eventually arrested and starved to death in prison. It is said that a search of his house turned up 'illustrated holy books' and a number of idols. The combined presence of illuminated scriptures, suggesting Manichaean sympathies, and 'idols', associated with Buddhism, is not particularly surprising, since the Sogdian approach to religion had long been eclectic and non-exclusive. During the ninth and tenth centuries this would change, as Sogdian identity – like that of the heavily Buddhist Bactrians further south – progressively dissolved into the strictly Muslim character of the Tajiks.

3

The Samanid Empire and the New Persian Renaissance

Agar Sāmāniān nabūd, Īrān nabūd
(Without the Samanids, there would be no Iran)
Sa'īd Nafīsī (1895–1966)

Imrūz ba har hālī Baghdād Bukhārā'st
Kujā mīr-i Khurāsān ast, pīrūzī ānjā'st
(Today in every way Baghdad is Bukhara
Wherever the Prince of Khurasan is, success is there)
Rūdakī (858–941)

The ninth century was a rich period in the development of Islamic civilization. From the Maghreb to Central Asia, a new cosmopolitan culture was taking shape, with many diverse peoples – each with their own languages and religions – coming to take their place under the Islamic umbrella. The Abbasid Revolution, which unfolded from 747 to 750, transformed Islam from the ethnic religion of the Arabs into a universal system which all could play a role in shaping; in the course of this process, Iranians would prove to be the outstanding figures.

Arabic was the lingua franca of this emerging society, but non-Arabs were the principal contributors to the Islamization of intellectual and artistic traditions, as well as to the formation of Islamic law. The new Abbasid capital of Baghdad, built near the site of Ctesiphon which had been the Sasanian capital in pre-Islamic times, was the centre of this civilization-building activity, drawing scholars from all across the Muslim world. Of these none left more of a lasting legacy than a certain Muḥammad b. Ismāʿīl (810–70), a tireless researcher who hailed from Bukhara.

'Bukhārī', as he was known throughout the Muslim world, spent his life collecting *hadīths* – reports about the words and deeds of the prophet Muḥammad – which Islamic scholars had begun to use as a source of law as they worked to construct a unified legal code that could be applied to Muslims everywhere regardless of their cultural background and differing norms. Bukhārī's *Ṣaḥīḥ*, or 'sound' collection, came to be acknowledged by Sunni jurists as the single most reliable assemblage of hadiths, and as such it played an unrivalled foundational role in the formulation of Islamic law. Another of the six hadith collections that were eventually confirmed as canonical by the Sunni tradition was that of Bukhārī's student and colleague Abū ʿIsā Muḥammad of Tirmiẓ (824–92), who was, like him, a product of the former Sogdian lands and likely a native speaker of Sogdian.

Muslim scholars of the formative period were engaged in the full range of academic pursuits, from interpreting the Qur'an and hadiths (which presupposed an intensive study of Arabic) to applying rational methods of argumentation – largely borrowed from the ancient Greeks – for purposes of theological elaborations or philosophical speculations within an Islamic framework. Contrary to the notions of many Muslims and non-Muslims alike, Islam, like any religion, was not delivered ready-made; it had to be developed and articulated over a period of several centuries before it could begin to assume its definitive shape.

But one should not lose sight of the fact that just like today, scholars of the formative Islamic period often spent their lives within ivory towers, communicating primarily amongst themselves whether in the context of personal discussions or through their writings. Islamic notions percolated down to ordinary citizens indirectly, and often only partially, as academic debates slowly but systematically generated some degree of consensus on what defined Islam and how it should be practised.

It should also be remembered that Islam during the early period was very much an urban phenomenon. Meanwhile, more than 90 per cent of the population lived in rural villages, where their traditional routines, languages and religious practices proved stubbornly resistant to change. From its very beginnings Muslim rule under the Caliphate consisted primarily of control over trade networks. All throughout the conquered lands, the merchant classes – along with government employees (*dabīrs*) and landowning families (*dihqāns*) in the countryside – were the first to embrace the process of Islamization. In this way the economic, political and intellectual elites were able to hold onto their privileged positions in society. Leaving their Sogdian identity behind, they became the original 'Tajiks', Persian by language and Muslim by confession. Sogdian language and religion did not disappear overnight, but became less and less visible as the new Perso-Islamic Tajik culture spread throughout Central Asian society.

As the cases of Tughshada, Devashtich and the Afshins of Ustrushana show, in Sogdiana as elsewhere throughout the Caliphate the local nobility was often able to retain their status through political manoeuvring. The extent of their power at any given time was dependent on the relative strength or weakness of the central authorities in far-away Baghdad. Realistically speaking the Caliphs could maintain the Empire only by ensuring the ongoing loyalty of regional governors. As time went on the latter became increasingly bold in asserting their independence, even while remaining nominal servants of the Caliphate.

Already prior to the Abbasid Revolution, a landowner and regional chieftain (*k͟hudā*, literally 'lord') in the Bactrian district of Saman (near Tirmiẓ) had professed loyalty to the Umayyad governor of Khurasan, Asad Qasrī. As a demonstration of his sincerity this 'Sāmān-k͟hudā' gave his son the Arabic name 'Asad' ('Lion') in honour of his friend the governor. Raised as a Muslim, Asad Sāmānī went on to have four boys of his own: Nuḥ, Aḥmad, Yaḥyā and Ilyās.

In 819 the young Samani brothers joined a government campaign to suppress a nativist rebellion in Samarkand. In recognition of their service each of the four was awarded a deputy governorship by the Abbasid administration, which had superseded the Umayyads seven decades previously. Nuḥ was given Samarkand, Aḥmad the Ferghana Valley, Yaḥyā the region around Chach (modern Tashkent, pronounced 'Shash' by the Arabs) and Ilyās Herat in eastern Khurasan. In this way the Samani family came to exercise control over the northeastern lands of the Caliphate to the north and south of the Oxus River. Hence, the year 819 is generally taken as the beginning of the Samanid dynasty.

Nuḥ was able to expand his territory by seizing the market town of Isfijab (modern Sayram in southern Kazakhstan) from the Turks, which he then fortified against further invasions from the north. After Nuḥ's death in 841 his position in Samarkand was taken over by Aḥmad, with Yaḥyā continuing to govern from Chach and Ilyās from Balkh. Yaḥyā died in 855, at which point Aḥmad controlled all the Samanid lands north of the Oxus. After Ilyās died the following year, however, his son and successor Ibrahīm lost the southern territories after failing in an assignment from the Caliph's Ṭāhirid vassals in Nishapur to put down the resurgently Iranist Saffarid rebellion that had erupted in the southeastern province of Sistan. Ibrahīm was captured by the Saffarids and his lands taken over by the Ṭāhirids.

The Saffarid revolt in the south can be seen in some ways as a nativist reaction to Arab rule, in that its leader, Rādmān pūr-i Māhak – better known by his Arabic name, Ya'qūb b. Layth – restored Persian to the status of official court language, as the Samanids would later also do. Ya'qūb is famous for having reprimanded his court poets for eulogizing him in Arabic, a language he did not understand, insisting that they compose instead in Persian.

The Saffarid rebellion severely weakened the Ṭāhirid governorship of Khurasan, allowing the sons of Nuḥ Sāmānī – Naṣr, Ya'qūb (not to be confused with Ya'qūb Saffārī), and Ismā'īl – to rule Transoxiana virtually without interference. As the eldest brother Naṣr was based in Samarkand, with Ya'qūb seated in Shash. Bukhara had been subjected to repeated attacks from Khwarazm, and in 874 the city's Ḥanafī clerics wrote to Naṣr asking for assistance. The Samanid Amir sent a detachment led by his brother Ismā'īl, who was received by the Bukharans as something of a saviour although the Bukhār-khudā technically remained in charge.

Before long Ismā'īl's popularity – enhanced by his successful defence of the city against several further raids – enabled him to consolidate the support of the local nobles, including even the Bukhār-khudā himself. By 885 Ismā'īl's prestige had grown to the point that he could challenge Naṣr (presumably over the remittance of taxes), which led to a three-year conflict between the two brothers. This came to a head in 888 when Ismā'īl managed to defeat and capture Naṣr in battle. Ismā'īl chose the course of magnanimity, restoring his elder brother to the family throne in Samarkand, but his reputation as the real power behind the throne was now clear. Naṣr reciprocated by naming Ismā'īl as his designated successor, and upon the former's death in 892 Ismā'īl was recognized as the formal head of the Samanid state.

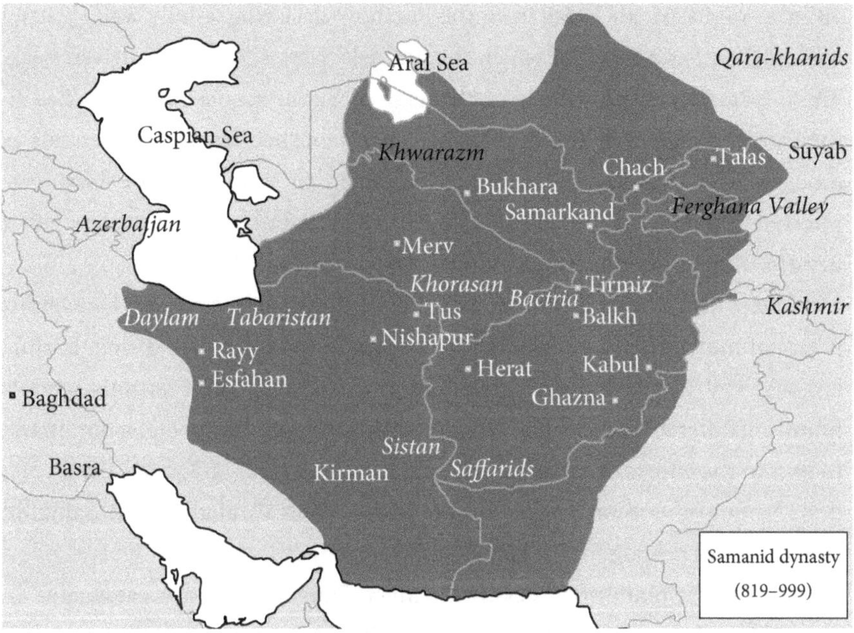

Map 2 The Samanid Empire, tenth century CE.

Further south, Ya'qūb Saffārī died the same year and was succeeded by his son Amr. The Abbasids in Baghdad lent their support to their new Saffarid 'vassal', who was thereby emboldened to challenge the Samanid position over the next several years. Amr, however, despite some initial successes, was ultimately defeated in a battle against Ismā'īl in 900. This led the Caliph to switch sides and confirm Ismā'īl as ruler not only of Transoxiana but also of Khurasan, as well as the regions of Ṭabaristān (modern Māzandarān, on the south Caspian coast), Rayy (the north central Iranian plateau, near present-day Tehran) and Esfahan in the Iranian heartland. In practice, by this point none of these territories was really within the Caliph's jurisdiction, so his gesture appears to have been an attempt to maintain the fiction of a united Caliphate by sanctioning a shift in power that had already occurred.

The Zaydī Shī'ites of Daylām (modern Gīlān province, on the Caspian shore west of Mazandaran) resisted Samanid suzerainty from the outset, but by 900 Ismā'īl had brought them under his control. Then, in 904 he responded to an invasion by pagan Turks from the north by declaring a 'holy war' (*ghazw*) against them, as a result of which the 'infidels' were successfully driven back. These victories, along with his patronage of Sunni scholars who flocked to the Samanid capital in search of positions, established Ismā'īl's credentials as a defender of 'orthodox' Sunnism. Ever since that time pious Muslims have referred to the city as 'Bukhārā-yi Sharīf' – 'Noble Bukhara' – a tendency that persists even to the present day.

Matters of the heart are difficult for the historian to judge, but whatever his personal motivations Ismā'īl's attachment to Sunni Islam was strong. Islamic law was still in the process of formation, with scholars of various schools following different approaches. In Bukhara the Ḥanafīs had become dominant, thanks to the efforts of a jurist by the name of Abū Ḥafṣ 'al-Kabīr' ('the Great'; d. 832). But other Sunni schools were also present throughout the Samanid lands, as were proponents of Ismā'īlī Shī'ism.

Against this pluralistic backdrop, Ismā'īl Sāmānī's military campaigns in ostensible defence of 'true' Sunni Islam against the perceived threats posed by 'heretical' Shī'ism and the 'infidelity' of the pagan Turks set a precedent that would be followed by many later Central Asian rulers, from Maḥmūd of Ghazna in the eleventh century to Muḥammad Shibānī Khān in the sixteenth century.

Thus, the focus of *ghazw* campaigns, which attracted young fighters from all across the Islamic world, shifted from the Byzantine frontier to Central Asia due to Ismā'īl's policy.[1] At the same time Sufi missionaries, possibly including such figures as Abū'l-Ḥasan Muḥammad b. Sufyān al-Kalamātī of Nishapur and Abū'l-Ḥasan Sa'īd b. Ḥātim of Usbānīkath, actively worked to propagate Islam amongst the Turks, just as Sogdians of various faiths had done during the preceding centuries. The Samanids also revived the earlier Sogdian practice of establishing merchant colonies along the nomadic frontier, for example at Jand, Khuvara and Yangikent along the Syr Darya.

During his last years and up to his death in 907 Ismā'īl Sāmānī exercised control over most of the Iranian world. One may, as modern Tajiks emphatically do, consider him to be a 'Tajik' in the sense that he was a Persian-speaking Muslim – Persian being, as we have noted, the primary language through which Central Asia was Islamicized by Iranian converts from the West. The original language of the Samanid family remains a mystery; mere geography would suggest that it was Bactrian. The family claimed descent from the Parthian

Mihrān clan that had been one of the pillars of Sasanian power in pre-Islamic times, but this may have merely been an attempt to provide themselves with noble credentials. One Samanid figural presentation coin seems to follow a Hephthalite, rather than a Sasanian, model. This raises the possibility that the Samanids may have been of Hephthalite origin, which would make geographic sense since the nomadic Hephthalites had a strong presence in Bactria.[2]

In any case, the Samanids' use and promotion of Persian, along with their adoption of many pre-Islamic administrative titles, was most likely intended to convey the notion that their rule was a continuation of the Sasanian imperial tradition, which in a sense it was. The claim is eloquently expressed in the following verse by the poet Mujalladī Gurgānī:

Az ān chandān nā'im-i īn jahānī
Ki mānd az āl-i Sāsān va āl-i Sāmān
Sināyi Rūdakī mānda'st va madhat
Navā-yi Bārbad mānda'st va dāstān.

From those blessing in the world that remain
From the House of Sasan and of Saman
Rudaki's refined verse remains
[and] Borbad's songs and tales.

Persian also served another political purpose for the Samanids, however, which was to unite the various Iranian peoples living throughout their empire, providing an easily learned lingua franca for speakers of related languages such as Khwarazmian, Sogdian and Bactrian.

Assuming no greater title than Amīr (literally, 'Commander'), Ismā'īl paid lip service to the Caliph in Baghdad but no taxes, and was for all intents and purposes an independent ruler. Medieval Muslim writers from Narshakhī to Niẓām ul-Mulk praise him as a just and capable sovereign. As the latter wrote late a century and a half later: 'He had pure faith in God (to Him be power and glory) and he was generous to the poor – to name only one of his notable virtues.'[3]

By now both fully Islamicized in religious terms and completely Persianized in regard to language and cultural traditions, Ismā'īl's administration not only confirmed the Islamic character of the newly evolving Tajik culture but also laid the foundation for the so-called 'Persian Renaissance' that took place

Figure 3.1 Mausoleum of Ismoil Somonī, Bukhara. Tenth century CE.

throughout the tenth century. The city of Bukhara, which Ismā'īl had made his capital and where his impressive mausoleum still stands today, would become the centre of this cultural revival (see Figure 3.1).

In modern-day Tajikistan Ismā'īl Sāmānī (written 'Ismoil Somonī' in Tojikī) is considered to be the 'Founder of the Tajik Nation'. He is commemorated by a massive statue in central Dushanbe facing the National Library (see Figure 3.2), and by another that towers massively over the northern city of Khujand amidst a park bearing his name. His likeness adorns Tajik currency (the 100-*somonī* note) and many other national symbols. The highest mountain in Tajikistan, standing at 7,495 metres (24,590 feet), known in Soviet times as Communism Peak, has been rechristened in his honour.

Ismā'īl was succeeded by his son Aḥmad, who soon added Sīstān to the provinces under Samanid control. Probably at the instigation of Islamic clerics within his circle of advisors Aḥmad attempted to change the court language from Persian back to Arabic, but this policy proved so unpopular that he was forced to back down. As numerous sources make clear, while the

Figure 3.2 Modern statue of Ismoil Somonī, Dushanbe, Tajikistan.

Sogdian population seemed to have no problem with adopting Persian, few, if any, Central Asians – with the notable exception of the clergy and some government administrators – knew Arabic or showed any signs of wanting to learn.

In 914, amidst the struggle to suppress an ongoing insurgency from the Zaydī Shī'ites in Tabaristan, Aḥmad was murdered by a group of his own slaves. He was succeeded by his son, Naṣr II, who was only eight years old at the time. Naṣr's reign went on to endure for three decades, but it was plagued throughout by rebellions from the intractable Zaydīs and from within his own family.

By this time in northern Africa the Fatimid dynasty – followers of another Shī'ite branch, the Ismā'īlīs – had established a state based in Cairo, from which they sent out missionaries to Iran and Central Asia. They succeeded in converting a Samanid general, Ḥusayn Marwāzī, who became the head of the Ismā'īlī mission in the East even while managing to secure for himself a place as one of Naṣr's courtiers.

Marwāzī was succeeded as chief missionary by Muḥammad Nakhshābī, one of the seminal figures in formulating the neo-Platonic Ismā'īlī philosophical system, who often participated in royal debates. Nakhshābī's intellectual arguments persuaded a number of key officials to embrace Isma'ilism, eventually including the sovereign himself. The Amīr's internal enemies, supported by Bukhara's Sunni jurists, used this as a pretext to intrigue against him, and Naṣr was finally forced to abdicate in 943 following an attempted plot on his life. It is remarkable that amidst all this continuing political unrest Naṣr nevertheless managed to preside over the greatest flowering of Persian cultural revival ever seen.

Since Sasanian times one of the principal means for Iranian rulers to demonstrate their importance and legitimacy was by inviting poets, musicians and scholars to be part of their elite circle at court. Under Naṣr Sāmānī this practice flourished, and a number of leading cultural figures were brought to Bukhara, where they enjoyed government patronage. Naṣr himself seems to have been a weak figure, as the repeated rebellions against him suggest. Accordingly, credit for the cultural revival at his court is usually given to his prime ministers, Muḥammad Jayhānī (from 914 to 922, removed due to accusations of Isma'īlism), Abū'l Faẓl Bal'amī (922 to 938, known as the

Elder) and, finally, Jayhānī's son Abū 'Alī (938 to 941). Thanks to the efforts of these capable officials Bukhara became, in the words of the eleventh-century Khurasani writer Abū Manṣūr Tha'ālabī, 'the focus of splendor, the shrine of empire, the meeting place of the most unique intellects of the age, the horizon of the literary stars of the world, and the fair of the greatest scholars of the field'.[4] The legacy of Hanafī theologian Abū Manṣūr al-Māturīdī (853–944) was particularly enduring: His theological approach (*kalām*) became and has remained preeminent throughout Central Asia up to the present day.

The intellectual liveliness of tenth-century Bukhara had its downside, however. The sectarian struggles between Ismā'īlī sympathizers and the Sunni jurists (who were largely of the Ḥanafi school) led to Naṣr's downfall but were not resolved by it. His son and successor, Nuḥ II, appointed a very conservative Ḥanafī jurist as prime minister in order to distance himself from his father's pro-Ismā'īlī religious policy. This conflict had a dampening effect on cultural production, as well as on effective governance.

The cultural flourishing of the Samanid realms during the mid-tenth century drew the admiration of travellers from all across the Muslim world. Ibn Ḥawqal, a native of northern Mesopotamia, wrote that

> The people of Bukhara are distinguished by all others of Khurasan for their culture, their religious sciences, their knowledge in the juridical field, their devotion, their faithfulness, their sober habits, the perfection of their social relationships, the absence of mean intentions, the propensity to good, their zeal for positive actions, and the purity and openness of their feelings.[5]

Of the physical setting, he states that

> I have not seen nor heard in the Islamic territory about a region more beautiful than Bukhara. From the heights of its citadel anywhere the sight is worth the looking, and there is a great extension of vegetation which is mixed with the blue of the sky as if the firmament was a blue cover above a green carpet.[6]

In a similar vein Ibn Ḥawqal praises the beauty of Samanid Samarkand:

> From the top of [the] citadel – where I have been – one can enjoy the best show ever imagined or dreamt about: green trees, resplendent castles, fast-flowing small rivers and wonderful cultivations. There is no point at which

> the eye is not satisfied, there is no garden where beauty is not evident: the whole is divided by well-designed buildings and the splendour is infinite. The cypresses have been cut in order to look like animals such as elephants, camels, oxen, confronting beasts as if they were talking to each other or fighting.[7]

The exotic image of these Central Asian cities in the minds of Middle Eastern Muslims – a kind of early Islamic Orientalism – was projected back even to the time of the Prophet. A hadith, almost certainly spurious but illustrative nevertheless, has Muḥammad predicting that

> There shall be conquered a city in Khurasan beyond a river which is called the Jayhun; which city is named Bukhara. It is encompassed with God's mercy and surrounded by His angels; its people are Heaven-aided; and whoso shall sleep upon a bed therein shall be like him that draweth his sword in the way of God. And beyond it lieth a city which is called Samarkand, wherein is a fountain of the fountains of Paradise, and a tomb of the tombs of the Prophets, and a garden as the gardens of Paradise; its dead, upon Resurrection Day, shall be assembled with the martyrs.[8]

Neo-Persian literature

Following the Sasanian model, from the beginning of the Islamic period elite Muslims of all kinds – rulers as well as wealthy businessmen, military officers and rural landowners – competed amongst themselves to employ the best poets, whose job was not only to entertain but also to memorialize their patrons by composing memorable panegyrics in their honour. Arabic poetry, inherited from pagan times and reworked to suit the Islamic context, was highly sophisticated; it possessed a complex repertory of structures, themes and symbols that took enormous skill to master.

In the Iranian East, however, few people outside religious circles had sufficient knowledge of Arabic to appreciate these subtle refinements. The following lines, composed for the eighth-century Saffarid ruler Yaʿqūb b. Lay<u>th</u>, clearly express the claim that local leaders such as he were restoring Iran to its rightful glory after a humiliating interlude under the barbarian Arabs:

> I am the son of the noble descendants of Jam[s͟hīd – the mythical first Iranian king], and the inheritance of the kings of Persia has fallen to my lot ... I am reviving their glory, which has been lost and effaced by the length of time ... Say then to all sons of Hās͟him: 'Return to your country in the Hijaz, to eat lizards and to graze your sheep.'[9]

Thus, through the support of court patronage first by the Saffarids and then by the Samanids, use of Persian for official purposes became respectable again after having been displaced by Arabic for more than a century. Usually called *darī* ('court language') in the sources of the period, this 'New Persian' differed considerably from the 'Middle Persian' form found in the Zoroastrian 'Pahlavi' texts. Written in a modified Arabic alphabet that was a huge improvement over the deliberately obscure Aramaic-based Pahlavi writing system, its grammar was much simpler – the result of the language coming to be used by a range of peoples who learned it as a second tongue – and many Arabic loanwords had entered the vocabulary. In Central Asia, a number of Sogdian words survived in local dialects of New Persian as well.

The first major poet to become known for writing in New Persian was Abū 'Abdullāh Ja'far b. Muḥammad Rūdakī, a native of the village now known as Panjrūd in the Zarafshan Valley of northern Tajikistan. Although earlier poets such as Abū Ḥafs Sug͟hdī (d. 902) are known to have composed in New Persian, their work has been largely lost. Rūdakī is thus recognized in Iran as the 'founder of New Persian poetry' and in modern Tajikistan as the 'Father of Tajik Literature' – the claims are not mutually exclusive. Today there is a large statue of Rūdakī in one of Dushanbe's main parks and a monument to him in his native village of Panjrūd.

Since Sasanian times, it had been usual at court for poems to be performed as songs set to music. A successful minstrel in his home region, Rūdakī was called to Bukhara some time during the reign of Naṣr II. He became the poet laureate of the Samanid court where he was very highly paid for his services, especially for the panegyrics (a form called *qaṣīda*) which he composed in honour of his patrons. Contrary to the florid verse that had become popular among poets expressing themselves in Arabic, Rūdakī's Persian style was simple and unadorned, appealing directly to the listener's emotions. A composer of melodies as much as words, Rūdakī is credited with inventing the musical forms known as *tarāna* and *c͟hama* which came to be widely used in Tajik music, although in reality they likely predate him.[10]

Perhaps Rūdakī's most famous couplet came to him while accompanying Naṣr on campaign in Herat, at the instigation of army officers who were anxious to return home. Evoking the aroma of Bukhara's celebrated garden district, the line can be rendered in English as follows: 'The scent of Jū-yi Mūliyān comes to mind/The memory of dear friends left behind' (*Bū-yi jū-yi mūliyān āyad hamī/Yād-i yār-i mihrabān āyad hamī*).[11] Naṣr's nostalgia awakened, he gave the order to return to Bukhara and the poet was generously tipped by the grateful officers.

Like his patron the Amīr, Rūdakī is said to have been an Ismāʿīlī, and as an old man he was apparently arrested and tortured during the course of the anti-Ismāʿīlī backlash that led to Naṣr's abdication. Blinded and crippled, he returned to his native village where he died several years later.[12] Sadly, the vast bulk of his work has been lost, including a New Persian rendering of the classic collection of animal fables *Kalila and Dimna*.

Rūdakī is said to have written more than a million lines during his lifetime, but of these only fifty-two poems have come down to us today. Like his somewhat lesser known contemporaries who served at the Samanid court – among whom one can mention Abū S͟hakūr Balḵẖī, author of a lost wisdom collection entitled *Āfarīn-nāma*, and the early Sufi poet S͟haḥīd Bal̲k̲h̲ī – mere fragments of Rūdakī's work survived only because they were included in anthologies and reference works compiled by later writers.[13]

The Samanids' support of Persian literature was in some ways a continuation of the eighth-century Baghdad-based literary movement known as the *s͟huʿūbiyya* (roughly, 'nationalists'), made up of court bureaucrats who sought to demonstrate the cultural superiority of Iranians over Arabs by translating great works from pre-Islamic Iran – including not just *Kalila and Dimna* but also the *Thousand Tales* later known as *A Thousand and One Nights*, as well as the legendary Pahlavi history of Iran's kings and heroes called the *Book of Lords* (*K̲h̲wadāy-nāmag*) – into Arabic so that non-Iranians might be able to read and appreciate them for the masterpieces they were. In most cases the Middle Persian originals were then lost, so the Samanid approach was to have this body of literature retranslated into New Persian so that Iranians themselves (most of whom didn't know Arabic) could rediscover their own literary heritage.

The most enduring result of this effort began when Nuḥ b. Manṣūr assumed the throne as Nuḥ III in 976. He immediately commissioned the poet Abū Mansūr Daqīqī to put into New Persian verse the Arabic translation of the *Book of Lords* (or *Book of Kings*) that had been carried out more than two centuries previously by the most accomplished of the *shu'ūbiyya* scholars, Rūzbih pūr-i Dādboy known as Ibn Muqaffa'. Daqīqī died prematurely the following year having barely begun the massive project. It was then assigned to another poet, Abū'l-Qāsim Firdawsī from the city of Tūs, who spent the next thirty-three years versifying what would go on to become the Iranian national epic.

Firdawsī incorporated a thousand lines of Daqīqī's work into his final version of the *Book of Kings* (called the *Shāh-nāma* in New Persian), a section dealing with the appearance of Zarathushtra and his conversion of King Gushtasp (Vishtaspa) to his new religion. Unfortunately for Firdawsī by the time he completed his oeuvre in the year 1010 his Samanid patrons were no longer in power, and the recompense he received from his new patron, the half-Turk warlord Maḥmūd of Ghazna, left him bitterly disappointed.

Whatever the reception of Firdawsī's *Shāh-nāma* during his own lifetime, the 60,000-line epic has endured over the past thousand years as the greatest single monument to Persian literature ever written. It is recognized as one of the most celebrated poetic compositions in the world, on a par with the works of Homer or Indian classics such as the Mahabharata and Ramayana. By glorifying the Iranians' pre-Islamic past, the *Shāh-nāma* has remained central to the very definition of Iranian – and, by extension, Tajik – national identity.

Iranians everywhere know the *Shāh-nāma*'s many stories by heart, as do a wide range of other peoples from the Balkans to all the way to China that have come under the sway of Iranian cultural influence over the centuries. Its unrivalled status as a model of pure Persian has kept the spoken language conservative enough that even after a thousand years, modern-day Persian-speakers can understand it with little difficulty. Within a few centuries it became the most oft-illustrated work in all Persian literature, inspiring miniature paintings that are considered to be some of the finest works in the history of art. To this day it is second only to the Qur'an as a source of names given to children across the Iranian world and beyond.

The Samanids' translation initiatives were not limited to secular literature, however. Even religious texts, in principle far more tightly bound to the Arabic language, were translated into Persian so that the non-Arabic-speaking majority could have access to them. This included the Qur'an itself, as well as a Persian redaction of the ninth-century Iranian scholar Muḥammad b. Jarīr Ṭabarī's Qur'anic commentary (*tafsīr*) supervised by the Samanid prime minister Balʿamī the Younger during the reign of the usurper Manṣūr I (r. 961–76). The junior Balʿamī also oversaw the translation of Ṭabarī's monumental *History of the Prophets and the Kings*; it is to him we attribute the statement quoted in our Introduction that 'Here, in this region, the language is Persian, and the kings of this realm are Persian kings'.[14]

Philosophy and science

The Samanids employed not only theologians, poets and musicians but philosophers and scientists as well at their court. Notable among these was Muḥammad b. Aḥmad Khwārazmī (d. 977), who authored an Arabic encyclopaedia entitled *Mafātīḥ al-ʿulūm* ('Keys of the Sciences') at the request of Nuḥ II's prime minister Abū'l-Ḥusayn ʿUtbī sometime around 980. Considered a pioneering work in its vast scope, the *Mafātīḥ al-ʿulūm* covered everything from Islamic disciplines such as law and theology to the 'Greek' subjects of philosophy, logic, mathematics, geometry, astronomy, music, ethics and medicine. A vast array of other fields are also discussed, including grammar, literary composition, history (including the history of religions), mechanical engineering, alchemy and the secretarial profession.

Khwārazmī's work had been anticipated a generation earlier in a taxonomical treatise entitled *Iḥṣāʾ al-ʿulūm* ('Enumeration of the Sciences') by the celebrated polymath Muḥammad Fārābī (d. *c.* 950), whom medieval Muslim philosophers referred to as 'the Second Master' (Aristotle being 'the First'). Fārābī was a native of the northern Samanid lands whose native tongue may well have been Sogdian. His writings, in any case, contain some Sogdian words. Unfortunately he cannot be counted as playing any part in the Samanid Renaissance, since he migrated westwards in his youth and spent his career amongst the Arabic-speaking intelligentsia of Baghdad and Damascus.

Fārābī's books were available in the well-stocked bookshops of late Samanid Bukhara, however. Such places were frequented by a brilliant local youth named Ḥusayn b. 'Abdullah, who would later gain fame throughout the world as Abū 'Alī ibn Sīnā, or Avicenna, one of the greatest and most influential minds that ever lived. A voracious reader, the young Avicenna made ample use of the wealth of international scholarship available at the time, including translations from Greek, Syriac and Sanskrit that were readily found in the Samanid capital. He took advantage as well of any opportunity to study with scholars from abroad who had been attracted by Bukhara's cosmopolitan environment, even learning mathematics from a well-educated Indian grocer.

The son of an Ismā'īlī government official, Avicenna's personal religious beliefs continue to be contested up to the present day. Most likely his intellectual mindset took him beyond the boundaries of sectarian thinking, and at the end of his life his enemies considered him to have abandoned Islam altogether (a charge levelled at many of the great philosophers of Islam's 'Golden Age'). His early studies of medicine enabled him to earn a government appointment – and more importantly for him, perhaps, access to the royal library – by successfully treating an illness suffered by the Samanid ruler Nuḥ II in 997. It was during this period at Bukhara that Avicenna wrote his first books.

With the final extinction of the Samanid regime in 1007 Avicenna lost his government support, forcing him to spend the next several years wandering in search of employment. He eventually settled in Rayy and went on to spend the rest of his career in Iran, where he produced his most significant works, including the encyclopaedic *Canon of Medicine*.

As in the case of Farābī, modern nation-state thinking would be hard put to count Avicenna as a 'Tajik' scholar since he spent his career outside the present-day Tajik lands, although he could perhaps be considered as an ethnic Tajik based on his birth and upbringing. Beyond the fact of his being a Persian-speaking native of Central Asia, he spent his formative years in Bukhara, and it was the rich intellectual climate of that place which provided him his education as well as his first professional experiences. Avicenna's deep and enduring legacy can thus be at least partially credited among the great and lasting contributions of the Samanid state to the development of Islamic civilization. Even today many hospitals, pharmacies and medical schools across the Muslim world bear his name.

Sufism

As more and more people spanning the vast territories of the Caliphate came to identify as Muslims, often bringing many of their prior notions and customs with them, Islamic scholars – the Ulema – were constantly challenged in their attempts to develop and articulate a code of social norms that could apply to everyone. These efforts were never fully successful, as attested by the fact that even today Sunnis are free to follow any one of four recognized schools of law (Ḥanafī, Shafī'ī, Mālikī or Ḥanbalī) while Shī'ites, who follow their own Ja'farī legal tradition, are themselves internally divided amongst several sects, including the Twelvers, the Ismā'īlīs and the Zaydīs.

Thus, while in theory – at least in their own minds – the Ulema were the rightful custodians of religious leadership over Muslims, in practice this authority was always contested amongst a broad range of actors. In real terms there has never been a universally acknowledged overriding authority in matters pertaining to Islam, and throughout history this or that group was able to exercise its legal weight only by winning the support of whichever political figures held power at the time.

The struggle for religious authority within Muslim societies was complicated by the emergence of mystical movements that formed around the esoteric teachings of charismatic spiritual masters (called 'shaykhs' in Arabic, or *pīrs* in Persian – both terms literally mean 'old men'). Some of these individuals, who came to be referred to as Sufis – most likely due to the self-mortifyingly scratchy woollen garments (Ar. *ṣūf*) worn by some early mystics – were able to attract huge followings. This eventually led to the development of brotherhoods whose members professed absolute obedience to their chosen guide. Naturally, such loyalty to the religious teachings of a particular individual figure posed a threat to the influence of the Ulema.

A Sufi master was doubly empowered if his unique spiritual insight was backed up by traditional learning so that he could stand his own ground amongst the Ulema. In Central Asia one early such figure was Muḥammad b. 'Alī (d. 869), who came to be known as 'the Sage (*ḥakīm*) of Tirmiz' due to his mastery of all the established scientific disciplines. Like many scholars, Ḥakīm Tirmiẓī spent much of his life travelling in search of teachers, in his case both academic specialists and spiritual guides. His written work, of which several important examples have survived, is some of the earliest Islamic literature to combine mystical spiritual insights with scholarly methodologies, an approach that would be taken up and further developed by other notable personalities in the following centuries, including the influential theologian Muḥammad Ghazālī of Tūs (1058–1111) and the Andalusian mystical philosopher Ibn 'Arabī (1165–1240).

Trade and economy

Samanid merchants inherited the central role of their Sogdian ancestors in the trans-Eurasian trade networks which linked China and Europe. With the rise of the Kievan state to the west, Samanid trade with northern Europe grew exponentially via their Khwarazmian neighbours and the Turkic Khazars north of the Caspian Sea. Simultaneously Swedish Vikings – who had founded Kievan Rus during the late ninth century – were venturing eastwards into Central Asia, reaching at least as far as the Aral Sea.

Large quantities of Samanid silver coins have been found throughout Russia, Poland and Sweden, attesting to the importance of this expanding commercial network. East European products such as furs, amber, leather and honey reached Central Asia in this way. The Samanids, in turn, exported luxury items, not just Chinese silk but also jewellery, weapons and metalwork. Looking eastwards to China, in addition to silk the Samanid lands imported spices and ceramics. In exchange for these they continued the long tradition of providing the Central Asian horses so coveted by the Chinese, as well as high-quality glass products from Samarkand.

Trade and industry were supported by the Samanid regime and flourished in the cities, especially Bukhara and Samarkand, enriched by all this economic activity. As is so often the case, however, the benefits of this wealth remained concentrated within the upper echelons of society even as conditions worsened for the majority. This economic inequality drove a vicious cycle: The growth of the urban centres attracted landowning families (the *dihqāns*) to relocate from the countryside to the cities, which depleted the financial resources available in rural areas where most of the population still lived. At the same time, the trend towards urbanization favoured the established bureaucratic elites (the *dabīrs*), even as the shift towards dependence on Turkish mercenaries to staff the army reduced the political role of the *dihqāns* who had traditionally been responsible for raising local militias.

Many private lands were taken over by the government. They were then parcelled out in order to reward Turkish officers for service, to honour religious figures such as *sayyids* (individuals claiming descent from the Prophet) or Sufi masters, or to fund tax-free pious endowments (*waqfs*) such as mosques. These policies, exacerbated by the secession of the rich province of Khurasan during the reign of Nuḥ III, dramatically reduced tax revenues while adding pressure on thc pcasantry who were expected to make up the difference. Many peasants fled to the cities in search of better conditions, which they rarely found. This demographic shift placed additional burdens on government resources, which were now in steady decline.

Social conditions were further complicated by a growing influx of 'holy warriors' (*g͟hazīs*) from abroad, large numbers of zealous young men who had travelled to the Central Asian frontier zone from all over the Muslim world in order to fight the 'infidel' Turks. As the Turkish tribes increasingly came over to Islam, these fighters for the faith became redundant. Samanid cities were increasingly plagued by urban gangs of unemployed peasants and holy warriors who posed the constant threat of riots and other kinds of civil unrest.

The rise of the Turks

The Samanid state faced deteriorating conditions in both the urban centres and the countryside. This was exacerbated by ongoing discord and intrigue within the court. By the reign of Nuḥ II (r. 943–54) a major new external challenge had also emerged in the form of the Twelver Shīʿite Būyid family who were beginning to chip away at the Samanids' western territories. Originally from the Gilan region of northern Iran, the Būyids had consolidated their control over the central Caliphal lands in Iraq and were now threatening Samanid control in Khurasan. Just as in Baghdad where the Būyid militia had reduced the Caliph to little more than a figurehead, the Samanid government was becoming vulnerable to the wiles of Turkic mercenaries who increasingly made up their armed forces. The Turkic general Alptegin was arguably the most powerful figure in Bukhara at this time.

Nuḥ's son 'Abd al-Mālik, who succeeded him in 954, was even more beholden to his Turkic officers than his father had been. His reign, characterized by later writers as exceptionally corrupt, was cut short in 961 when he was killed in a horse-riding accident while drunk. 'Abd al-Mālik's untimely death led to an outbreak of public disorder during which his own newly built palace was looted and burned. The military officers at Bukhara tried to quell the civil unrest by appointing his brother Manṣūr as the new Amīr, but Alptegin, who was now serving as governor of Khurasan and charged with holding off the Būyids, refused his support.

Alptegin then marched his army to Ghazna in the southeast, where he seized power and set himself up as a semi-independent ruler beyond the reach of the new Samanid Amīr. The reign of Manṣūr, which lasted until 976, saw the gradual erosion of Samanid supremacy at the hands of the Buyids in Khurasan and the Ghaznavids in Seistan. The Turkic Ghaznavids, seeking political legitimacy through the patronage of established elite traditions, soon began to surpass the Samanids as the Muslim world's principal patrons of Perso-Islamic culture.

In Bukhara Manṣūr was succeeded by his son, Nuḥ II, but since the latter was still a teenager the reins of government were held by his prime minister, Abū'l-Husayn 'Utbī. A capable regent, 'Utbī sought to restore the position of the Tajik bureaucracy vis-à-vis the Turkish-run military. But after some initial success, he was ultimately assassinated by his own Turkish officers in 982 after losing a battle against the Būyids. Social and economic conditions in Bukhara and other cities continued to worsen, as the ongoing influx of rural migrants outpaced improvements in infrastructure. Writers of the time complain of smelly, garbage-strewn streets, unruly mobs and all manner of public health issues. As Richard Frye poignantly notes, 'Poems have been preserved which describe Bukhara in this period as a sewer, unfit for human life.'[15]

Plagued by a lack of capable leadership and an increasingly troubled economy, the Samanid government suffered a near-fatal blow when a confederation of Turkic nomads known as the Qara-khanids invaded the capital in 992. When the Qara-khanids returned to deliver the coup-de-grâce a few years later, in the fall of 999, it seems the population did little to support the Samanid regime which had become powerless to resist the Turkic onslaught.

For several years thereafter a son of Nuḥ II, Ismāʿīl Mustanṣir, travelled here and there throughout the region seeking military support from his neighbours and attempting to restore the Samanid state, but without success. Eventually in 1005 he was murdered by Arab tribesmen who had settled near Marv, and there were no further efforts to revive Samanid rule. The Tajik people – increasingly the majority as Central Asia continued to be Islamicized – would serve Turkic rulers for most of the next eight and a half centuries.

4

Tajiks and Turks

Bāš-sız börk bolmaz, Tāt-sız Türk bolmaz
(A hat won't be without a head, a Turk won't be without a Tajik)
(Old Turkic saying)

Turkic nomads referred to Muslim invaders as 'Tāzīk' from as early as 720, when the term appears in a Turkish inscription from southern Kazakhstan.[1] Initially, the word was applied indiscriminately to Muslims in general, although with the gradual entrenchment of Muslim power in the region the majority of immigrants into the region – and, with time, local converts – were Iranians, not Arabs.

Within the ever-shifting alliances and confederations among the various Turkic tribes, it had long been a trend for ambitious Turks to assume the cultural trappings of the civilizations they came to rule. This strategy had the dual purpose of facilitating their integration into existing international trade networks on the one hand, and making them more acceptable as rulers in the eyes of the general population on the other. In China this meant embracing Chinese culture and traditions, while in the West it entailed adopting Iranian norms. (In the same way, in later centuries some Turkic groups interacting with Russia would become largely Russified.) The Qara-khanids, who brought an end to Samanid rule at the end of the tenth century, had formally adopted Islam *en masse* beginning in around 960.

The Turk–Tajik symbiosis

For Central Asian Turks accepting and promoting Islam was only one aspect of claiming to be 'civilized'. Going back to the Sasanian model of pre-Islamic times, having a 'high' culture was also defined as knowing and supporting the

Persian language and its literature, as well as art, courtly music, food, dress and ceremony. Over the next eight centuries successive waves of nomadic invaders from the steppes, mostly Turkic-speaking, would continuously move in and take over the Central Asian oases one after the other, each following in the steps of their predecessors by embarking on this process of acculturation.

Obviously as one Turkic tribe after another became Islamicized and Persianized, their previous use of the term 'Tajik' to denote Muslims in general – as a group distinct from themselves – was no longer meaningful. Moreover, in taking over the reins of government the Turks, similar to the Arabs, tended to leave local bureaucracies in place. These consisted largely of Tajik *dabīr*s, who maintained their own particular (often chauvinistic) mindsets even as they came to serve new masters. Thus, from the time of the Qara-khanids onward the Turk/Tajik dichotomy came to acquire a more socio-genealogical meaning, evoking an essentialized difference between the refinements of the urban, literate Persian-speakers and the rough, battle-hardened qualities of the Turkic ruling class.

Like all stereotypes, these caricatures masked a considerable degree of ambiguity. Since Turkic men often 'married up' and started families with Tajik women, the bloodlines tended to become increasingly mixed over the generations. (Recent DNA studies in Uzbekistan and Tajikistan have shown no notable genetic difference between modern Uzbeks and Tajiks.[2]) And since children typically spent their first years within the harem, the influence of Tajik mothers in constructing the identity of their mixed-race children was surely much greater than is admitted in the patriarchal written sources of the time. Military figures in particular often made much of their tough Turkic heritage, even as they sought to demonstrate their own cultivation by speaking Persian and patronizing Persian courtly culture. The Tajik scribes, for their part, were naturally required to flatter their patrons, but they flattered themselves as well in whatever subtle ways they could.

The dependency of the Turks on Tajik support was widely acknowledged, as evidenced by a popular Turkish saying from the eleventh-century dictionary compiled by Maḥmūd of Kashgar and quoted at the beginning of this chapter. Kā<u>sh</u>garī also highlights the ambivalence this reality provoked among the Turks, expressed in another telling verse: 'When a sword becomes rusty (*tāt-ïqsa*), the job begins to suffer; When a man becomes Tajikified (*tāt-ïqsa*), his flesh begins to stink.'[3] ('Tāt' was a somewhat pejorative synonym for Tajik. It was still used in the Caucasus in modern times, especially for Iranian-speaking Jews.)

Kāshgarī, who was perhaps history's first pro-Turkish linguistic purist, confirms the tendency towards bilingualism that was prevalent in his time. In his opinion, Turks who stayed aloof from the urban Tajik population retained 'the most elegant speech', in contrast to those who mixed with them. It is worth noting that according to Kāshgarī, in frontier towns such as Talas, Isfijab and even the Qara-khanid capital of Balasaghun, this bilingualism was Turkish and Sogdian rather than Turkish and Persian,[4] suggesting that the Islamization process there was still far from complete.

The Ghaznavids

No figure better represents this sometimes tense symbiosis of identities than the founder of the Ghaznavid Empire, Maḥmūd b. Sebüktegīn (r. 998–1030). Maḥmūd was the son of a former slave soldier who rose to become the semi-independent governor of Ghazna under the Samanids. His mother, however, was a Tajik woman from a wealthy landowning family in the region of Zābulistān, the legendary birthplace of *Book of Kings* hero Rustam. Thus, while Maḥmūd's reign is generally taken to mark the beginning of Turkic rule over the Muslim world, he himself was half-Tajik. In fact he did as much to foster the spread of Iranian culture as he did the Turkic, and in some ways more so. It is one of the ironies of history that from the eleventh century and even up to the twentieth century, Turk-led governments from Anatolia to India would become the world's principal promoters of Iranian civilization, a process that began with Maḥmūd.

The reasons for this have already been stated: Persianization was a way for Turkic elites to demonstrate their legitimacy as imperial rulers, even though the administrators who ran the Turkic empires – and also the scribes who memorialized them – were mainly Iranians. Persian was thus confirmed as the language of culture and prestige. As Maḥmūd's poet laureate, Abū'l-Qāsim 'Unṣurī (d. 1039), wrote in one of his couplets, *Cho bā ādamī juft gardad parī/ Nagūyad parī juz ba lafs-i darī* (When a fairy couples with a human, the fairy won't speak but in Persian). Among the other important Tajik lyric poets employed at the Ghaznavid court one may count such figures as Abū'l-Hasan Farrukhī (d. 1038) and Abū Najm Manuchehrī (d. 1041). Maḥmūd, moreover, was the final patron of that unsurpassed repository of Iranian culture, the *Book of Kings*, although its author, Firdawsī, was left bitterly disappointed by the miserliness of this patronage.

Notwithstanding Maḥmūd's lukewarm reception of Firdawsī's masterpiece centuries of Turkic sovereigns after him would commission lavishly illustrated copies of the *Book of Kings* for their royal libraries. Often they would have their painters depict the epic's many heroes with Turkic facial features, reflecting the ruling elites' persistent desire to write themselves into the ancient Iranian royal tradition with all that it entailed. Maḥmūd's successors sought to do this through patronizing historiographical works as well, notably the *Zayn al-akhbār* of Abū Sa'īd Gardīzī (*c.* 1050) and the *Tārīkh-i Mas'ūdī* of Abū'l-Fazl Bayhaqī (d. 1077). Another important work giving insight into the elite culture of the time, dating to the later Ghaznavid period, is the *Four Discourses* of Aḥmad b. 'Umar, known as Niẓāmī-i Arūẓī of Samarkand. In this work the author offers prescriptive discussions of four professions considered 'indispensable' for the running of a civilized society: the Secretary (*dabīr*), the Poet, the Astrologer and the Physician. All were vocations that the Turkic rulers found themselves entirely dependent on educated Tajiks to fill.

Maḥmūd is best known as the conqueror who permanently established Muslim dominance in northern India, which – apart from a brief period of Tajik rule under the Ghurids during the late twelfth and early thirteenth centuries – remained under the control of Turkic dynasties all the way up to 1857. Maḥmūd was accompanied on his Indian campaigns by the great Khwarazmian scholar Abū Rayḥān Bīrūnī (973–1048), whose encyclopaedic study of India's religions and scientific achievements, the *Book of India* (*Kitāb mā fī li'l-Hind*) is still a useful resource for scholars today. In an earlier work, the *Remaining Traces from Past Centuries* (*Al-Āthār al-bāqiya 'an al-qurūn al-khāliya*), Bīrūnī assembled a uniquely informative catalogue of social and religious customs, including those of pre-Islamic Central Asia, in many cases based on primary research: In addition to Arabic, Persian and his native Khwarazmian, he knew Sogdian as well.

By bringing the land routes out of India under Muslim control, the Ghaznavid presence facilitated the movement of people and goods between the subcontinent and the Middle East. Transoxiana lay outside Ghaznavid control and remained part of the Qara-khanid sphere. No longer the centre of a powerful empire, Bukhara continued to be a hotbed of Ismāʿīlī activism until its Ḥanafī scholars finally succeeded in persuading the Qara-khanid sultan Bughrā Khān to order a general massacre of Ismāʿīlīs in 1044. With the Ismāʿīlīs at last removed from the scene, the Ḥanafīs became the undisputed religious authorities of Transoxiana. In Bukhara, a family of jurists called the Burhāns combined this with their extensive business connections to assert virtual control over local politics. Their prominence frequently brought them into conflict with their nominal Qara-khanid overlords, and a succession of Burhān family leaders met violent deaths.

Notwithstanding the efforts of Ismāʿīlī proselytizers – who mainly targeted people that were already Muslim and whose sophisticated esoteric teachings held a special appeal for the intellectual classes – Sufi mystics can be considered the Muslim world's first true missionaries in the sense that they actively sought to bring non-Muslims into the Islamic fold, not for economic or political reasons but primarily for spiritual ones. Among the Sufis who travelled to India during the Ghaznavid period the best known is ʿAlī Hujwīrī, a native of Ghazna who, like many scholars and mystics of the time, spent his youth travelling throughout the Islamic lands in search of teachers and books. Sometime during the reign of Sulṭān Masʿūd (1030–40) he travelled to Lahore in the Punjab, where he remained for the rest of his life. Hujwīrī's mystical treatise *The Unveiling of Mysteries* (*Kashf al-maḥjūb*) was the first major Sufi manual to be composed in Persian. A slightly later Sufi writer of Ghazna, Majdūd Sanā'ī, wrote the first Persian Sufi didactic epic, *The Walled Garden of Truth* (*Ḥadīqat al-ḥaqīqa*), using the *masnavī* format of rhymed couplets that would be adopted two centuries later by the unsurpassed mystic poet Jalāl al-dīn Rūmī, the inspiration for the so-called 'Whirling Dervishes' of Konya.

Maḥmūd's forays into India were essentially plundering raids – large Hindu temples, such as the one at Somnath pillaged by Maḥmūd and his forces in 1025, were known to be vast storehouses of treasure. Thus, as with the Arabs four centuries earlier, the principal driving force for his campaigns was economic rather than religious. Also like the Arabs, however, Maḥmūd's soldiers were emboldened by the rhetoric of the holy warrior (*ghazī*), fighting in the name of orthodox Sunni Islam with all the zeal of the recently – and no doubt sometimes superficially – converted.

Throughout the centuries to come many subsequent Turkic leaders would wage wars in the name of 'restoring Sunni Islam', but in most cases this was little more than propaganda. Turkic fighters were famously fond of such things as heavy drinking and pederasty, among other vices, and one can imagine the quandary of their religious advisors who often had to turn a blind eye to their patrons' behaviour even as they egged them on in their endless efforts to 'crush the infidels'.

A militant, if perhaps somewhat cynical, pro-Sunni ideology also served to justify Maḥmūd's attacks on Iran to the west, where he could present himself as ridding the largely Sunni Islamic heartlands from the unjust rule of the Shīʿite Būyid 'heretics'. He died shortly after his last successful Iran campaign in 1029, by which point the extent of his empire practically matched that of the Abbasids at their height. The following decade saw internecine struggles for power between Maḥmūd's twin sons Muḥammad and Maʿsūd. Even so, the Ghaznavids managed to persist in their military tug of war with the Iranian Būyids in the west and the Turkic Qara-khanids in the north for some years to come.

The Seljuks

During this period yet another rival appeared on the scene, a newly formed Turkic confederation from the steppes known as the Oghuz Turkmen with the Seljuk clan at its head. Bands of Oghuz raiders began attacking the caravans and trade centres of Transoxiana and Khurasan, and neither their Qara-khanid overlords nor the Ghaznavids proved able to stop them. One sees a recurring pattern here, where no sooner does a Turkic group settle into administering a settled territory than their 'swords begin to rust', as the saying went – a sign, no doubt, that they have become 'Tajikified' and are hence due to be replaced by another, more 'authentic' Turkic ruling tribe.

The main Ghaznavid army under Masʿūd was decisively defeated by Oghuz cavalry near Marv in 1040, opening the way for the Seljuks to move into Iran proper and eventually in 1055 to Baghdad. There, playing the familiar 'champions of Sunni Islam' card, they received the Caliph's support in expelling the Shīʿite Būyids. They then continued their campaigns westward towards Anatolia, where they enjoyed a hugely symbolic victory over the Roman imperial forces at the Battle of Manzikert in 1071. This landmark success marked the beginning of the Turkification of Asia Minor, a process that continues even up to the present day.

With their capital now at Baghdad, the Seljuks under Sultan Malik Shāh fell into the established pattern of adapting themselves into an Iranian polity, relying on Persian bureaucrats to run things and adopting all the trappings of Iranian monarchs. Sunni orthodoxy remained an ideological bulwark of the state, with covert Ismāʿīlī missionary activity superseding Būyid political power as the major perceived threat. The most famous Ismāʿīlī propagandist of the time was Nāṣir-i Khusraw, who kept a record of his peregrinations in a travelogue that is still widely read today.

Nāṣir was born in 1004 in what is now southwestern Tajikistan. While young he acquired the kind of comprehensive knowledge that characterized the great minds of classical Islam, encompassing not just Islamic Studies but also philosophy, mathematics, medicine, astronomy and a number of foreign languages. He was able to secure employment first under the Ghaznavids and then under their successors the Seljuks, but at the age of 42 he abandoned his professional career and set off on a pilgrimage to Mecca.

For the next six years Nāṣir travelled about the Near East. Much of this time he spent at Cairo, where the Ismāʿīlī Fatimid state was at the height of its power. He studied at Al-Azhar (today the most highly regarded centre for Sunni learning, the institution was in fact originally founded by the Fatimids as a training centre for Ismāʿīlī missionaries), where he mastered the esoteric doctrine to such an extent that he was made chief missionary for the region of Khurasan, for which he set off in 1052.

Unfortunately for Nāṣir eastern Iran at the time was very much under the control of the vigorously pro-Sunni Seljuks, who were allocating significant state resources towards the violent suppression of Ismāʿīlīs. He therefore found it more prudent to confine his activities to the mountain regions of Badakhshan, beyond the reach of government agents. In 1060 he settled in the Yamghan region of what is now northern Afghanistan, where he remained and carried out his mission for the next twenty-eight years until his death. Nāṣir's mission seems to have enjoyed remarkable success since today much of the population of Badakhshan, in both Afghanistan and Tajikistan, are Ismāʿīlīs who consider Nāṣir-i Khusraw as the founder of their community.

By the late eleventh century the Seljuks, now in firmly in control of the Islamic heartlands, were faced with a new distraction in the form of the Frank-led Crusades. Throughout the twelfth century the Seljuks' eyes were to the west. The Tajiks of Transoxiana were left at first under nominal Qara-khanid rule, then as vassals to an emerging steppe power from the east known as the Qara-khitai – but with the Burhān family continuing to run Bukhara and a Qara-khanid governor still in Samarkand. From the 1180s the Shah of Khwarazm – himself of Turkic origin but ruling over a region that was still Iranian-speaking – became an additional active competitor for hegemony in the region.

The twelfth century saw the growth and spread of Sufism in Central Asia, due largely to the missionary activities of Yūsuf Hamadānī (1062–1141), a scholar from Baghdad who settled in Marv, and his disciples Aḥmad Yasavī (1093–1166) and ʿAbd al-Khāliq Ghidjuvānī (d. 1179). Part of a chain known as the Khwājagān ('the Masters'), these spiritual teachers laid the foundations for a Sufi order that would be established two centuries later by Bahā al-dīn Naqshband of Bukhara. From the fifteenth century onwards the Naqshbandiyya would dominate the spiritual life of Central Asia.

The Ghurids – a Tajik dynasty

Amidst the ascendancy of Turkic tribes that had been steadily taking place all across Central Asia another pocket of Iranian rule still survived in the isolated, mountainous Ghur region east of Herat. This was an area populated mainly by Tajiks, many of whom had not yet fully embraced Islam. (It had long been a stronghold of Buddhism.)

Beginning in the middle of the twelfth century the Ghurid Tajiks, under the leadership of the brothers Muʿizz al-dīn and Ghiyās al-dīn, took advantage of the ongoing struggles between the Ghaznavids and Seljuks to seize the territories of Bamiyan and Tukharistan for themselves. Then, having made an opportunistic alliance with the Seljuk authorities in Herat and Balkh, the

Ghurid brothers took Ghazna itself from the Ghaznavids. While Ghiyās turned his attention to the west, Mu'izz set his sights on the Punjab, conquering Multan in 1175 and Lahore in 1186.

The Ghurids remained in control of northwestern India until the death of Mu'izz in 1206, after which one of his Turkish slave soldiers, Quṭb al-dīn Aybak, seized power and went on to establish the Delhi Sultanate. Despite their relatively short reign, the Ghurids can be credited not only with consolidating Muslim rule in north India but also with fostering the establishment of a Persian court culture that would be maintained by subsequent Turkic dynasties there well into the nineteenth century. Also, while the Ghurid sultanate did not endure more than a few decades as an imperial entity, in a certain sense it can be considered the last independent Tajik state of the pre-modern period. The Ghurids left a number of significant architectural remains, the best known of which is the Jām minaret in west-central Afghanistan (see Figure 4.1).

By the early thirteenth century most of the Iranian world from the Zagros Mountains to the Hindu Kush had come under the rule of Khwarazm, south of the Aral Sea. In 1207, when the Khwarazmians were at the height of their power, the mystical poet Jalāl al-dīn (later known as Mawlānā or Rūmī) was born in the town of Vakhsh beside the river of the same name, near the modern village of Sangtuda in southern Tajikistan. At age 5 young Jalāl al-dīn accompanied his father, Bahā al-dīn Valad, himself a respected theologian and mystic, to Samarkand. A few years later they fled westwards to escape the Mongol armies that were advancing into the region. After sojourns in Nishapur and Baghdad, they eventually settled in the western Anatolian city of Konya which the Seljuks had recently taken from the Byzantines or eastern Romans – hence the sobriquet 'Rūmī' which the poet acquired in his adulthood. Nominal founder of the Mevlevi Sufi order, Rūmī is claimed by the Turks on the basis of his residence, by the Persians because of his language and by Afghans due to his father's origins in Balkh. By birth and upbringing, however, he may rightly be considered a Tajik.

Many Central Asians fortunate enough to escape before the Mongol onslaught chose to head south rather than west, seeking refuge under the Mamluks of Delhi. This included a scholar from Ghur by the name of Minhāj al-din Juzjānī, who became the court historian of Sulṭān Nasīr al-dīn Maḥmūd

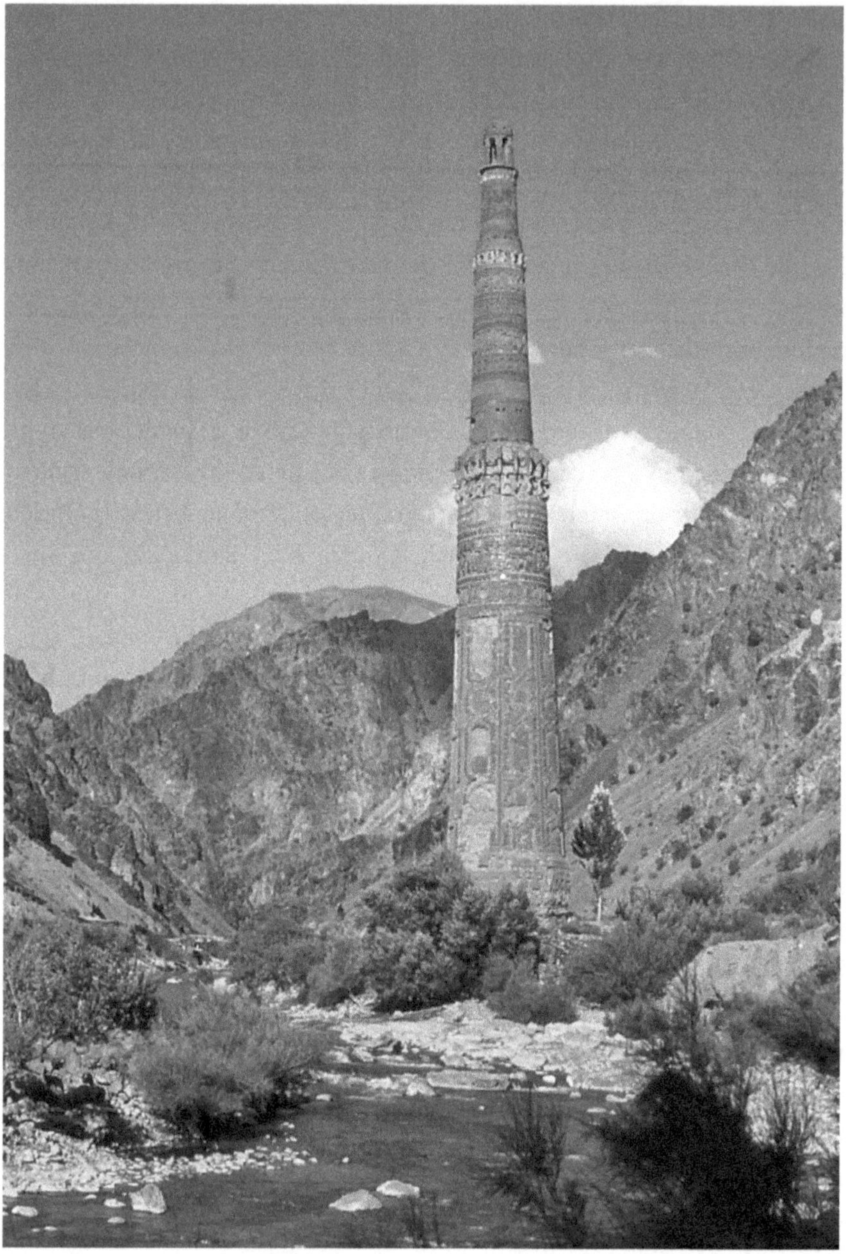

Figure 4.1 Ghūrid minaret, Jām, Afghanistan. Late twelfth century. Photo courtesy of Wiki Commons.

(r. 1246–66). Juzjānī's best-known work, the twenty-three-volume *Tabaqāt-i Naṣīrī*, is the major historical source for the Ghurid dynasty.

The Mongols

Mongolia had historically been mainly a concern for the Chinese, who, like their Tajik analogues in Central Asia, had a long history of tense relations with nomadic tribes to the north. (The Great Wall was built in stages beginning in the seventh century BCE in an attempt to keep the nomads out, but it never succeeded in doing so.) During the second half of the twelfth century the eastern steppelands were under the control of the Qara-khitai, a nomadic confederation linguistically related to and most likely including many Mongol tribes.

Within the ever-shifting realignments of tribal alliances that make steppe politics so maddeningly difficult to follow, an unusual event took place in 1206. A young, charismatic man by the name of Temüjin, who had spent the past two years waging battles and winning followers, succeeded in gathering the loyalty of all the Mongol tribes – similar to what Muhammad had done in Arabia six centuries earlier – and had himself crowned as their supreme leader, or *khāgān*. The assembly of elders (*quriltai*) that had gathered for this purpose gave him the title Chinggis Khan, meaning 'universal ruler'. With the Mongol tribes now united, they could no longer attack each other and had to direct their raids further afield.

For the next decade Chinggis was preoccupied with subduing various neighbouring powers such as the Uighurs and the Qarluqs into tributary status. He then turned his attention to the Qara-khanids, whose capital at Balasaghun (near modern Tokmak in Kyrgyzstan) was captured by a Mongol detachment in 1216. By this point a number of Tajik communities bordering the southern steppes were now living under Mongol sovereignty.

During the same period, the Shah of Khwarazm, Muḥammad II, had been expanding his territory at the expense of the Qara-khanids in Transoxiana and of the Seljuks in Iran. Most of the Tajik-inhabited lands had come under his control, including Bukhara, Samarkand (despite a failed rebellion in 1212), Ferghana, Balkh and Herat. In 1217 the Khwarazm-Shah tried to march on Baghdad so as to force the submission of the Caliph, but he and his army were turned back by a snowstorm in the Zagros Mountains.

Despite this failure, the Khwarazmian state now encompassed most of the Iranian world and had become the immediate neighbour of the Mongol confederation to the east. Chinggis acknowledged this new relationship by sending an embassy to the Khwarazm-Shah seeking to open trade relations, but the arrogant Muḥammad II rebuffed this overture and had the Mongol ambassadors killed.

An infuriated Chinggis retaliated by launching an invasion of Khwarazmian territory. Unfortunately for the Tajiks their lands lay directly in the Mongols' path, and Samarkand and Bukhara were among the first cities to experience the full force of Mongol brutality. This included the massacre of entire populations and the wholesale destruction of cities down to the last brick. In the wake of all this devastation Khwarazm became largely Turkified as the bulk of the settled, Iranian-speaking population were either annihilated or driven into exile and Turkic nomads moved into the region to take their place. The Khwarazmian language appears to have died out at this time.

Some Tajik merchants, on the other hand, having had the prescience to attach themselves to the Mongols early on, now prospered in the aftermath of all this initial destruction, and within twenty years or so Bukhara and Samarkand were once again functioning as important centres of trans-Asian trade. In fact, the ensuing *pax mongolica* proved to be enormously beneficial in the long run for both trade and cultural exchange since the entire region from Eastern Europe to China was now under a single government: Caravan routes were well policed, and tariffs were regularized. Moreover, the Mongols typically spared skilled workers from their horrific ravages. Once the dust of destruction had cleared, Tajik craftsmen and other professionals were sent to practice their expertise all throughout the Mongol Empire. This included wine-making, which was introduced to northern China by Tajik viniculturists transplanted from Samarkand.

Upon Chinggis' death in 1227 his empire was divided among his four male offspring, with the lands from Transoxiana to Kashgar falling to his second son, Chaghatay. Over the following century Chaghatay's successors ruled and added to these territories, forming an increasingly independent khanate. The Chaghatayid ruler 'Alā al-dīn Tārmāshīrīn adopted Islam in 1329; this was a key step, demonstrating that the Central Asian Mongols would follow the historical pattern of steppe conquerors gradually assimilating themselves into the local culture where they ruled. (The Il-khan Mongols in Iran had already done this at the end of the thirteenth century, while the Kublaiyids who founded the Yüan dynasty in China had embraced Buddhism.) The Islamization of the general population met with some resistance, however, especially in northern towns such as Talas and Almalik (near modern Khorgos) where Nestorian Christianity – established since pre-Islamic times through the connections of Sogdian Christian traders with the Middle East – had a strong presence.

Throughout this time the Chaghatay lands were plagued by more or less continuous infighting amongst various Chinggisid claimants, leading to a constant cycle of annihilation and reconstruction. The Moroccan traveller Ibn Baṭṭūṭa, who visited Samarkand in 1333, praised it as 'One of the grandest and finest cities, and the most perfect of them'. Yet he noted that the city walls and gates were no longer functional, though there was much activity in the bazaar.[5]

It was during the turbulent period following the Mongol conquest that a Tajik Sufi master, Sayf al-dīn Bākharzī (1190–1261), returned to Bukhara from Khwarazm where he had been a disciple of Najm al-dīn Kubrā and was appointed to run an important pious foundation (*waqf*) which included a Sufi lodge. His reputation spread throughout Central Asia and the religious complex became a well-known and prosperous centre for Sufi pilgrimage.

Throughout the fourteenth century Central Asian Sufism expanded even further through the efforts of Bahā' al-dīn Naqshband (1318–89), eponymous founder of the Naqshbandī order that would come to dominate Central Asian society and politics up to the modern period. Bahā' al-dīn was born near Bukhara and spent most of his life there. Influenced by the teachings of earlier Sufi masters Yūsuf Hamadānī and 'Abd al-Khāliq Ghijduvānī who had been active in Central Asia, Bahā' al-dīn taught such techniques as silent *ẓikr* (meditative repetition of the divine names). Ghijduvānī's methods also included attention to one's breathing (*hūsh dar dam*), a practice that is sometimes considered to be a sign of Indian influence having penetrated Central Asia's spiritual circles.

One of the important Tajik Sufi poets of the fourteenth century was Kamāl Khujandī, who was born in Khujand and educated in Samarkand but went on to spend his life in Tabriz. The following *ghazal*, in the style of Kamāl's more celebrated contemporary Ḥāfiẓ of Shiraz, emphasizes the poet's feeling of spiritual alienation and yearning. Soviet scholar Bobojon Ghafurov interprets this on the most literal level, as nostalgia for his 'Tajik' homeland.[6] But serious poetry isn't generally intended to be taken literally, and separation is a standard theme in Sufi literature. More likely, Kamāl means here to evoke the soul's suffering due to estrangement from the Divine Beloved. The absent subject of longing is symbolized by 'dear ones' (*jānān*, a code word for fellow seekers who would unite in Sufi gatherings):

Dil muqīm-i kū-yi jānān ast va man īnjā gharīb
chūn kunad bīchāra-yi miskīn-i tan tanhā gharīb
dar gharībī jān ba sakhtī mīdihad Kamāl
Vā gharībī, vā gharībī, vā gharībī, vā gharīb!

The heart resides in the street of the dear ones, and here am I here estranged
What can this wretched, helpless body do alone, estranged
In estrangement Kamāl will give up the ghost with difficulty
Oh estrangement, oh estrangement, oh estrangement – alas for the estranged!

The Timurids

Central Asia under the Chaghatayids was less a unified khanate than an assemblage of squabbling statelets. Beginning in about 1370 the leader of the Turkic Barlas tribe, an ambitious young man by the name of Tīmūr (Tamerlane, 'Timur the Lame', referring to a childhood injury that left him with a limp), began to unify the region under his control. From his native Kish south of Samarkand, he first seized Balkh and then Khwarazm. Tīmūr aimed to restore the vast empire of Chinggis Khan, but because he was not a direct descendant of that fearsome Mongol conqueror he claimed instead to rule in the name of a Chinggisid puppet. Notwithstanding this he proved to be one of the most brutal, uncompromising and authoritarian sovereigns in Central Asian history.

Over a thirty-five-year career Tīmūr forced most of the Islamic lands into submission, from Mesopotamia to the frontiers of India. In 1398 he even penetrated as far as Delhi which he ruthlessly sacked. His hold on India proved temporary, however, as did his presence in Anatolia after defeating the Ottoman sultan Bāyazīd I Yıldırım ('the Thunderbolt') in 1402. In the Caucasus he justified mass killings and enslavement of the Christian Georgians and Alans by using the premise of holy war, and the once-prosperous Nestorian communities of Central Asia did not survive his reign. He was equally merciless in persecuting Ismāʿīlīs and other Shīʿite 'heretics'.

On the other hand, the Tajiks of Tīmūr's native Transoxiana fared rather well under his rule, as he built up Samarkand into the most fabulous city of its time. Foreign visitors, including a number of Europeans, were awestruck by its opulence. The Bibi Khanum mosque, erected in honour of his wife, boasted the largest dome ever constructed, and the Gūr-i Amīr mausoleum, built for Tīmūr's heir apparent who died prematurely and in which he himself was later buried, was in some ways the architectural forerunner to India's Taj Mahal. Tīmūr also commissioned the construction of a massive palace in his native town of Kish (modern Shahri Sabz), although today only the two sides of the main entry gate have survived.

Tīmūr was surely one of Central Asia's most effective empire-builders, but his achievements did not long outlast him. The usual internecine disputes followed his death in 1405, with various relatives holding onto whatever fragments of territory they could. The strongest of these claimants was Tīmūr's youngest son, Shāhrukh, who had been given the governorship of Herat; this city displaced Samarkand as the Timurid capital following Tīmūr's demise.

Shāhrukh proved himself a great patron of culture and his reign witnessed an impressive flourishing of literature and the arts. He also oversaw many important building projects, including the shrine of the Sufi saint 'Abdullah Ansārī (d. 1088) and major renovations to Herat's bazaar, while his wife, Gawharshād, funded the construction of mosque/madrasa complexes both in Herat and in the Shīʿa shrine city of Mashhad further west. A son of Shāhrukh by Gawharshād, Prince Bāysunghur, established a library-cum-atelier at Herat where books were lavishly copied and illustrated. The best-known relic of this period is a copy of the *Book of Kings* now in the Golestan Palace in Tehran; it features paintings by the most skilled artists of the time. Also employed at Shāhrukh's court was the historian Ḥāfiẓ-i Abrū, whose *Collection of Histories* (*Majmaʿ al-tawārīkh*) was similarly embellished with beautiful miniatures. Tajik merchants and craftsmen profited from Shāhrukh's economic policies which included a revival of trade with China.

During this time the province of Samarkand was independently governed by Shāhrukh's eldest son, Ulugh Beg, who was every bit as active in promoting the sciences as his father was for the arts. Ulugh Beg commissioned the construction of a madrasa in Samarkand's Registan Square that still bears his name, and later an observatory where he could indulge his interest in astronomy. In 1437 he completed a star catalogue (*zīj*) which is considered by historians of science to have been the most accurate of its day.

Shāhrukh's death in 1447 was again followed by succession struggles. These were further complicated by interference from the Qara-Koyunlu (Black Sheep) Turkmens, who now controlled western Iran, and from nomadic Uzbek tribes from the north. Ulugh Beg, for all his scientific erudition, was no warrior, and he could not overcome the various factions fighting to take his father's place. He was eventually murdered on the orders of his own son 'Abd al-Latīf (d. 1450) who was serving as governor of Balkh. A religious reactionary in contrast to his scientifically minded father, 'Abd al-Latīf can nevertheless be credited with having commissioned the most impressive Timurid monument to be found in present-day Tajikistan, the Blue Dome (Kök Gumbaz) mosque and madrasa complex in Istaravshon, not far from Khujand at the western edge of the Ferghana Valley (see Figure 4.2).

In 1451 Samarkand was taken by Ulugh Beg's nephew Abū Sa'īd with help from a hitherto marginal western Turkic alliance known as the Uzbeks. The Timurid lands remained divided amongst rival claimants throughout the following decade, however, until Abū Sa'īd finally succeeded in subduing all his relatives. The Naqshbandī Sufi order, under the leadership of Khwāja 'Ubaydullah Aḥrār (1404–90), developed a policy of political involvement during this time. The Naqshbandīs became closely tied to the Timurid family, offering spiritual guidance and confirmation while receiving considerable state support in return. As Jo-Ann Gross has noted, 'Khwāja Aḥrār's leadership marked a turning point in the history of Sufi communities in the eastern Islamic world in which the Naqshbandīya of Mawarannahr penetrated the socio-economic and political fabric of Timurid society to an unprecedented degree. Sufis acquired great status, enjoyed remarkable benefits and established networks of philanthropy and economic activity that continued up to the Soviet period.'[7]

Over the following centuries Tajik Naqshbandī families such as the Juybārīs of Bukhara and the Dahbidīs of Samarkand would enjoy enormous wealth and

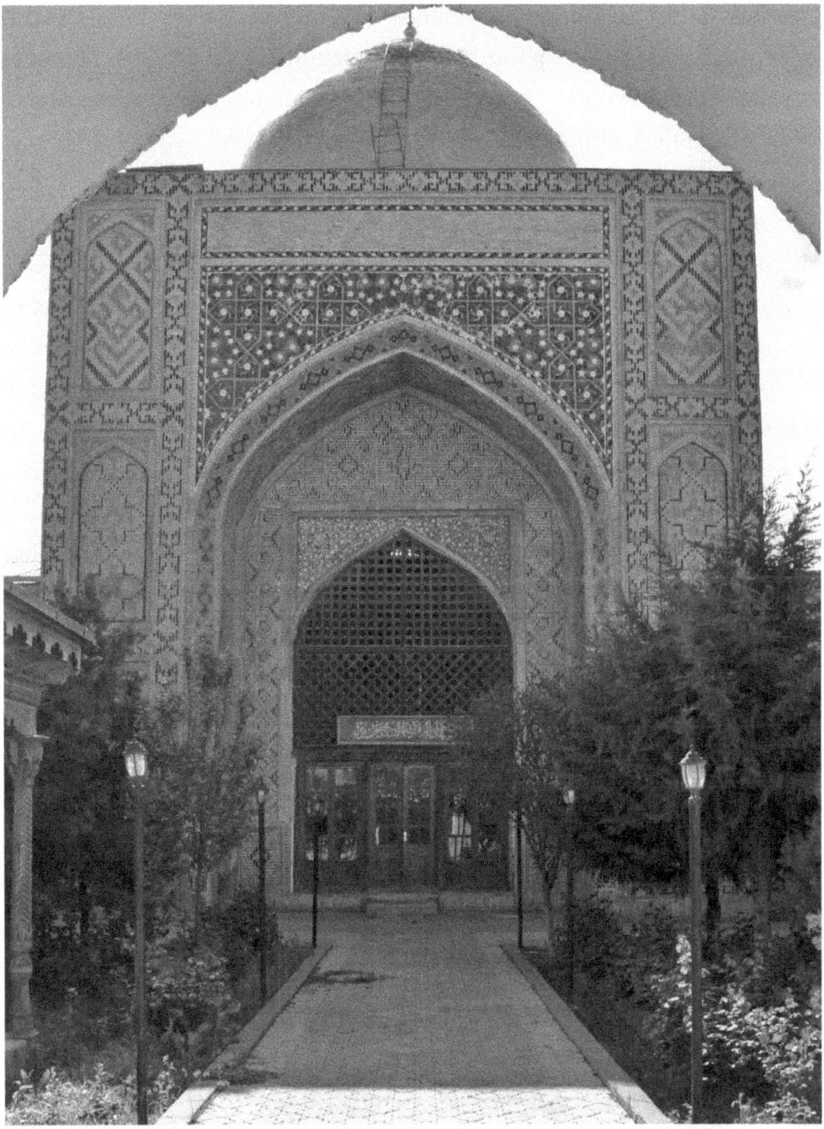

Figure 4.2 Kök Gumbaz madrasa complex, commissioned by the Timurid ruler Sultān 'Abdul-Latīf. Mid-fifteenth century. Istaravshon, Tajikistan.

influence.[8] Apart from receiving regular donations from their disciples, the shaykhs were enriched and empowered by the governing elites who assigned them custody over tax-free pious endowments (*waqfs*) which 'provided a secure economic base to the religious class and its institutions'.[9] These *waqfs* included mosques, madrasas, *k͟hānqāhs* (Sufi lodges), shrines, farms, irrigation networks, shops, caravanserais, bathhouses and other public infrastructure. Such custodianships were passed on within families, enabling them to amass vast economic and political power over the generations. One can see lingering traces of this effect within Tajik (and Uzbek) society even today.

The hagiographer ʻAbd al-Razzāq Samarqandī goes so far as to credit Khwāja Aḥrār with 'plant[ing] the thought of ruling the world in the mind of Mīrzā Sulṭān Abū Saʻīd', stating that the latter always considered himself to be [Khwāja Aḥrār's] agent, and if it were ever possible to do anything against his wishes, he would still not do it.'[10] With the firm support of the Naqshbandī networks Abū Saʻīd went on to rule as unrivalled head of the Timurids until 1469, when he was captured in a battle against the Aq Qoyunlu Turkmens (the 'White Sheep', successors to the 'Black Sheep' in Azerbaijan), who turned him over to one of his Timurid cousins for execution.

Abū Saʻīd's death left a power vacuum that was eventually filled by his cousin Sulṭān Ḥusayn Bāyqarā ('the Eagle'), a capable leader who restored Herat as the Timurid capital and reigned there for the next thirty-eight years. Under Sultan Ḥusayn's patronage Herat became an unrivalled centre for the production of art and literature. The city was home to the legendary miniature painter Bihzād and to the last of the great classical Persian poets, the Naqshbandī shaykh ʻAbd al-Rahmān Jāmī, author of the *Seven Thrones* (*Haft awrang*) which includes his retellings of the popular romances *Laylā and Majnūn* and *Yūsuf and Zulaykha*.

Sulṭān Ḥusayn himself claimed that he had nearly 1,000 poets in his service, with Jāmī at their head.[11] Mīr Khwānd, a Sufi scholar from Bukhara who authored a universal history entitled *The Garden of Purity* (*Rawżat al-ṣafā*), was employed by Sulṭān Ḥusayn as well, as was his grandson Muḥammad Khwānd Amīr who would also go on to make his mark as a historian years later in India. Another important literary figure of the period was Ḥusayn Wāʻiz Kāshifī, author of a 'Mirror for Princes' work on ethics as well as a retelling of the *Kalila and Dimna* stories which he titled *The Lights of Canopus* (*Anwār-i Suhaylī*).

The Turkic language was promoted at Sulṭān Ḥusayn's court by the poet ʻAlī Shīr Navā'ī, a Turk by ethnic origin who could compose in Persian but also wrote in his native tongue, called Chaghatay or simply Turkī; this was the literary ancestor to modern Uzbek. Sulṭān Ḥusayn himself wrote in both languages, and his reign marked a turning point where Turkī was no longer necessarily seen as a rough, military idiom but capable of literary expression as well. Among urban Tajiks and Turks of different classes – merchants and craftsmen as well as scholars and bureaucrats – bilingualism was becoming the norm, so the Turk/Tajik distinction remained most pronounced in the countryside.

Sulṭān Ḥusayn and his family sponsored many important building projects, not just in Herat but also at Mazar-i Sharif further east where he funded the restoration of a shrine to the fourth Caliph (and first Shīʿa imam), ʿAlī b. Abī Ṭālib. During this period the Naqshbandīs maintained their powerful involvement in Central Asian politics: Jāmī, Navāʾī, and even the Sultan himself all counted themselves among Khwāja Aḥrār's disciples. The Timurid tomb complex in Samarkand where Khwāja Aḥrār is buried has remained a site of pilgrimage for Naqshbandī devotees up to the present day, as has that of his teacher and predecessor Yūsuf Charkhī (1360–1447) in the southern suburbs of Dushanbe.

The Uzbeks

The nomadic Uzbek tribes of the western steppes had been peripherally involved in Central Asian power struggles throughout the post-Mongol period, whether as mercenaries or as temporal allies. Around the turn of the sixteenth century, under the strong leadership of the Chinggisid governor of Tashkent, Muḥammad Shībānī Khān, the newly emboldened Uzbeks began to challenge Timurid power directly. They took Samarkand in 1501 and the Ferghana Valley a year later, followed by Khwarazm, Balkh and Bukhara in 1505–06. Sulṭān Ḥusayn finally marched from Herat at the head of a Timurid army to meet the Uzbek threat. He died along the way, however, and Shībānī Khān entered Herat the following year.

Meanwhile a young Timurid prince, Bābur, whom Shībānī Khān's forces had previously expelled from Samarkand on two occasions, gave up trying to hold onto his ancestral legacy and retreated to Kabul. Bābur governed there for another twenty years, launching periodic raids into northern India, before eventually settling in Delhi following a victory over the Afghan Lodis at the Battle of Panipat in 1526. This marked the establishment of a neo-Timurid state in India: within a few short decades the Mughal Empire, as it is known in the West, rose to become the wealthiest country in the world and the envy of Europe.[12]

The sudden expansion of the Uzbeks, meanwhile, was a source of worry to the recently established Shīʿite government of the Safavids in Iran. Led by their charismatic king Ismāʿīl I, the Safavids' Turkmen army defeated the Uzbeks at Marv in 1510. Shībānī Khān was executed, and following an old steppe tradition Shah Ismāʿīl had his head made into a drinking cup. The Uzbek polity in Central Asia survived, however, governed by a succession of Shībānī Khān's relatives. Bukhara once again acquired the status of capital, and the city flourished under Shibanid patronage.

In Iran, the Safavid policy of forced conversions to Shīʿism caused a large number of Sunni scholars, poets, artists and men of science to flee to Central Asia, India and other lands; many entered the service of the Uzbeks. This influx of talent greatly enriched the urban culture of Bukhara, Samarkand, Herat and Balkh. Prominent among these political refugees was the Shirazi scholar Faẕlullah Rūzbihān, who composed an important manual on governance, the *Sulūk al-mulūk* (The Conduct of Kings) for the Shibanid ruler ʿUbaydullah Khan during the 1530s. The local Naqshbandī shaykhs, meanwhile, survived the transition from Timurid to Uzbek power and maintained their status as 'spiritual preceptors' to the governing class, continuing to enjoy the economic benefits concomitant with their political position.

The dynamics of the global economy were changing during this period. The expansion of sea trade across the Indian Ocean and the increasing role of Europeans there enriched India even as the Central Asian overland routes declined. The Uzbek territories saw a realignment of trade oriented towards Russia,[13] a change in which even England played a role. The head of the English Muscovy Company, Sir Anthony Jenkinson, travelled through Russia to Bukhara on two occasions, the second time as ambassador of the Russian tsar Ivan IV in 1562. Russia had begun its long eastward expansion, having recently conquered two Muslim Turkic khanates to the southeast: Kazan in 1552 and Astrakhan in 1556.

In northern India, meanwhile, the cosmopolitan meritocracy of Akbar I (r. 1556–1605) had built the Timurid Empire of the Mughals the richest state the world had ever seen. As the global economy's centre of gravity shifted towards Delhi, so did the migration of ambitious men from all across the Muslim world.

The Uzbeks lost much local talent to their erstwhile Timurid rivals, as Turk soldiers and Tajik scholars, poets, Sufis, administrators, artists and businessmen all followed the money and sought their fortunes in the Mughals' employ. The Tajik poet 'Abd al-Raḥmān Mushfiqī of Bukhara (1525–88) travelled on two occasions to India where he was richly rewarded by his Mughal hosts. 'The land of Hind is a sugar field,' he wrote; 'its parrots all sell sugar'.[14]

There was a major influx of skilled migrants from Iran and the Arab world as well, but due to their own Central Asian origins the Mughals had maintained an exceptional level of contacts and networks with their homeland, which they referred to as the *gūrkhāna-yi ajdād* ('graveyard of [our] ancestors').[15] Sufi shaykhs of the Naqshbandī order were particularly favoured and could expect to be rewarded with lavish gifts and important positions upon their arrival in India.[16] The Mughals never really gave up their claim to the former Timurid lands, symbolically expressing their enduring attachment by a range of means which even included sending money for the restoration of their founding ancestor's mausoleum, the Gūr-i Amīr in Samarkand.[17]

The Timurids' tradition of patronage, particularly apparent in the realm of architecture, was nevertheless contested by the Uzbeks who built stunningly beautiful monuments of their own. These included the Lab-i Hawz ensemble in Bukhara – incorporating the spectacular Kukultāsh and Nādir Dīvān Begī madrasas – and the imposing Shīr-Dār and Tilla-Kārī madrasas in Samarkand's Registan Square. One of the most accomplished architects of the time was Mīrak-i Sayyid Ghiyās, originally from Herat. He designed a number of important of buildings and gardens for the Uzbeks at Bukhara before moving to India to work for the Mughals. His son Muḥammad, born in Bukhara, relocated to India as well. There, he was commissioned by Emperor Akbar to draw up the plans for Humayun's tomb in Delhi – this monument was the architectural forerunner to the celebrated Taj Mahal. (When the latter building was erected during the following century, the chief draftsman was from Samarkand and the head sculptor from Bukhara.)

Tajik religious scholars had enjoyed a high level of prestige throughout the Muslim world since the Samanid era but they were known for their conservatism. In a telling case, Qāẓī Abū'l-Ma'ālī of Bukhara, an advisor to the Shibanid ruler 'Abdullah Khān, succeeded in having the 'infidel' subjects of logic and dialectics banned from the emirate's madrasas. He later travelled to India, where he joined a reactionary faction of clerics who were struggling, with limited success, to defend Sunni orthodoxy at Akbar's liberal court.

The Uzbek elites also competed with the Mughals in extending patronage to Sufi orders, especially the Naqshbandiyya, constructing for them a number of important lodges and appointing them to powerful administrative positions. The royal ateliers, meanwhile, supported accomplished painters such as Maḥmud Muẕahhib of Herat, known as Shaykh-zāda. Even so, artistic production under the Uzbeks remained overshadowed by that of India and Iran. In the minds of many art historians, the so-called 'Bukhara style' of miniature painting appears flat and overly stylized in comparison with the more refined Safavid and Mughal schools that were its contemporaries.

Despite many cultural achievements, by the seventeenth century Central Asia was in economic decline. This was due as much to internecine struggles as to shifts in global trade routes. Given the Mughals' extraordinarily successful situation in India, their ongoing preoccupation with Central Asia – a region that was becoming increasingly marginal and ever less prosperous – might seem somewhat surprising. Sentimentality aside there was little there that could rival the opulence and international stature the Mughals enjoyed in India, not that the Uzbeks didn't try. In 1599 the Shibanid dynasty was overthrown by the Janids – also known as the Toqay-Timurids – a rival Chinggisid group fleeing the Russian takeover of Astrakhan. A branch of the Shibanids, however, retained control of Khwarazm for another century.

The Uzbeks practised an 'appanage' system of inheritance, which, in place of primogeniture, involved the distribution of lands amongst the males of the ruling family – a tradition inherited from the Mongols.[18] This meant that the various Uzbek princes were always in competition with each other to enlarge their respective territories. Such a system did not lend itself to economic or political stability. Many parts of the Hindu Kush and Pamir mountain regions, meanwhile, thanks to their virtual inaccessibility, remained for all practical purposes independent, only rarely remitting any form of tax to the Uzbeks. The Mughals, sensing the Uzbeks' limitations, launched a grand attempt to retake Central Asia in 1646–47 under the emperor Shah Jahan (builder of the Taj Mahal), but they got no farther than Balkh and the expedition turned into a humiliating failure.

Central Asia's brain drain towards India persisted throughout the seventeenth century. The anthologist Malīhā Samarqandī mentions twenty important Tajik poets who had left the Uzbek lands to seek their fortunes in India.[19] One, however, did not: Mīr 'Abid Sayyid of Nasaf (historic Nakhshab, modern-day Qarshi), known as Saido (d. *c.* 1710), who apparently contemplated emigration but in the end decided to stay in Bukhara. The most popular Tajik poet of his time, Saido wrote lyric odes (*ghazals*) in the classical Persian style, but with strikingly new subject matter. Instead of roses and nightingales, Saido's work addressed injustices perpetrated by society's elites and the hardships faced by ordinary working people. In the following passage he plays on the well-known Sufi motif which likens the lover's attraction to the beloved to that of a moth for the candle flame:

Sham' ba'd az kushtani parvona qasdi khud kunad,
Khuni nohaq shu'lai domoni qotil meshavad.
Dar jahon az himmati piron biju rohi najod,
Qomati khamgashta bar darioyi otash pul shavad.
Zi dunyo har ki shud labrez, umrash bebako gardad,
Chu kishti pur shavad az ob, girdobi fano gardad.
Shudam piru nemeoyad burun gahvora az yodam,
Qadam dar mulki hasti to nihodam, khonabardusham.[20]

The candle, having killed the moth, turns on itself
The blood of the victim will stain the killer's garments
Seek justice from the sages of the world
The one who prostrates before the sea of fire will be a bridge
Whoever is filled with the world, his life will not persist
A ship filled with water will sink in any storm
I've become old and can't forget the cradle
From the moment I set foot in this world, I cannot settle down.

Saido's popularity was rivalled throughout the eastern Muslim world by that of his contemporary, 'Abd al-Qādir Bīdil (1642–1720), who was of Central Asian Turkic origin but born in Delhi, where he spent his career at the court of the Mughals. Bīdil's poetry, written on the so-called 'Indian style' (*sabk-i hindī*) of literary Persian, explored existential themes using obscure language and innovative wordplay, departing from the classical style even while working within its established structures. Bīdil was not a Tajik and never lived in Central Asia, but he remains quite well known among the Tajiks of Central Asia today.

In 1709 the governor of Kokand in the Ferghana Valley rebelled against Bukhara and succeeded in establishing an independent state. Janid amirs continued to rule the remainder of the Uzbek khanate up to 1740, when they were forced to submit to the Persians under the Afsharid emperor Nāder Shāh. Transoxiana was thus reintegrated into the Iranian world, but this reunion proved ephemeral as Afsharid rule quickly disintegrated following Nāder's murder in 1747.

One of Nāder's generals, an ambitious Pashtun warrior by the name of Aḥmad Durrānī, seized this occasion to declare himself as the independent sovereign of Kandahar. Supported by the majority of Pashtun tribes as well as Tajiks, Aḥmad went on to take control of territories from the Oxus to India, thereby laying the foundations of modern Afghanistan. The resulting political bifurcation between the Uzbek and Afghan states has endured to the present day, dividing the Tajik world into two adjacent, but separately evolving, spheres.

In Transoxiana the power vacuum left by the collapse of the Afsharid regime was quickly filled by an Uzbekified family of Mongol origin, the Manghits, who established an Emirate in Bukhara. (The Manghit rulers took the Islamic title 'Emir' (Amīr) as opposed to the Mongol designation of 'Khan' because they could not claim Chinggisid descent.) Khwarazm meanwhile remained under the rule of a Chinggisid dynasty based in Khiva, as did Kokand in the east.

Kokand soon entered into an alliance with the Chinese Qing Empire, which, following their defeat of the Mongol Jungars – 'the last great Inner Asian nomadic state'[21] – absorbed the Altishahr ('Six Cities') region of the Tarim Basin during the mid-eighteenth century. Merchants based in the Ferghana Valley benefitted greatly from increased opportunities to trade with China. One assumes that these merchants were mainly Tajiks, though by this stage they would have been bilingual in Turkī and were coming to be known by the generic term 'Sart' – the designation 'Tajik' being used increasingly for rustic mountain-dwellers who did not necessarily speak Persian.

At the beginning of the nineteenth century the Kokand ruler, 'Ālim Khān (r. 1799–1811), departed from longstanding tradition by breaking the Turkic monopoly over the armed forces. Perhaps modelling the Ottoman policy of building the Janissary corps out of kidnapped Balkan Christians who lacked

Turkic tribal loyalties, 'Ālim Khān created a new military body, known as the Ghalcha, consisting of Pamiris whom he relocated to the Ferghana Valley; they were part of his 'New Army' (*sipāh-i jadīd*) intended to complement and counterbalance his 'Old Army' (*sipāh-i kuhna*). Turkic soldiers mocked these 'Tajik' newcomers by calling them 'donkey jockeys ... good only for digging'. The Pamiris were able to show their stripes however in 1806, when, led personally by 'Ālim Khān dressed in Pamiri clothing, they managed to penetrate the defences of Ura-teppa (modern Istaravshon) in under an hour.[22]

Notwithstanding Kokand's improved trade relations with China, the division of Central Asia into petty states contributed to the economic decline and increasing political vulnerability of the region as a whole. During the nineteenth century Kokand, with a mushrooming population thanks to the development of irrigation networks in the Ferghana Valley, succeeded in dramatically increasing its territory across the steppes to the north and the northwest. This expansion, however, ensured that Kokand would remain in conflict with the neighbouring khanates of Bukhara and Khiva from which it was siphoning off Russian trade. Internecine tensions, moreover, simmered between Turkic nomads and the settled bilingual Sarts. Finally, the commercial routes going west were not secure and many travellers were being kidnapped and sold into slavery. These were primarily Persian merchants, but there were Russian victims as well and also some British.

The Russian push to the east, which had begun in the sixteenth century with the conquest of the Turkic khanates of Kazan and Astrakhan, proceeded apace. Attracted by the discovery of gold in the lower Amu Darya basin but using as its pretext the desire to free Russian slaves, the tsarist empire tried on two occasions to conquer the Khivan khanate during the eighteenth century; both forays ended in failure. The British, meanwhile, were slowly consolidating their control over the Indian subcontinent. Now three separate Uzbek states – Bukhara, Khiva and Kokand – along with the newly established kingdom of Afghanistan all found themselves caught up in a vise grip between the two converging European imperialist powers: Britain and tsarist Russia.

British imperialists, with typical glibness, came to refer to this geopolitical manoeuvring as 'the Great Game'.[23] As games go, the nineteenth-century struggle for supremacy in Central Asia was blood sport in the extreme. The

British tried to take Afghanistan on two separate occasions, from 1839 to 1842 and again from 1878 to 1881 (the First and Second Afghan Wars). Both times they were repulsed by fierce resistance from the Pashtuns, an experience that the Soviets would repeat in the late twentieth century and the Americans in the early twenty-first. Thomas Barfield notes that the Afghan Durrānī leadership was able to succeed in defending their lands against the British by mustering the support of local militias, but fell into conflict with their domestic allies after refusing to share power once the invaders were expelled. A similar pattern emerged following the Soviet occupation in the 1980s, after which Afghanistan's various Mujaheddin groups, led by rival warlords each with their own regional power bases and personal militias, turned their weapons against each other.[24]

The British did succeed in preventing Qajar Iran from reintegrating the largely Tajik province of Herat in 1838, but they received a setback when their agent Colonel Charles Stoddart was arrested and imprisoned by the Emir of Bukhara during the course of a diplomatic mission the same year. Another agent sent to secure his release, Captain Arthur Conolly, was promptly imprisoned and tortured as well. Eventually, charged with spying and declining to save themselves by converting to Islam, the two were publicly beheaded in 1842. The event was witnessed by another Englishman, the missionary Joseph Wolff, who somehow managed to escape.

Even as the British found themselves bogged down by their first attempt to take Afghanistan in 1839, a Russian invasion of Khiva from the opposite direction was thwarted by an especially severe winter. Undeterred, tsarist forces continued to make forays into the region. Starting in 1847 the Russians began building a series of forts along the Syr Darya, from the Aral Sea all the way to the Tian Shan Mountains in the east – a massive project which the Khivans proved unable to forestall. From these new regional bases the Russians finally succeeded in conquering Tashkent (at that time part of the Khanate of Kokand) in 1865, under General Mikhail Grigorievich Cherniayev. The Emir of Bukhara had sent a contingent to Tashkent to help the resistance effort, but to no avail.

Russians took Khujand the following year and soon forced the Emir of Kokand, Khudāyār Khān, to accept protectorate status. A new 'Turkestan Governorate' was established at Tashkent under the command of General

Konstantin Petrovich von Kaufmann. The duly intimidated Emir of Bukhara, Muẓaffar al-dīn, began to negotiate for peace, but many of his subjects took affairs into their own hands and launched defensive raids against the Russians. Von Kaufmann finally settled the matter by attacking Samarkand in the summer of 1868. The city submitted, and Muẓaffar al-dīn formally became a Russian vassal.

Afghanistan's survival as an independent entity throughout the tumultuous nineteenth century perhaps owed something to its status as a buffer zone between the Russian and British spheres of influence. However, one unfortunate effect of this reality was a permanent rupture between Tajik populations living on opposite sides of the Oxus River (the Amu Darya), as well as a cutting off of the Tajiks as a whole – the Iranians of the East – from Iran proper. This three-way geopolitical division of the Persian-speaking peoples has persisted up to the present day.

Still, despite nearly a thousand years of Turkic rule in Central Asia in the nineteenth century Persian still enjoyed the status of court language, and the scribal class still consisted mainly of Tajiks. A notable figure from this period is Ahmad Donish (1826–97), a precociously modernizing scholar and artist who served several successive Bukharan Emirs. Dissatisfied by the level of education offered in Bukhara's traditional institutes of Islamic learning, he became an autodidact and taught himself the full range of academic disciplines, from math and science to philosophy and literature.

Donish was initially hired by the court as a painter and architect. He soon won the respect of Emir Naṣrullah (r. 1827–60) who sent him on a delegation to St. Petersburg in 1850. Impressed by what he saw in Russia Donish encouraged the Emir to implement a number of modernist reforms, but without success. Even so the subsequent ruler, Muẓaffar al-dīn, sent him on a second mission to the Russian capital in 1869–70. This time upon his return to Bukhara he was better received, treated by the Emir as someone uniquely knowledgeable about Russian and Western society and politics. Donish was offered an administrative position, but instead chose to work on a treatise which analysed the workings of the Bukharan government. He recommended substantial changes, including the establishment of a Parliament to counterbalance the absolute authority of the monarchy and a redesigning of the educational system to incorporate European methods.

Not surprisingly these suggestions were roundly rejected by the Emir. Donish spent the last years of his life writing works critical of the Emirate in general and in particular of its backward-looking Muslim clergy. Today the Institute of History, Archeology and Ethnography of the Tajikistan Academy of Sciences is named in his honour, preserving his legacy as the first great Tajik modernist intellectual.

Growing Russian influence in Central Asia

The Turkestan Governorate of the Russian Empire continued to expand throughout the last quarter of the nineteenth century. This included the annexation of the Amu Darya Administrative Division (*otdel*) in 1873 and, following an unsuccessful uprising in Kokand, of Bukhara's Ferghana Province (*oblast*) in 1876. By 1894 the lands to the east of the Caspian Sea had been added to the territories of the Governorate, leaving the Khanate of Khiva and the much-truncated Emirate of Bukhara both surrounded by Russia.

At the turn of the twentieth century the Russians were focusing their development efforts primarily on Tashkent, Samarkand and the rich agricultural lands of the Ferghana Valley. Khiva and Bukhara, with their relatively large populations of highly traditional Muslims, seemed not worth the trouble and were left nominally independent at least for the time being. As a Russian geographer noted at the time, 'The economic management of Bukhara is carried out in a predatory way and has deplorable consequences … The government sucks the blood of poor Bukharans and if some time Bukhara is attached to Russia, we will literally acquire a bunch of mendicant people.'[25]

Communications with European Russia were strengthened with the building of the Trans-Caspian Railway, which reached Samarkand in 1877. This facilitated the arrival of small numbers of European settlers including Mennonite farmers. The influx of settlers increased after 1906 when a direct rail line was completed linking Tashkent with Orenburg south of the Ural Mountains. This led to a competition for resources that caused native resentment towards the European newcomers. The Russians built European-style satellite cities adjacent to the major Central Asian towns so as to minimize their interactions with the local populations. In the countryside the Russian government focused on developing the production of cotton, which raised agricultural revenues but largely benefitted settlers at the expense of native farmers. Many local peasants became unemployed, especially in the Ferghana Valley, and some turned to criminal gang activity in order to survive.

By this time the urban population of Central Asian cities had evolved a distinct hybrid identity through years of interaction between Turks and Tajiks. Bilingualism had so long been the norm that it was hardly possible anymore to say whether urban-dwellers belonged specifically to one language community or the other. As evidence of this widespread phenomenon one may point to the prevalence of leather-bound private notebooks of poetry called *bayāẓ* (lit., 'white'), dating from the sixteenth through the nineteenth centuries, in which Persian and Turkī verses are often bound together in the same volume. While the more opulent manuscripts commissioned for the elites give an indication of the tastes of officialdom, *bayāẓ* notebooks can be taken as a reflection of readers at a more popular level. Jāmī appears to have been the most popular poet throughout this period, followed by Ḥāfiẓ of Shiraz and Amīr Khusraw of Delhi, but the Turkī poets Navā'ī and Fuẓūlī are also frequently present.[26]

Central Asia's bilingual city folk were most often referred to as 'Sarts', a somewhat pejorative term that had been in use for centuries and implied that one was a Persian-speaker.[27] By the turn of the twentieth century, however, the sense was no longer linguistic, since Sarts typically spoke both languages interchangeably. When they spoke Turkī (more often referred to as Turkestānī), it was in a highly Persianized form that drew the disdain of Kazakhs, Qara-Qyrgyz and Turkmen who remained proudly attached to their rural, nomadic lifestyles and values – an echo of the prejudice shown by Maḥmūd of Kashgar towards 'Sogdianized' urban Turks a millennium before. At the same time, the Tojikī dialect had been diverging from standard Persian through the adoption of Turkic vocabulary and syntax, and, now, with an infusion of neologisms from Russian as well.

We have noted that the Russians in Central Asia, following four centuries of interactions with the Turkic-speaking Muslims of Kazan and Astrakhan, used Tatar interpreters. This privileged their interactions with Turkic speakers even as it undermined the use of Persian. This tendency was particularly detrimental to the Muslim clergy, who were primarily Tajiks.[28]

The Jadidist movement

Central Asia in the nineteenth century was in many ways isolated from world events, and when modernity began to penetrate the region it was primarily via Russia. This was true even in the case of Islamic reformist ideas, which arose first amongst the so-called Jadidist Tatars and others who had been subjects of the Russian Empire for several centuries already. The cornerstone of Jadidist thought was education. As the Jadidists saw it Muslim communities, including the Tajiks and Turks of Central Asia, had for too long been held back by conservative religious scholars who jealously guarded their monopoly on knowledge and resisted any form of education beyond the rote memorization of the Quran and prophetic traditions taught in their *maktab*s (elementary schools) and *madrasa*s (colleges). The most prominent Tajik Jadidist, Sadriddin Ainī (1878–1954), recalled his own traditional education in a village near Bukhara: 'I completed school, but I was still illiterate. I could read things I had read in school, and from the same book I had used at school, but I couldn't read things I hadn't read before, or even things I *had* read before but from a different book.'[29] As one of the most active Central Asian Jadidists Ainī went on to become an iconic cultural figure of Soviet Tajikistan (see Figure 5.1). Growing up in Bukhara he received a traditional Islamic education, about which he had little positive to say in his many writings. Ainī eventually became a communist and played a major role in spreading Bolshevist ideas amongst Central Asians during and after the Russian Revolution in 1917.

Jadidist reformers argued for improved literacy and access to modern curricula especially in the sciences, and they promoted their ideas through the circulation of newspapers.[30] With the support of the Russian authorities who saw them as a useful counterbalance to the continuing influence of the traditional Ulema, the Jadidists managed to set up more than 5,000 new schools by the eve of the Revolution. This was at a time when 98 per cent of the native population of Central Asia was illiterate.

In the early stages of the Revolution the Jadidists and Bolsheviks found much common ground. Both sought radical social reform, and believed in education, media and the arts as means for improving the conditions of the masses. At the same time, the Bolsheviks aimed to build a unified, multinational secular state, whereas many of the Jadidists remained attached to their Islamic identity and saw themselves as religious as well as political reformers. Pan-Turkic ideas were also widespread within the Jadidist movement, although a few of its members – most notably Ainī – identified more strongly as Tajiks.

The settled Tajik and Sart populations of Central Asia were not directly involved in the Kazakh uprising of 1916, which was largely a response to Russian attempts to sedentarize and control the Turkic populations that were still nomadic. However, this conflict more generally fanned the flames of animosity against the Russians, who were seen as imperialist and anti-Islam – which of course they were. After the first Russian Revolution in February 1917 some Jadidists established a formal Islamic Council (*s̲h̲ūrā-yi islām*) with the stated goal of working towards an autonomous, democratic Muslim state within a federated Russia. Meanwhile another organization, the Society of Scholars (*Ulema Jamiyati*), was formed by religious leaders aiming to maintain their traditional institutions (i.e. mosques, madrasas and various other *waqf*s) and to reverse the steady encroachment of the Russian legal system which had begun to displace Islamic law.

At first the two organizations worked together against the tsarist regime, but following the October Revolution later in the year the Jadidists broke the coalition and offered their support to the Bolsheviks. The Jadidists were bitterly disappointed, however, when the Bolshevists in Tashkent banned Muslim participation in the new government. Outraged by this betrayal they rejoined the Ulema to form an autonomous Islamic polity based on Kokand.

After some initial back and forth with the Bolsheviks in Tashkent, the latter decided to invade and put a bloody end to the short-lived 'Kokand Autonomy' in early 1918. Muslims throughout the region were further incensed by the Russians' brutality and duplicity, as well as in some cases by their clear anti-traditionalism. Thousands rallied to join the emerging rural-based resistance movement of the 'Basmachis' (Turkic for 'raiders' or 'bandits'). The Basmachi movement had no real alternative programme for Central Asian society, but it continued to be a thorn in the side for Soviet nation-building efforts for the next two decades.

5

The Soviet Period

There were Tajiks who didn't even know that the Iranians spoke the same language as us until they heard Googoosh!

Muhiddin Olimpur, Tajik journalist

The year 1917 saw the establishment of a new modernist political party calling themselves the Young Bukharans, a transparent reference to the Young Turk movement then operating in the Ottoman Empire. They were led by Faizullo Khujaev (1896–1938), a native of Bukhara whose businessman father had sent him on a trip to Moscow as a boy. Deeply impressed by what he saw there, young Faizullo – who as a native Bukharan probably grew up speaking Persian but quickly absorbed the bilingualism of his family's merchant milieu – soon came under the sway of Jadidist and pan-Turkic ideas.

In early 1918 and with the Russian Revolution in full swing, the Young Bukharans encouraged the Bolsheviks to seize control of Bukhara and to depose its puppet Emir, Alim Khan. The attempt proved premature. The Young Bukharans' reformist agenda was too radical for Central Asians, a majority of whom remained overwhelmingly conservative and traditional, and their secular values made them bitter enemies of both the established (largely Tajik) Sunni clergy and the emerging anti-Russian Basmachi movement (who were mostly, but not exclusively, ethnic Turks). The rapacious behaviour displayed by the Red Army on entering Bukhara in March of that year further mobilized the population into fierce resistance and the Russians eventually had to withdraw.

With the Bolshevik forces tied up in fighting a civil war on many fronts across Russia the Bukharans enjoyed a two-year respite from further aggression. Eventually, however, Red Army forces under General Mikhail

Frunze captured the city in September 1920 and deposed Alim Khan. The Emir escaped, eventually fleeing to Kabul, where he remained until the end of his life in 1944. The Bolsheviks abolished the Emirate of Bukhara once and for all and the Bukharan People's Soviet Republic (BPSR), with Faizullo Khujaev at its head, was established in its place. In response to this development many conservative Bukharans – especially those living in the countryside – joined up with the Basmachi rebels.

Others, however, particularly in the cities, chose instead to side with the victors. In fact thousands joined the communist party, likely in hopes of securing protection and positions. Many of these converts were rightly perceived by the new Soviet government as the opportunists they were and quickly stripped of their membership. The loosely organized Basmachi movement, meanwhile, now led by the former Ottoman Minister of War Enver Pasha, remained a major threat. (Enver had come to Central Asia on the premise of aiding the Soviets, but once there he defected and joined the rebels.) The Basmachis briefly controlled much of the eastern BPSR in early 1922, but by the end of that summer the Red Army had crushed the movement and Enver Pasha was killed.

Soviet control now assured, in February 1925 the nominally independent BPSR was formally incorporated into the USSR. Its borders were redrawn and its territories divided between the newly created Uzbek and Turkmen Soviet Socialist Republics.

The redesigning of national identities

The 'national delimitation' strategy, first envisioned by a youthful Joseph Stalin prior to the Revolution[1] and put into practice by the Soviets during the 1920s when redrawing the political geography of Central Asia, was presented as a way of empowering the various 'brother nations' of the Soviet Union within their own semi-autonomous lands, 'freely choosing' to associate themselves with the USSR. In reality, power remained in the hands of the Russians and their local allies and most of the important decisions were made in Moscow.

The attempt to create 'nation-states' on the European post-Enlightenment model was vastly complicated by the broad diversity of languages and ethnicities spread across the region, which in most cases were inconveniently integrated with each other rather than falling within neat boundaries. Linguistically most urban-dwellers could communicate in either 'Turkistānī' or Persian, the Central Asian version of which was re-christened as 'Tojikī' only in 1924. Both were to some degree koine forms since the many local dialects of each sometimes differed to the point of mutual unintelligibility. In urban areas, meanwhile, the bilingual norm made it difficult to accord an 'ethnicity' to the Sarts who were the predominant group.

Language, in any case, was only one distinguishing factor in Central Asian societies, and in reality it was not the most operative. Amongst the Turkmen, Kazakh and Kyrgyz – all of whom were still largely nomadic – the differences were not just dialectal but in many respects cultural as well, based on centuries of proud tribal identities. Generally speaking Central Asians prior to the Soviet period tended to identify themselves primarily in terms of their religious affiliation (Sunni, Isma'ili, Sufi or Jewish), their social class or professional guild, their extended family or tribe, as settled or nomadic, mountain-dwelling or lowlander, or by their place of origin. Neither language nor what we would call 'ethnicity' played any definitive role in peoples' self-identification.

In practice, the Soviet approach to ascertaining 'nations' and attaching them to specific territories paid little regard to historical connections and social relations. Instead, Soviet ideologues – along with the linguists and anthropologists they employed to serve them – took the approach of seeking out maximal differences to use as baselines for constructing distinct 'national' languages and ethnicities. As a result of this method, a dialect spoken by a relatively small number of people in a remote location could become the basis for a new national language standard merely because its differences from other dialects were the most extreme.

This was done not just for the Turkic languages but for the newly christened 'Tojikī' as well, so as to separate it as much as possible from Persian and Darī with which it was easily mutually intelligible and from which it had never been considered distinct. Hence, whereas previously most people could communicate across and beyond the region by resorting to a historically standard form of either 'Fārsī/Darī' or 'Turkī/Turkistānī' in their relations with people outside their native locale, subsequent generations of Central Asians would grow up learning a single, idiosyncratic new 'standard language' that was of little value beyond the borders of their own 'national republic'. This was not considered a problem, however, since the medium of higher education and inter-republic communication would be the new lingua franca, Russian.

The creation of Soviet Tajikistan

Within this vast scheme of social re-engineering in which a number of historically marginal tribal identities became redefined as 'nations', the Tajiks were the great losers. First, the 'Tojikī' language was forcibly divorced from Persian, and thus from the common literary culture of Persian-readers from Istanbul to Calcutta.[2] This was accomplished by making a particular local spoken dialect, with all its deviations in pronunciation and vocabulary from formal literary Persian, the new official standard language of the 'Tajik nation'. It also entailed creating a new phonetic alphabet – first Latin-based beginning in 1928, then Cyrillic from 1940 – in which it would be written, thereby cutting off Tajiks from the vast, rich, international universe of Persian letters both past and present. (Of course, many works selectively culled from this rich heritage would eventually be re-printed in Cyrillic as 'Tajik' literature.)

To this day many Tajik intellectuals see the artificial severing of their literary language from Persian as a highly damaging mistake. The late, much-loved Tajik poet Loiq Sheralī wrote not long before his death

Yaki guftī tu eronī, digar guftī tu tojikī
Judo az asli khud mirad kase moro judo kardast

(Once you said 'You are Iranian,' then you said 'you are Tajik'
May he die separated from his roots, he who separated us)[3]

Still today calls persist for abandoning the label 'Tojikī' in favour of simply acknowledging that the language of the Tajiks is Persian[4] – just as Americans speak English, Austrians speak German, Argentines speak Spanish and so on.

But there was more to the weakening of Tajik cultural identity than merely severing the language from its broad Iranian heritage. In the initial structuring of the Soviet Union into constituent national republics in 1924, the Tajik 'nation' was left out entirely. Instead, Tajiks were accorded a mere administrative subdivision called the 'Tajik Autonomous Soviet Socialist

Republic' within the newly created Uzbek SSR. This arrangement left the Tajiks entirely under Uzbek control, giving them nominal autonomy over a much-truncated territory consisting largely of mountainous, marginally productive lands that were sparsely populated. None of the regional urban centres – including Bukhara, Samarkand, Tirmiz, Qarshi and Khujand – was included in the areas allotted to Tajiks, despite their historical character as Tajik cities and the fact that most of them still had strong Tajik-speaking majorities. Instead, Dushanbe, then no more than a mountain village of some 1,000 inhabitants, was made the administrative capital.

It is easy to imagine that this extraordinary marginalization of the Tajiks to the benefit of the Uzbeks was the result of a calculated policy on the part of Soviet decision-makers. In a 1997 book the Tajik academician Muhammadjon Shakurī (1925–2012) argued that the Russians preferred to give Samarkand and Bukhara to the Uzbeks because 'the Tajiks were too religious'; that is, they possessed a system of traditional institutions – considered as threatening as they were 'obsolete' – that the Uzbeks did not:

> Russian colonialists … viewed the Turkification of the population as being in their own interest, because Tajiks were more religious and the majority of the Ulema of Islam were Tajiks … whereas, among the Turks – especially the Turks of the steppes – religiosity was weak … [And thus] the Turkization of the Tajiks could serve this purpose, that little by little amongst them as well Islam would grow weaker.[5]

Shakurī's fellow academician Rahim Masov, meanwhile, in a series of very angrily written books on the subject, places the blame not so much on the Moscow-based Russian party cadres but more on the machinations of 'Tajik traitors' such as Faizullo Khujaev, Abdurauf Fitrat and Mahmudkhoja Behbudī, abetted by an overly passive and apolitical Tajik population.[6]

Adeeb Khalid, a specialist in Uzbek history, attempts to clarify the matter by arguing that that 'While the Jadids were discovering the Turkic roots of Central Asia and an affinity with Turkic populations elsewhere, there was no parallel discovery of Iranian roots or an affinity with Iran, and Persian never became a locus of national mobilization'. Khalid therefore suggests that 'Tajikistan emerged the way it did because there was no Tajik nation in 1924. Persian-speaking intellectuals and political actors did not identify themselves as Tajiks and did not therefore seek rights for a Tajik nation.'[7] But Muhammadjon Shakurī contests this view, stating, 'It is completely wrong to say that, in the 1920s, the Tajiks had no national leader, that the intellectuals failed to shoulder the responsibilities of national leadership, and so on. No, it was never so!' He goes on to mention Sadriddin Ainī, Abdulqodir Muhiddinov, Nusratullo Lutfulloev and Abdurrahim Hojiboev as examples of intellectuals who claimed and defended Tajik identity.[8]

Either way, 'Tajik' voices were largely absent from the discussions on national delimitation despite the fact that in the now-defunct Bukharan People's Soviet Republic Persian-speakers had made up 31 per cent of the total population. Their exclusion is not surprising when one considers that Tajiks constituted a mere 0.7 per cent of the membership of the Bukharan Communist Party – formed by Jadidists in 1918 – as opposed to 49 per cent who identified as Uzbeks.[9]

Ironically the strongest and most effective voice demanding political recognition for Tajiks was himself a Shughni-speaking Pamiri, a young activist by the name of Shirinsho Shotemur who is heralded today as a 'Tajik' national hero even as the Pamiris seek to assert their own distinct identity.[10] It was largely through Shotemur's continuous lobbying throughout the 1920s that the Tajik ASSR was elevated to a full union republic in 1929. (He later served as head of the Tajik Soviet but fell victim to Stalin's purges in 1937.)

Not only was the Tajik ASSR in 1924 deprived of an important urban centre, about half of all Tajiks – including most of the educated urban professionals – actually lived within the territory of the Uzbek SSR proper outside the boundaries of their own nominally 'autonomous' republic. During the next few years many Tajiks living in the Uzbek Republic began to complain about this, until eventually a committee was formed to look into a possible redrawing of borders. The 'Tajik Project Commission' concluded with the recommendation that the northern province of Sughd (including the city of Khujand), plus Samarkand, Bukhara and the districts of Surkhondaryo and Qashqadaryo, all be added to the Tajik ASSR. But in the end, only Sughd was added.[11] The Tajik polity was elevated to a full union republic in 1929, with Dushanbe being renamed 'Stalinobod' to mark the occasion (Khujand was renamed 'Leninobod' in 1936).

Even after the inclusion of Sughd the Tajik SSR was the smallest in Central Asia. With only 7 per cent of its land suitable for cultivation it was impoverished, underdeveloped and bisected by one of the world's highest and most impenetrable mountain ranges. The Tajik SSR was left utterly dependent on the surrounding republics, in terms of infrastructure as well as economy. The main road and railway linking the northern and southern parts of the Republic could not pass over the lofty Zarafshon Mountains and had to be routed through the Uzbek SSR. (Direct year-round road access between the two major cities of Dushanbe and Khujand was ensured only as recently as 2015 with the opening of the Iranian-built Anzob Tunnel.)

Moreover, the meagre agricultural terrains left to the Tajik SSR were separated from each other by high mountain ranges that covered over 90 per cent of the republic. The Gorno-Badakhshan Autonomous District – home to only 3 per cent of the population, the religiously and linguistically distinct Pamiri Ismāʿīlīs, but representing 45 per cent of the republic's territory – contained even less arable land. This unforgiving geography seriously hindered the development of the Tajik SSR at both the social and economic levels.

It turned out to be seriously detrimental to political development as well, since the regional divisions were reflected in mutually antagonistic clan-run power bases that extended patronage largely within their own respective spheres. Tajiks who lived in Samarkand, Bukhara and elsewhere in the Uzbek SSR came under strong pressure either to identify as Uzbeks (and many were forcibly registered as such), or else migrate to the Tajik SSR and accept the challenges and difficulties of life there.

Reform and reaction in Afghanistan

In the wake of the Bolshevik takeover in Central Asia, the Afghan king Amānullah Khān seized the opportunity to invade the Pashtun lands of British India in May 1919. This initiative proved unsuccessful and had to be abandoned several months later, but it had the effect of demonstrating Afghanistan's non-aligned status vis-à-vis the regional designs of Britain and the newly formed Soviet Union. Over subsequent decades the Afghan government would be able to exploit this intermediary position to play off the rival imperial powers against each other to its own benefit.

Amānullah K͟hān enjoyed wide popularity among Afghanistan's diverse ethnic groups, including the dominant Pashtuns, the Persian-speaking Tajiks and Hazaras, and the Turkic-speaking Uzbek and Turkmen minorities. Encouraged by his Westernizing foreign minister, Maḥmūd Tarzī, the king sought to modernize the country by implementing a series of policies, including a revitalization of the armed forces, the secularization of education, the emancipation of women, the abolition of slavery and rationalizing the taxation system.

Amānullah K͟hān's radical attempts to modernize Afghan society mirrored those being undertaken by Atatürk in Turkey and Reza Shah in Iran. In Afghanistan these efforts were met with strong resistance by traditional elements such as the Ulema, as well as by various tribal leaders throughout the country who feared the centralization of state power. In late 1928 two separate rebellions converged on Kabul, one led by Pashtuns from Jalalabad in the east and the other by Tajiks from the north. The Afghan Tajiks, under the leadership of Ḥabībullah Kalakānī, quickly overran the capital. The king abdicated in January of 1929, and Ḥabībullah seized control of the government a few days later. Amānullah K͟hān eventually fled to Europe, where he lived until his death in 1960.

Ḥabībullah's rule was not welcomed by the Pashtun tribes, however, and the Tajik-led government was overthrown by a subsequent rebellion in October 1929. An ethnic Pashtun, Nādir K͟hān of the royal Bārakzay tribe, was crowned as the new king. Ḥabībullah was captured and hanged, and the conservative Nādir quickly rescinded or watered-down most of Amānullah's modernizing reforms. Tajik rule had lasted a mere nine months.

Development in the Tajik SSR

While the Tajik republic's central government was based in Dushanbe with its shallow historical roots, powerful clan-based networks from the Khujand region in the north dominated the political structures of the Tajik SSR throughout the Soviet period, at the expense of those based in Kulob and Gharm south of the Zarafshon Mountains that bifurcated the republic. These regional coteries remained in place even as many Tajiks were forcibly relocated throughout the country, whether to the capital or, for example, to the Vakhsh Valley in order to provide labour for the construction of irrigation networks or other projects. Kirill Nourzhanov and Christian Bleuer note the implications of this phenomenon:

> An official position gave a person access to resources and jobs that they could then distribute. Losing one's position meant far more than one disappointed Communist Party cadre; an entire network would then be at risk of losing benefits such as jobs, university acceptance, equipment, fertilisers, and other political and economic goods.[12]

In other words, the traditional Central Asian structures of social and economic power – residing largely in independent actors who ensured for themselves a loyal support base by means of patronage – survived by insinuating themselves into the emerging Soviet system which proved unable to eliminate them. The endurance of such dispersed, camouflaged and uncontrollable forces throughout the Soviet period had much to do with to the eruption of civil war following the breakup of the Soviet Union in 1991.

The collectivization programmes that took place between 1927 and 1934 caused great hardship to peasant farmers in the Tajik SSR as elsewhere throughout the Soviet Union. These were accompanied by campaigns to suppress religion and emancipate women, which exacerbated popular animosity towards the regime. Any attempt at resistance was violently crushed, however, and many people were forcibly relocated so as to meet the demands of central planners. The transition to a cotton monoculture begun in the tsarist period was accelerated, entailing major investments in irrigation systems that siphoned off the flow of the Amu Darya and other rivers. During this difficult time as many as 240,000 Tajiks fled across the border to Afghanistan, but the Soviet reach extended there as well. Across the border, the swampy region around Kunduz was also converted to cotton production with most of the harvest being exported directly to the Soviet Union.

Throughout the 1930s political purges resulted in the removal of many Tajiks from government positions, to be replaced by Russians. This demographic transition was augmented by an influx of settlers from the European parts of the USSR, who came to comprise 13 per cent of the population by the 1950s and 46 per cent of the industrial workforce. The urban and rural populations of the Tajik SSR lived largely in parallel universes, greatly divided by lifestyle, living standards, ethnicity and cultural values. Even the local secret police was staffed mainly by Europeans who did not know Tojikī and could not really penetrate the society or understand its dynamics.

Although fighting during the Second World War did not reach Tajik territory, around half of the quarter million Tajiks conscripted into the Soviet army were killed, representing 8 per cent of the total population. Tajik interpreters were sent to Iran, where they served in the 'Persian corridor' project by which the Allied powers channelled supplies to the Soviet Union. Within the Tajik Republic itself, the war economy and lack of male labourers created numerous hardships for those left behind.

Despite rebuilding efforts after the war, conditions in the Tajik SSR remained the most backward of all the Soviet republics. The water- and labour-intensive cotton monoculture made Tajiks reliant on food imports from other parts of the Soviet Union, even as it damaged the environment and kept large numbers of peasants trapped in physically exhausting work conditions.

In many respects the Tajik economy retained the essentially extractive character that had marked Central Asia during the colonial period. Newly established mining industries exported their gold, silver, lead, mercury, zinc and uranium to other parts of the USSR. Moscow's policy of industrial interdependence among the republics meant that factories could only produce parts, not finished products – even the raw cotton produced locally was sent to the European republics for processing.

Nevertheless, while economic and social conditions in the Tajik SSR lagged behind the rest of country, the achievements of the Soviet system should not be overlooked. Housing, employment, education, health care and women's rights (in theory, at least) were all now universal, so that Tajiks as a whole enjoyed a much higher average standard of living than in any of the neighbouring countries outside the Soviet Union – including Afghanistan, Pakistan, China and even in many respects Iran.

Still, the Soviet effort to transform the Tajiks into a modern nation ultimately fell short of its goal, as events following independence in 1991 would tragically demonstrate. For years before the collapse of Soviet power revealed the persistent fault lines within Tajik society anthropologist Sergei Poliakov had argued that 'harmful' traditions – especially ruinous expenditures on huge celebrations (generically referred to as *tūys*) marking the occasion of circumcisions and weddings – had yet to be eradicated from amongst the Tajiks.[13] An inward-looking regionalism continued to characterize the mentality of many, who remained more attached to the distinctive features of their home provinces than to a sense of belonging to any putative 'Tajik nation'. The endurance of traditional values, identities and social networks was perhaps largely due to the fact that organs of state control – from local party branches to the secret police – had little presence in the rural areas, where more than two-thirds of the Tajik population still lived.

The extended family (*avlod*) remained the fundamental social unit, and birth rates stayed high – more than double those elsewhere in the Soviet Union. *Avlod*s provided advice and counselling for their younger members, in terms of marriage and career choices, and often gave financial support as well.

During the forced collectivization of the late 1920s and early 1930s many *avlod*s managed to reconstitute their prior structures within the new Soviet format of the collective farm (*kolkhoz*). Within this parallel system largely hidden from the eyes of non-native officials the selling of homegrown produce from family gardens remained an important source of revenue, its distribution determined by the all-powerful patriarch of the *avlod*. Following the breakdown of the integrated Soviet economy after 1991, these small, private orchards became the principal means of subsistence for many Tajik families. In the mountainous, almost entirely rural east-central province of Gharm, where Basmachi rebels had held out until the late 1930s, farms avoided conversion to the cotton monoculture (since cotton cannot be grown in the mountains). This situation enabled farmers to maintain a level of private enterprise by selling their own fresh produce, especially citrus fruits. Large numbers of Gharmis, however, were forcibly relocated to the Vakhsh Valley to work in cotton production, setting the stage for the horrific outbreaks of inter-communal violence that would occur there after independence.

Related to the *avlod* structures in the villages are those of urban neighbourhoods (*mahalla*s), where a range of traditional social interactions – including the organization of life-cycle ceremonies such as circumcisions, weddings and funerals; the collection of taxes on behalf of the government and resolving local conflicts – persisted in parallel to the new Soviet institutions. Neighbourhood councils, overseen by an elected *Raisi mahalla* (neighbourhood head), also assumed responsibility for the maintenance of water channels and other public infrastructure, as well as cleaning the streets and restoring public buildings. All residents of a *mahalla* were encouraged and expected to participate in such voluntary social work, known as *ha<u>sh</u>ar*. As Saidbek Goziev has poignantly observed in a book devoted to the subject, during the Soviet period 'the entire corpus of Tajik culture [was] preserved in the *mahallas*'.[14]

Within these *mahalla*s an all-male group culture akin to professional guilds, called *ga<u>sh</u>tak*, provided (and continues to provide) the principal context for socializing among many Tajik men. *Ga<u>sh</u>tak* meetings centre around a shared meal and offer a setting where members can discuss problems and give each other mutual support. If someone is in financial need, funds can be pooled to assist them. *Ga<u>sh</u>tak*s thus often serve to help out with marriages, funerals and building their members new houses.

The *mahalla* councils also oversaw sports activities such as *gu<u>sh</u>tingirī* (traditional wrestling) and *buzka<u>sh</u>ī* (lit., 'goat-pulling', a kind of polo played with the headless carcass of a goat). In the absence of *madrasa*-trained Islamic clergy the *mahalla*s provided a context for the surreptitious passing on of popular religious knowledge (*odat*) by unofficial *mullo*s. The centrality of *mahalla* organizations to Tajik life quickly surged back into evidence with the fall of the Soviet Union – proof that they had never gone away in the first place.

One of the remarkable features of Tajik society in the twentieth century was that, contrary to the rest of the USSR and indeed the developing world as a whole, the transition from a largely rural to urban society did not occur. In fact, by the late Soviet period this process was actually reversing itself, with people moving back from the cities to the countryside. A number of factors would seem to account for this, including a superior quality of life, lower living costs, greater independence and, perhaps most of all, the persistence of traditional clan-based support networks.

Beginning in the early 1960s Moscow invested huge amounts of money in an attempt to industrialize southern Tajikistan, a project called the 'South Tajik Territorial Industrial Complex'. This included the construction of a massive hydroelectric plant on the Vakhsh River at Norak (as well as laying plans for an even larger one at Rogun not far away) and nearly fifty factories throughout the region, dedicated to everything from smelting aluminium to producing chemical fertilizers. Inefficiency and waste, however, exacerbated by rampant corruption, led to a situation where the costs of running these enterprises exceeded the revenues they generated. By the 1980s crime had increasingly become a problem, whether systematic fraud at the government level or hooliganism in the streets.

It is hardly surprising that most Tajiks preferred village life over what was offered in industrialized towns, where salaries were low, expenses high and conditions stressful. At the same time, while even younger generation Tajiks continued to show a preference for farm jobs over factory work, agricultural production could not keep pace with the rising birth rate – the highest in the USSR – which translated into an overall decline in living standards at the national level. By the end of the Soviet period more than 87 per cent of Tajiks lived below the poverty line – an astonishing figure.

Environmental degradation also became a major problem by the 1980s, especially in areas of intensive cotton-growing such as the Ferghana Valley in the north and the Vakhsh Valley in the south, as well as the entirety of the Amu Darya and Syr Darya basins in neighbouring Uzbekistan and Turkmenistan. Apart from the depletion of precious water resources siphoned off for irrigation which would soon lead to the virtual disappearance of the once-vast Aral Sea downstream, the excessive use of chemical fertilizers and pesticides – including the infamous DDT – poisoned the water and the soil, causing a massive increase in cancer and other diseases such as anaemia and intestinal disorders across all the Central Asian republics. Children were worst hit by these epidemics and infant mortality rose dramatically. Deforestation also accelerated during this period, especially in the upland regions, with a resulting loss of biodiversity.

Religion and popular customs

In the realm of religion, the atheist Soviet state failed spectacularly in its attempt to dislodge Islamic or para-Islamic customs and beliefs (*odat*) or the religious authority of the traditional Sufi families. Early on the Bolsheviks, needing to consolidate their support among Central Asia's Muslims, had allowed traditional Islamic institutions such as schools (*maktab*s and *madrasa*s) and other pious endowments (*waqf*s), as well as Islamic law courts, to continue functioning. In 1927, however, the state felt sufficiently confident that it abolished all of these and began a campaign of anti-Islam purges and persecutions.

The Ismāʿīlīs, who constituted most of the population of the Pamirs, were banned from sending their religious tithes to their spiritual leader, the Aga Khan, and were deprived of his guidance which – given his status as the Imam of the Age – they considered infallible. Ironically enough, the progressive outlook of the Bombay-based Aga Khan III, Sulṭān Muḥammad Shāh (1877–1957), coincided in a number of respects with that of the Soviets, in that his vision for the modernization of his community included women's rights and universal access to education.[15] Also, like the Soviets, he sought to break the power of Badakhshan's hereditary *pīr*s who, thanks to the region's remoteness, had exercised virtually independent religious authority for centuries. While the Aga Khan's close relations with Britain made Ismāʿīlīs potentially suspect in the eyes of the Soviets, in his communications to his followers he enjoined them to remain loyal subjects of whatever government they lived under, including the USSR.

Unofficial religious leaders in Muslim villages throughout the Tajik SSR would preside over weddings, circumcisions and funerals. In Pamiri villages, Ismāʿīlī 'caliphs' performed a surreptitious funerary ritual known as *chirāgh rawshan* ('lighting the lantern', a ceremony traced back to Nāṣir-i Khusraw), risking imprisonment and even execution if they were caught. Pamiri Ismāʿīlīs also practised a religious dance called *haqthed*, a kind of blend between the ecstatic Sufi *samāʿ* and Shīʿite mourning ceremonies associated with ʿĀshūrā.[16]

For the Sunni majority, by closing the madrasas and drastically reducing the influence of formally trained Ulema the Soviets unwittingly cleared the field in favour of the Sufi masters. Relieved of the opposition they had long faced from traditional religious scholars, Sufi shrines (*mazor*s) retained their importance in Tajik society as pilgrimage sites, under the guise of tourist attractions where local 'tourists' could surreptitiously receive instruction – or, more often, 'miraculous mediation' – from shaykhly 'tour guides'. Rural villages and urban *mahalla*s all maintained unofficial mosques and religious instructors (*mullo*s), who for the most part operated under the government's radar.

By the 1970s the Soviet authorities came tacitly to accept Islamic practices as being 'personal' rather than state business, and slowly loosened the prohibitions on Islamic institutions. Nevertheless, only a minority of Tajiks regularly performed such pious duties as daily prayers and the Ramadan fast, preferring to express their religiosity through lavish expenditures on ostentatious weddings and circumcision ceremonies (*tūyi khatna*) for young boys. I once stumbled accidently into a large neighbourhood circumcision feast during a visit to Samarkand in the summer of 1990, near the end of the Soviet period. Tents and tables were set up in the middle of the street across an entire city block and the spread included a full bottle of Russian vodka for each guest. The centre of attention was an apprehensive-looking seven-year-old boy dressed in expensive purple silk. His family presented him to my friend and me, the fortuitous foreign guests, with the proud words, 'Today he will become a Muslim!'[17]

The persistence of popular religious culture throughout the Soviet phase became abundantly clear immediately upon Tajikistan's independence in the fall of 1991, when traditional institutions and their hereditary custodians could once again function openly. However, the decapitation of traditional Islamic scholarship – a domain in which Tajiks had made such enormous contributions over the course of some twelve centuries – meant that ordinary Tajik Muslims were almost entirely deprived of trained religious leadership. This left them vulnerable to the influence of cash-wielding organizations from Saudi Arabia and Qatar, who have been steadily sponsoring the building of thousands of new mosques and the dissemination of Wahhābī propaganda over the past three decades. The Islamic Republic of Iran, playing the language card, made some early attempts to counteract this activity by setting up 'Iranian cultural centres' promoting their own Twelver Shīʿite views on Islam, but this had little impact among Tajikistan's largely Sunni population.

Meanwhile, for the Ismāʿīlī inhabitants of the remote, underdeveloped and underpopulated Pamir region the collapse of Soviet power opened up access to a worldwide Ismāʿīlī community of some 15 million largely prosperous and educated co-religionists. The Tajik Ismāʿīlīs would henceforth have access to the rich resources administered by the Aga Khan Development Network as well as to the spiritual guidance of their Imam, Prince Karim Aga Khan IV (b. 1936). In 1995 'His Highness', as he is known by his followers, would become the first Ismāʿīlī Imam personally to travel to the Pamir region, and he has returned on several occasions since. Foreign Islamicists were amazed to discover that Tajik Badakhshan contained great troves of Ismāʿīlī texts in libraries hitherto unknown to them, a huge boon to the field of Ismāʿīlī Studies.

Parallel to Islamic practices, and sometimes conflated with them, many Tajiks continued to seek the services of shamanistic spiritual masters adept in such matters as fortune-telling and healing. As in many other settings throughout the Muslim world, belief in Islam was not seen as incompatible with a fear of spirit beings (*arvoh*) or the need for specialists (*ishon* – a term also applied to Sufi masters, who often fulfilled shamanistic functions as well) able to deal with them.

Change and continuity in women's roles

Improving the status of women – already a cornerstone of the reforms promoted by Jadidists prior to the Revolution – came to be emblematic of the changes brought about by Soviet socialism. Laws were passed banning child marriage, forced marriages, polygyny, payment of bride price and mistreating, insulting or forcing a woman to wear the veil. Tajik women, like others across the USSR, enjoyed free access to education and entry into the public workspace, as well as new legal rights such as the option to initiate divorce. The establishment of state-sanctioned women's organizations also provided the possibility for expanding social networks, which offered additional channels of solidarity and support. By the 1930s Soviet Tajik women – at least in theory – enjoyed many more rights and opportunities than their Muslim peers in neighbouring countries such as Iran, Afghanistan and British India.

Inherited attitudes towards gender relations could not be so easily overturned, however. Many women continued to be subject to pressures from their fathers or husbands, and a family's honour was still seen as dependent upon the chastity of its female members. Marriages continued to be arranged in most cases by the parents, and underage girls were often given away in 'Islamic' weddings (*nikoh*) which were then registered with the state authorities at a later time once they reached majority.

Cooking, housecleaning and child-rearing all remained primarily, if not exclusively, women's responsibilities, so that it was common for a woman who found full-time employment in her chosen career to come home from a long day's work only to begin her 'second job', namely taking care of domestic duties. Many women thus learned consciously to perform two distinct identities: a liberated, professional, 'Soviet' one in public, even as they maintained ostensibly submissive ones at home.[18] Some ambitious men, on attaining positions by joining the Communist Party, increased their own income by taking on additional unofficial wives and mistresses whom they then sent out to work on their behalf.[19]

For much of the Soviet period a pronatalist policy was in place, according to which a woman having more than ten children was given the title 'Hero Mother' and provided with an extra pension. Among Tajiks this policy reinforced the traditional emphasis on woman's maternal role, ensuring that their republic maintained the highest birth rate in the entire USSR. Even today it is not uncommon for rural families in Tajikistan to have ten or more children.

The traditional *mahalla* social networks maintained gender divisions by separating male and female leadership within the community. The *Bibiotin* (or *Bibimullo*) held religious authority over the women of the neighbourhood, providing them with moral instruction – mostly consisting of teaching them their place in patriarchal society – and reciting Islamic prayers at religious ceremonies. For day-to-day matters, women were represented by the *Raisi zanon* (Head of the Women) who would intercede for them with the male elders led by the *Raisi mahalla*.[20]

Cultural production during the Soviet period

Those striving to advance the cause of Tajik literature and the arts during the Soviet period had much to overcome. The Tajik SSR lacked a historical centre of cultural production, since those centres had been primarily Bukhara and Samarkand which were now under the control of a neighbouring regime charged with promoting the culture of the Uzbeks. Uzbek intellectuals, many of whom had been active in the pan-Turkist movement prior to the Revolution, put forward the historically baseless argument that Tajiks were simply Turks who had forgotten their native language and should now adopt it once again. Ironically most Tajik intellectuals lived within the Uzbek SSR, where Tajik culture was not something that could easily be promoted or even talked about.

Living in the smaller, less developed Tajik SSR, on the other hand, at least had the virtue of allowing the people of Dushanbe, Khujand and the Pamirs to assert their respective heritages within the framework of Soviet cultural institutions. Also, with the more repressive political climate taking shape under Joseph Stalin during the 1930s many scholars and professionals from European Russia migrated to the Tajik SSR as a way of staying off the tyrant's radar. Politically harmless fields such as archaeology and linguistics enticed a number of great minds to leave Moscow and Leningrad for the peaceful mountain air of Stalinobod (as Dushanbe was then known), turning the Tajik capital into a kind of academic refuge.

The Jadidist teacher, poet, journalist and revolutionary Sadriddin Ainī is generally considered to have been the originator of modern Tajik literature (Figure 5.1). Commissioned by the Tajik government to prepare an official volume of representative 'Tajik' (that is to say, Persian) literature from the classical period to the present (*Namunai Adabiyoti Tojik*), Ainī worked as a consultant at the Tajik Publications Centre established in 1926. The following year he published his first novella, *Odina* (aka 'The Story of a Poor Tajik') in the new Sovietized Tojikī language which he himself had played a central role in shaping. He then began work on a full-length novel, entitled *Dokhunda* (1931), the story of a poor Tajik who falls in love with a girl from a wealthy family. This was followed by three further novels (one of them written in Uzbek) and a four-volume collection of memoirs. *Dokhunda* was made into a film in 1956 but was banned soon after by Soviet censors as 'too formalist' and its footage destroyed.

Ainī was the first president of the Tajik Writers' Union, founded in 1934. In 1947 he was elected to the Supreme Soviet of the Tajik SSR, and when the Tajik Academy of Sciences was established in 1950 he was named its first president. Three times awarded the Order of Lenin, Ainī died in Stalinobod in 1954 at the age of 76.

Another key figure in the development of modern Tajik literature and a close friend of Ainī was the Iranian Marxist poet Abū'l-Qāsim Lāhūtī (Toj. Abulqosim Lohutī). After surviving many difficulties in his native Iran due to his politics, Lohutī immigrated to the Soviet Union and settled in Dushanbe in 1924. Author of the lyrics to the national anthem of the Tajik SSR, he served as Minister of Education as well as president of the Tajik Writers' Union. Like

Figure 5.1 Portrait of Sadriddin Ainī. 1978. By Ivan Lisikov (1927–86). National Museum of Tajikistan, Dushanbe.

Ainī, Lohutī is credited with helping shape the new modern 'Tojikī' literary language. A member of Stalin's inner circle, he was also instrumental in protecting Ainī from the infamous purges of the 1930s which decimated the communist intelligentsia.

Mirzo Tursunzoda was another prominent Tajik literary figure of the twentieth century. After his death in 1977 the town of Regar in the Hisor Valley was renamed in his honour, and his image was emblazoned on the one-somonī banknote. Loiq Sheralī (1941–2000), who devoted much of his life to the study of classical Persian literature, is also considered one of the major modern Tajik poets.

Figure 5.2 Traditional painted wood ceiling. Dushanbe, Tajikistan.

In the realm of fiction one may mention Fazliddin Muhammadiev (1928–86), whose novel *In That World* (*Dar On Dunyo*, 1965) provides an atheist's view of the Islamic Hajj pilgrimage. Another of his well-known works, *Hospital Ward* (*Palatai Kunjakī*, 1974) is a biting social commentary aimed at highlighting ways that the USSR's socialist society could be improved. He also wrote film scripts and served as chief editor for the Tajik State Committee for Cinematography. In 1986, the year of his death, he was awarded the title 'Writer of the People of the Tajik SSR'.

Sotim Ulughzoda (1911–89) is known for historical novels such as *The Morning of My Youth* (*Subhi javonii man*, 1954) which evokes the hardships of Tajiks living under Manghit rule during the time of the Bukharan emirate. He also wrote biopics on Firdawsī and Ibn Sino (Avicenna).

The works of Sattor Tursun (b. 1946), exemplified in novels such as *Silence of the Peaks* (*Sukuti kullaho*, 1974) and *The Snow Will Also Pass* (*Barf ham biguzorad*, 1983), focus on current 'real-life' issues facing Tajiks during the late Soviet period. His novel *Rustam's Rainbow* (*Kamoni Rustam*, 1976) was made into a successful feature film.

The importance accorded within the Soviet system to supporting the (approved) arts extended to music as well. The Tajik symphonic *shashmaqom* (six modes) style, historically passed on by ear from master to student, was now formally transcribed, studied and taught in conservatories, along with European classical music theory, performance and composition. Russian ballet also became popular. Tajik composers trained in Dushanbe and Moscow often blended eastern and western musical traditions, and their works were performed on state radio and in official venues such as the Ainī Theatre in the Tajik capital and the Rudakī Music and Drama Theatre in Khorugh.

Cinema, seen as a direct and effective way of propagating socialist ideals, enjoyed a particularly privileged status during the Soviet period. The first feature-length film to be produced in Tajikistan was *When the Emirs Die* in 1932. However, with the notable exception of Komil Yarmotov, a native of the Ferghana Valley who produced the first Tajik documentaries in 1932, few ethnic Tajiks were actually involved in the 'Tajik' film industry. As elsewhere in the Soviet Union, Tajik movies were usually done in Russian (ensuring their exportability to other republics) and told morally instructive stories.

Beginning in the 1960s Tajiks began to play a larger role in their own cinema. One who would rise to prominence was the Pamiri director Davlat Khudonazarov (b. 1944) who collaborated with Boris (Ben Zion) Kimiyogarov (1920–79), a Bukharan Jew from Samarkand, to produce several cinematic renderings of stories from Firdawsī's *Book of Kings*. Another important Tajik filmmaker, Tohir Sobirov (1929–2002), also drew inspiration from Persian literature, producing a trilogy based on the *Thousand and One Nights*. The most popular films produced in Tajikistan during the 1960s and 1970s, however, were modelled after American Westerns. These shoot-'em-up epics typically featured heroic Bolsheviks battling Basmachi bandits, giving rise to a genre that came to be known as 'Basmachi-kino'.

Cultural production throughout the Soviet period was formally required to reflect official, party-approved perspectives, emphasizing the backwardness of the pre-communist era and the great advances made since by noble Marxist heroes. Beginning in the 1930s Tajik writers and artists trod a delicate and sometimes schizophrenic balance between trying to sustain their cultural past – especially the literary tradition as expressed through poetry – and celebrating the modernizing accomplishments of socialism. By the 1960s nationalistic themes were becoming more prominent, portraying the Tajiks as purveyors of one of humankind's great civilizations – a mindset that required the conflation of 'Tajikness' with the whole of Iranian culture from Mesopotamia to China.

This approach was most fully expressed in the work attributed to (but perhaps largely produced by others on behalf of) Bobojon Ghafurov (b. 1909), a politician and historian who served as First Secretary of the Central Committee of the Communist Party of Tajikistan from 1946 to 1956 and thereafter as Director of the Institute of Oriental Studies of the Academy of Sciences of the Soviet Union up to his death in 1977. Ghafurov's book *A Short History of the Tajik People* (*Ta'rikhi Mukhtasari Khalqi Tojik*, 1947) was the first Soviet work to treat a specific Central Asian nationality.

Together with Russian Orientalist A.A. Semënov, Ghafurov oversaw the publication of a three-volume *History of the Tajik People* in Russian which was published from 1963 to 1965, and later signed a work entitled *The Tajiks: Archaic, Ancient and Mediaeval History* published in 1970.[21] These writings, reinforced by the work of later scholars such as Rahim Masov, Muhammadjon Shakurī and Numon Negmatov, laid the foundation for the broad historical claims that continue to characterize Tajik self-identity up to the present day.

War in Afghanistan 1979–89

Tajiks have historically occupied the lands both north and south of the Oxus River (today's Amu Darya), their identity having emerged from among the Sogdians and the Bactrians as part of the process of Islamization. With the creation of Afghanistan in the mid-eighteenth century they became once again divided by political boundaries, even as they retained a common Perso-Islamic language and culture.

A comparison of the experiences of Tajiks living under Soviet rule with those of their cousins to the south in Afghanistan shows some marked advantages to the former. The Soviet Union may not have provided freedom of expression but it did create universal access to education, employment, housing and health care – benefits most Afghans enjoyed to a very limited extent, if at all. Little surprise that throughout the twentieth century in Afghanistan as elsewhere in the developing world, the promises and achievements of socialism held a strong attraction for many intellectuals concerned with improving conditions in the societies in which they lived.

Intellectuals are never more than a small minority in any society, however, and their views are often at odds with deeply held traditions and values. Virtually every socialist revolution of the twentieth century, once conceived by the intellectual class, had to be imposed on the masses by force, often resulting in much bloodshed. Even so many did succeed, from Latin America to Africa and Asia, and the Afghan visionaries who brought about a Marxist coup in April 1978 no doubt imagined theirs would follow the established pattern.

Under the rule of Muḥammad Ẓāhir Shāh who reigned from 1933 to 1973, Afghanistan had remained a backward country with little infrastructure and a mostly illiterate rural population engaged primarily in subsistence agriculture. What little development there was, through the assistance of French, German and Soviet agencies, was largely restricted to the cities of Kabul, Mazar-i Sharif, Herat and Kandahar. The vast majority of the population – about a third of whom were Tajiks – continued to live in impoverished villages much as they had for centuries.

A Marxist political party, the People's Democratic Party of Afghanistan (PDPA), was established in 1965, at a time when Marxist movements all across the developing world were flourishing. In 1973 a military coup led by former Prime Minister Muḥammad Dāwūd Khān, a cousin of the king, abolished the monarchy, accusing it of corruption and inefficiency. The coup had much popular support but it was opposed by the PDPA, which obviously would have preferred to see itself in power. The new government under Dāwūd Khān launched a campaign to suppress the PDPA and its supporters, but in 1978 the Marxists, buttressed by the army, overthrew their oppressors. They promptly executed Dāwūd Khān and declared the establishment of the Democratic Republic of Afghanistan, with party secretary Nūr Muḥammad Tarakī as its first president.

The PDPA swiftly embarked on a series of major economic and social reforms based on the Soviet model. These included land redistribution, literacy campaigns and women's rights. As under Amānullah Khān in the 1920s, for the vast majority of Afghans such a dramatic overhaul of their traditional society was too much, too soon. Local rebellions rose up almost immediately and within a year and a half, amidst widespread unrest which included the assassination of the US ambassador, Afghanistan's socialist government was asking the Soviet Union to provide military support.

In September of 1979 Deputy Prime Minister Ḥāfiẓullah Amīn carried out an internal coup and took over the position of Tarakī, who was arrested and later executed. Meanwhile, across the country popular resistance assumed the form of Muslim 'holy warriors' – *mujāheddīn* – fed by the anger traditional Afghans felt towards the government's secularist agenda. The Amīn government, no more able than its predecessor to subdue the rebel threat, increased its demands for Soviet intervention. Amīn's ruthless persecution of internal rivals, however, caused the Soviets to fear he was making things worse and not better. On 27 December 1979 Soviet forces invaded the country, but with the primary aim of removing Amīn, an ethnic Pashtun, from power. He was replaced by Babrak Kārmal, a Soviet favourite and leader of a rival branch of the PDPA. Kārmal publicly downplayed his Tajik background but his Parcham faction was more Darī-speaking, educated and urban than the rural, Pashtun-dominated Khalq group that had been led by Tarakī and Amīn.

The Soviet army rapidly moved to support Kārmal by occupying the major cities and strategic installations throughout the country, hoping to pacify an increasingly tense situation. In fact, the opposite happened: the appearance of foreign invaders caused the diverse rebel groups across the land to rise up and unite against the outside enemy and its perceived internal puppets.

For the next nine years Afghanistan was embroiled in a vicious conflict of attrition. It soon degenerated into a proxy war between the two Cold War superpowers, the United States and the USSR, as the United States and its allies – mainly Pakistan and Saudi Arabia – sought to exploit the religious angle by arming and training resistance fighters, including many foreign volunteers. One, a Saudi engineer by the name of Osama bin Laden, would later emerge to lead a radical Islamist organization that would come back to haunt the world for years to come: Al-Qaeda (Arabic for 'the Base').

While the various armed resistance groups may have been united in their fight against the godless foreign enemy, they had no central leadership but were rather organized along regional, tribal or ethnic lines. The Tajik commander Aḥmad Shāh Mas'ūd, based in the Kohistan region in north of Kabul, was perhaps the most effective of the lot, while Pashtun groups operated in the south and Uzbeks in the northwest. Tajiks from opposite banks of the Amu Darya, as well as Uzbeks and Turkmens, often found themselves fighting on opposing sides, as the Soviet army included many conscripts from the Central Asian republics. Religiously minded Tajiks living in the USSR, notably Abdullo Nurī who would later lead Tajikistan's Islamic Revival Party, denounced the war as an assault on Islam. Nurī was arrested in 1986 and imprisoned for eighteen months, but for his followers this only served to enhance his credibility.

By 1985 the Soviets were looking for a way out. From the outset their strategy had been to gradually turn over the battle to pro-government Afghan forces, but these proved inadequate to the task. The Soviet withdrawal lasted from 1987 to 1989, after which Afghanistan's Marxist government was left to manage on its own.

The fall of the Soviet Union

The *perestroika* ('restructuring') reforms initiated by Soviet President Mikhail Gorbachev beginning in 1986 were intended to strengthen the Soviet system by making it more open and adapt to the changing conditions of the late twentieth century, as well as to consolidate control in the centre by taking it away from the republics. While the effect of these reforms varied throughout the Soviet Union, their ultimate result was the dissolution of the state. And while certain areas of the country – the Baltic Republics, for example – were able to make a rapid transition to Western-style capitalist democracies, in Central Asia the failure of the Soviet system over seventy years to transform traditional social structures and group identities into national ones meant that with perestroika these disparate, semi-covert forces could operate more freely and openly against the broader interests of the state.

More importantly, perhaps, changes brought about under perestroika had a distinctly harmful effect on the Tajik SSR's economy, which had been relatively healthy prior to Gorbachev's rise to power. Under the new system the transfer of resources and products from other republics declined, as did subsidies from Moscow. As one scholar has observed, 'Perestroika functionally meant that Tajikistan was left without both raw inputs and finished goods from other republics, and told to fend for itself economically, and yet was still required to deliver hundreds of thousands of tonnes of cotton each year for other republics' further use.'[22] This situation led to unemployment, inflation and a decrease in real wages, creating the feeling among Tajiks that their quality of life had become suddenly and dramatically worse.

Gorbachev's reforms conversely entailed a push towards a centralization of control, which included the transferring of many powers and functions from the republics to Moscow and the suppression of local languages in favour of Russian, thereby exacerbating the existing resentments of many Tajiks. Intellectuals such as the academician Muhammadjon Shakurī began calling for Russian to be replaced at the official level by Tojikī, which some feared was in danger of dying out. In 1987 Shakurī published an article entitled 'Who Knows His Own Language', which struck a chord with many non-Russian readers even beyond the borders of the Tajik Republic, and later inspired the poet Loiq Sherālī to write:

To naī sohibi zaboni khesh,
Nashavī sohibi jahoni khesh

(As long as you aren't master of your own language,
You won't be master of your own world).[23]

Shakurī went on to take a leading role in the drafting of a 1989 law that made Tojikī the official language of the Tajik SSR.

Soviet Central Asians who had been sent to fight in Afghanistan rediscovered their connections with peoples to whom they were culturally closer than to the Russians. One Tajik journalist, Muhiddin Olimpur, was so moved by the plight of his fellow Tajiks in Afghanistan that he stayed on there for seven years after completing his military service. Upon returning to Dushanbe he launched a new television programme called 'Stars of the East' (Sitorahoyi Sharq), featuring singers from Iran and Afghanistan – an effort to sensitize his Tajik audience to the cultural connections they shared with those two neighbouring countries.

Thanks to this initiative the Afghan singer Aḥmad Ẓāhir (1946–79) and the Iranian songstress Googoosh (b. 1950) became wildly popular throughout Central Asia, their pirated cassettes filling the bazaars. With the loosening up of press restrictions newspapers such as *Javonon* (Youth) joined in the campaign to educate Tajiks about their own history and culture. 'We talked about sending Persian books to Samarkand and Bukhara, where people had

Plate 1 6th century Sogdian wall painting from Panjikent, Tajikistan.

Plate 2 6th century Sogdian wall painting from Afrasiab, Samarkand.

Plate 3 Poi kalon complex, 12th to 16th centuries, Bukhara.

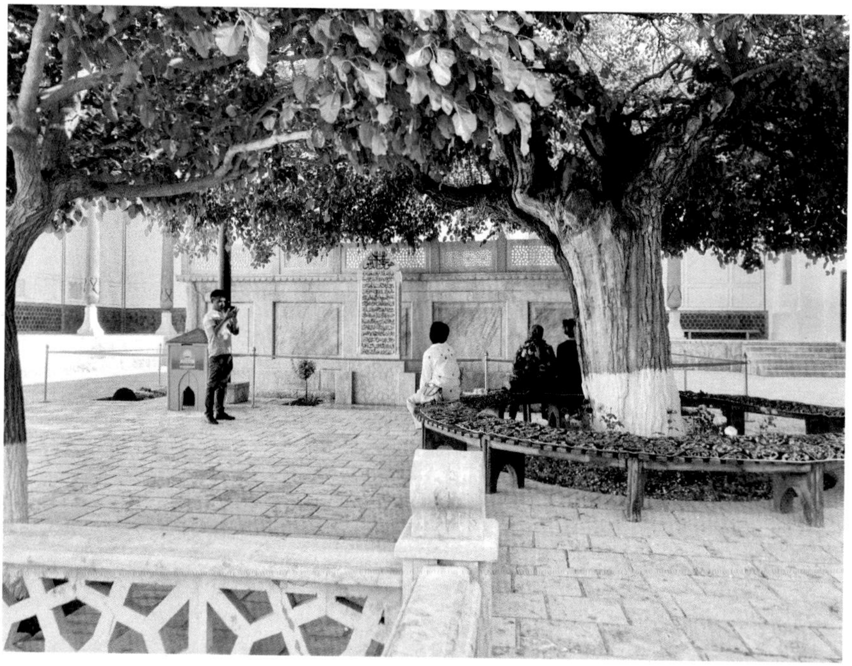

Plate 4 Tomb of 14th century Naqshbandi Sufi master Baha al-din Naqshband, Bukhara.

Plate 5 Shrine of 15th century Naqshbandi Sufi master Khwaja Ubaidullah Ahrar, Samarkand.

Plate 6 Registan, 15th to 17th centuries, Samarkand.

Plate 7 Rudaki Avenue, Dushanbe.

Plate 8 Persian literature class, Istaravshan.

Plate 9 Kamol Khujandi monument, Khujand.

Plate 10 Farm workers, southern Tajikistan.

Plate 11 Khorugh, Gorno-Badakhshan, Tajikistan.

Plate 12 Pamiri musician, Wakhan Valley.

Plate 13 Toqi zargaron bazaar, Bukhara.

Plate 14 Tajik musicians, Bukhara.

Plate 15 Hebrew wall inscriptions from a former Jewish mansion, now converted into a restaurant, Bukhara.

Plate 16 Afghan village on the Tajik border, Badakhshan.

been under Uzbek rule for so long,' recalled one reporter. 'We wanted to understand each other again.'[24]

Meanwhile, long-simmering tensions among various regionally based groups – primarily northerners from Khujand (then known as Leninobod) and southerners from Kulob – came to a head in early 1990 when elections were called for the Supreme Soviet, unleashing a competition among rival factions within the existing political hierarchy. These tensions were further complicated by the opening up of political discourse under perestroika, which allowed an unprecedented degree of space for non-governmental actors ranging from modernizing intellectuals to traditionalist Islamic groups to express themselves and mobilize support. The reduction of the republic's local powers vis-à-vis Moscow simultaneously weakened the Tajik SSR government's capacity to bring these diverse forces under control.

Gorbachev's *glasnost* ('transparency') policy had allowed for the formation of a number of new associations, marking the emergence of a new civil society in the Tajik SSR as elsewhere throughout the Soviet Union. These organizations were mostly urban-based, with the rural majority remaining largely detached from political events going on in the cities. On one side these new associations included the democratically minded Rastokhez ('Resurgence') movement, led by nationalist intellectuals such as the philosopher Mirbobo Mirrahim and the poet Bozor Sobir, and the youth-oriented Ru-ba-ru ('Face-to-Face') political club which shared much of their progressive agenda. On the other, there arose groups which sought to advance the interests of specific regions of the country, including Ihyoi Khujand ('Revival of Khujand') in the north and Oshkoro ('Transparency,' a calque on *glasnost*) in the southern city of Kulob, reflecting the ongoing rivalry of two regions that had long competed for political control of the Tajik SSR. At the same time a regional organization in the Pamirs, Lali-Badakhshon ('Ruby of Badakhshan'), called for more equal relations with the Tajik central government, asserting their cultural and linguistic differences from the rest of the country. Representing religious interests, the Hizbi Nahzati Islom – a Tajik branch of the all-Union Islamic Revival Party (IRP) – was established in 1990, but it was soon outlawed by the Tajik government who claimed it was made up of foreign-trained 'terrorists' in the pay of the Saudis or the CIA.

On 10 February 1990 there was a large public demonstration in Dushanbe. Ostensibly organized in opposition to rumours that Armenian refugees fleeing conflict in Azerbaijan were to be given priority for new housing, it was really motivated by a wide range of complaints. The following day violence broke out, including attacks on non-Tajiks, followed by looting and vandalism. Martial law was declared and troops were brought in from neighbouring republics to restore order. The demonstrators, represented by a group called Vahdat ('Unity'), called for the government's resignation and the dissolution of the Communist Party of Tajikistan along with other demands such as the freeing of political prisoners, a more equitable distribution of cotton profits and the closing of a heavily polluting aluminium plant in the western part of the republic. The government agreed to resign, but rescinded its resignation on February 15th once it became clear that the Soviet army had managed to bring the demonstrators under control.

The casualty count over a week of violence was an estimated 25 dead and 850 injured. Although most of those killed were Tajiks, a majority of the injured were Russians. Ongoing attacks by young Tajik thugs over the following months became an incentive for many Russians to emigrate to other parts of the Soviet Union. And yet, attempts in some circles to characterize the demonstrations as being anti-Russian or pro-Islamic may camouflage their real nature. It is significant that most of the demonstrators were from southern Tajik areas other than Dushanbe; in fact, much of the violence seems to have been perpetrated by youth gangs from Kulob.

While political scientists continue to debate the causes of the outbreak in February 1990, the events were clearly planned and organized. To a large extent they may be seen as representing an effort by marginalized elites to change the balance of power.[25] In this respect they were successful, in that politicians from the Kulob region were henceforth given more parity with their erstwhile rivals from Khujand/Leninobod. Elites from the east-central region of Gharm, on the other hand, were sidelined from this rapprochement, laying the foundations for future conflict. At the same time the Khujandi-Kulobi alliance meant a reconsolidation of authoritarian power, the unrest serving as justification for the heightened persecution of opposition figures (nationalists as well as Islamists) along with a tightening of censorship.

Apart from the Communist Party leadership whom a large proportion of Tajiks blamed for the February 1990 crisis, the big losers from this incident were the Rastokhez party who were seen as having cynically tried to misrepresent the nature of the unrest to their own advantage. Many of the party's best-known figures left to join the new Democratic Party of Tajikistan (DPT), which was formed in August of the same year. The DPT preserved much of the Rastokhez agenda, notably the call for building civil society, a free economy and national self-determination.

While it was the first formal political body in modern Tajik history to openly challenge the power monopoly of the Communist Party, the DPT was plagued from the outset by internal disagreements – and, being a party primarily of intellectuals, by a level of disconnection from the general population as well. The intellectual elite were of course themselves products of the Soviet system to which they owed their status and positions, and they were reluctant to share these privileges with the younger generation and its new ideas.[26] As for the CPT, despite the fact that it was no longer the sole actor in Tajik politics, it remained the strongest, and, to many, the most viable one. The Tajik SSR, still the poorest of all the Soviet republics, relied on Moscow for no less than 47 per cent of its annual budget. Not surprisingly, a referendum held in March 1991 showed strong public support – a resounding 96.2 per cent – for the preservation of the USSR.

Thus, while the Baltic and Caucasian republics during this period were actively seeking formal independence, the overwhelming preference among Tajiks at both the elite and popular levels was for the preservation of the status quo. On the eve of an independence few Tajiks really wanted, the Tajik SSR was more heavily dependent on Moscow – both politically and economically – than ever before.

Tajiks in the Uzbek SSR

The population of the Emirate of Bukhara, whose boundaries roughly corresponded with those that would be drawn for the Uzbek and Tajik Soviet republics, was about one-third Tajik, with the major urban centres of Samarkand, Bukhara, Qarshi and Tirmiz all having strong Tajik majorities. With virtually all urban Tajiks thus finding themselves living within the boundaries of the new, officially Turkic-speaking Uzbek republic, the future of traditional Tajik language and culture seemed doomed from the start. Indeed, by the end of the Soviet period there were no Tajik-language schools in the Uzbek SSR and virtually no publications in Tojikī.

Beginning in the 1920s Tajiks living in the Uzbek SSR were strongly encouraged to identify themselves for all official purposes as Uzbeks, so that government censuses throughout the Soviet period consistently and dramatically under-reported the proportion of the republic's population that were Tajik (officially less than 5 per cent, but the real figure was very likely three or four times that). Uzbek historiography claimed (and continues to claim) – spuriously but stubbornly – all of Central Asia's great historical figures for the Uzbeks, including the medieval scholars Khwārazmī, Farābī and Bīrūnī, with utter disregard for the fact that these individuals lived at a time when the region was culturally Iranian. It was against this fabricated historical backdrop that Tajiks were dismissed as being merely 'Turks who have forgotten their language'.

With the opening up of public discourse under perestroika came a revindication of identity from Tajiks living in the Uzbek SSR, voiced by new organizations such as Samarqand, Ihyoi Farhangi Bukhoro ('Revival of the Culture of Bukhara'), Oftobi Sughdion ('Sunlight of the Sogdians') and Oryoni Buzurg ('The Great Aryans'), demanding an end to language-based discrimination and even political autonomy for Tajik-majority regions such as Samarkand, Bukhara and Surkhondaryo.

Not surprisingly these demands were echoed and supported by Tajiks and their organizations in the Tajik SSR. A two-volume collection of articles entitled *Darsi Kheshtanshinosī* (Lessons on Self-Knowledge), edited by Qodiri Rustam and published in Dushanbe in 1989 and 1991, criticized the national delimitation of the 1920s and argued for reattaching Samarkand and Bukhara to Tajikistan, as did dozens of articles in newspapers such as *Rastokhez, Charoghi Ruz* and *Komsomoli Tojikistan.*[27]

In 1989 the Samarkand-based Tajik Cultural Society presented the government of the Uzbek SSR with three demands: (1) the right to freely choose one's nationality, (2) official status for Tojikī as the second language of the republic and (3) legal status for Tajik cultural and educational activities. These demands were ignored by the Uzbek government, which continued to pursue its policy of assimilation. The arguments of nationalist Uzbek scholars that Uzbeks were the region's original inhabitants, that the entirety of its history belonged to them and that Tajiks were merely Uzbeks who had forgotten their language became all the more insistent with the fall of the Soviet Union and the emergence of an independent Uzbekistan that desperately needed to construct a national narrative for itself. In a repeat of the 1920s, millions of Tajiks were marginalized amidst this Uzbek drive to consolidate their own national identity.

6

The Republic of Tajikistan

Giryai man na az on ast, ki bechora shudam
Na 'z on ast, ki farsuda buvad pirohanam
Giryam az on ki turo hukmi kushtan kardand
Ey tu, ham poya-vu ham moyai inson budanam

My crying is not because I have become wretched
Nor because my shirt is torn
My crying is because they sentenced you to death
Oh you, the foundation and substance of my being human.

Loiq Sheralī (1941–2000)

The fate of the USSR was sealed by an abortive coup in August 1991, after which the union that had endured for more than seven decades was widely seen as no longer viable. One by one the republics declared their independence, with Tajikistan reluctantly bringing up the rear on 9 September following the resignation of Tajik Communist Party leader Qahhor Mahkamov. The Tajiks had, in this willy-nilly fashion, achieved sovereignty for the first time since the fall of the Samanid dynasty in 999, nearly 1,000 years earlier. Unfortunately, the result of this newfound self-rule – 'a freedom', in the words of one scholar, 'more forced on them than acquired or won'[1] – was a rapid slide into five years of brutal internal conflict.

The Tajik civil war, which lasted from 1992 to 1997, has often been portrayed as a struggle between the old guard who were raised as communists versus a newly emerged Islamist opposition. This trope has been taken up by the Soviet successor regimes in all the former republics of the USSR where Muslims constitute a significant proportion of the population, and has served over the past quarter century to justify all manner of autocratic abuses and the stifling of human rights on the pretext of 'fighting against Islamic extremism', a kind of fear-mongering that has garnered much uncritical support from Western democracies. In this regard Adeeb Khalid has pointed out with irony a remarkable foreign policy about-face, whereby Western governments went from supporting Islamists against Communism during the 1980s, to supporting Communists against Islamism after 1991.[2]

A more careful analysis of the various participants and their stated programmes suggests a somewhat different picture. In fact, the crisis in Tajikistan – the roots of which were already present during the Gorbachev years – had more to do with competition among rival elites within the existing Soviet system. These elites and the patronage networks they controlled were often regional (Toj. *mahalgaroī*), but they could also be based on professional contexts such as the cotton industry, the transport sector, the security services, academia, sporting clubs and organized crime.[3] Angry public demonstrations and street gang hooliganism were definitely present during this turbulent period – along with rather vague calls for a revalorization of the Islamic components of Tajik identity – but such public agitations were most often either orchestrated or co-opted by elite actors for the promotion of their own immediate agendas. Tajikistan's crushing poverty rate was a major factor, in that many Tajiks saw civil disorder not as a means to political ends but simply as a cover for obtaining food and goods through looting.

Tajikistan's first elections as an independent nation were held on 24 November 1991. The ostensible victor was Rahmon Nabiev, an old-time Communist Party leader strongly rooted in the northern Khujandi (Leninobodi) clique which had recently allied itself with the Kulobis from the south. Many believed the election to have been rigged and that the reformist candidate, Pamiri filmmaker Davlat Khudonazarov, had actually received more votes. In a 2012 interview, Khudonazarov bemoaned the absence of foreign observers to monitor the process. 'This allowed the government in Tajikistan to falsify the elections,' he said. 'And I can add that within a week after the elections, they were using falsified elections ballots to wrap fruits and vegetables in the farmers market.'[4] Whether a Khudonazarov-led government would have been more successful in staving off civil conflict is doubtful, however, given widespread regionalist tendencies across the population and the strong Sunni sentiments of the majority.

Tajiks from the relatively less-developed and more tradition-minded Gharm and Pamir regions – representing the eastern and southeastern parts of the country, but also including many whose ancestors had been forcibly relocated to the Qurghonteppa region during the 1930s and 1940s to work on kolkhoz farms and in factories – were excluded from the winning Khujandi–Kulobi alliance, and by extension from the all-encompassing patronage networks they controlled. Nationalist, pro-democracy intellectuals saw in Nabiev's election a retrenchment of the former Soviet elites and their outdated system.

The neo-Soviet status quo represented by Nabiev was opposed by a range of groups, including the recently formed Islamic Revival Party of Tajikistan (IRPT), by secular reformists such as academics and journalists who figured prominently in the Democratic Party of Tajikistan (DPT), and by the Pamiris, represented by the Lali Badakhshon ('Ruby of Badakhshan') party which sought greater autonomy for their remote, sparsely populated, mostly Ismā'īlī region.

While the Islamic opposition in Tajikistan has long been treated both inside and out of the country as a potential threat, the IRPT – in its public rhetoric at least – did not advocate an Islamic government, but merely more rights for Muslims and a greater recognition of the historical place of Islam within Tajik society. (As late as 1989 there had been only seventeen legally registered mosques operating in the entire Tajik SSR, but an estimated 2,000 illegal ones were maintained by local *mahallas*.[5]) What the IRPT and the DPT shared was a nationalist agenda, which enabled them to cooperate despite many ideological differences. It is important to note that each of the three major opposition groups sought merely to *participate* in the government, not to overthrow it.

The masses of protestors who took to the streets of Dushanbe in the spring of 1992 were mostly bussed in from the countryside. In particular, the IRPT brought in large numbers of Gharmi demonstrators, both from Qurghonteppa[6] and from the Gharm region itself. The government, for its part, mobilized supporters from the district of Kulob. The demonstrations in Dushanbe's Martyr's Square – which coincided with the fall of the Marxist regime in neighbouring Afghanistan and the outbreak of civil war in that country – went on for fifty days. Many of those present found inspiration in the leadership model of the Afghan warlord Aḥmad Shāh Mas'ūd, seen as a Tajik 'national' hero.

A compromise proposal by Nabiev to form a coalition government – even as he surreptitiously ordered the distribution of arms to the main Kulobi militia – was inadequate to quell the growing civil unrest. Beginning in early May of 1992 a number of opposition paramilitary forces had converged on the capital. Fighting in the streets went on throughout the summer, causing many deaths. During this period it became apparent that the conflict was less about political ideologies than an opportunity for rival regional gangs – primarily Kulobis versus Gharmis in Qurghonteppa – to settle scores and to seize control of collective farms and other resources. For this reason, French political scientist Olivier Roy has labelled it 'the War of the Kolkhoz'.[7]

Many members of Tajikistan's large, mainly rural Uzbek minority – who constitute nearly a quarter of the country's total population – joined forces with the pro-government Kulobis, fearing the Tajik nationalist agenda of the reformists. Neighbouring Uzbekistan, having itself assumed the character of an authoritarian neo-Soviet state, sent military support as well, followed by Russia which already had a number of units stationed on the Afghan border. These interventions succeeded in securing Nabiev's government in place but they did not eliminate the ongoing factional violence throughout the country. Amidst the continuing unrest, Nabiev was ousted in an internal coup in early September. This was followed by renewed fighting as the various militias battled for power.

In November the Tajik Supreme Soviet, in the presence of no less than twenty-four militia leaders as well as official representatives from Russia and Uzbekistan, named a forty-year-old former kolkhoz director from Kulob, Emomali Rahmonov, as Chair of the Supreme Soviet. Rahmonov was supported by a militia calling itself the Popular Front of Tajikistan (PFT), comprised largely of career criminals such as the notorious Kulobi mafia boss Sangak Safarov as well as corrupt politicians, most notably Safarali Kenjaev who had previously been Speaker of the Tajikistan Supreme Soviet and – ironically – chairman of the parliamentary commission on human rights.

Assisted by forces sent in from neighbouring Uzbekistan, PFT fighters took control of Dushanbe in December 1992 and immediately embarked upon a massive campaign to expel opposition fighters from the capital. Many Pamiris and Gharmis were driven into Badakhshan, or even across the Amu Darya into Afghanistan. PFT soldiers burned some 55,000 homes, turning hundreds

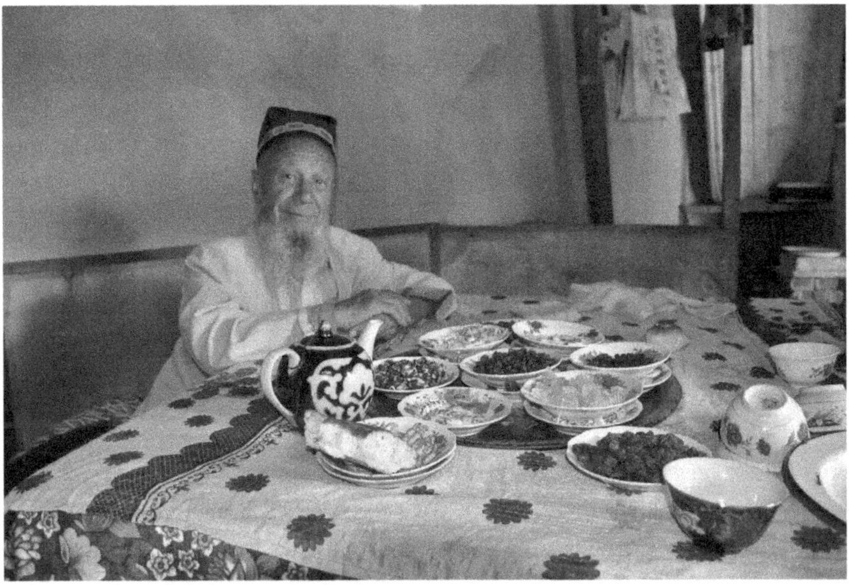

Figure 6.1 Caretaker of a neighbourhood mosque offering tea. Istaravshon, Tajikistan.

of thousands of non-combatants into internal refugees. (The leaders of these rapacious gangs would eventually meet violent ends themselves: Safarov and a fellow PFT leader, Fayzali Saidov, killed each other in a shootout in 1993, and Kenjaev was assassinated in 1999.)

Although Rahmonov was able to establish control over the capital, regional militias – including even those led by the very PFT warlords who had enabled his own rise to power – continued to operate according to their private agendas. These were often connected with the activities of organized crime networks, which operated with impunity and often government protection. The drug trade flourished as never before. Ordinary citizens, meanwhile, were subject to the constant threat of being robbed, raped, murdered or kidnapped for ransom. Legitimate forms of employment all but disappeared.

The Islamic opposition, now based in Afghanistan, reconstituted itself as the United Tajik Opposition (*Ittihodi oppositsioni Tojik* – UTO) under the chairmanship of Abdullo Nurī in 1994. They launched periodic raids into Tajik territory, allegedly at times with the assistance of Afghan troops loyal to Aḥmad Shāh Mas‘ūd or Gulbuddīn Ḥikmatyār. For the next four years much of eastern Tajikistan was under opposition control; cut off from the centre, most people suffered greatly from lack of food and other resources in this isolated region. The mostly Ismāʿīlī population of the Pamirs survived largely through food aid from the Aga Khan's charitable network, trucked in from Kyrgyzstan over difficult mountain roads.

The 'Islamist threat' was used by Russia as a pretext to provide military support to help prop up the fragile Rahmonov regime. This included policing Tajikistan's 1,344-kilometre southern border with Afghanistan, which was, in the opinion of Russia's then-president Boris Yeltsin, 'in effect, Russia's'.[8] (Russia does not in fact share any border with Tajikistan or Afghanistan.) Russia deployed some 11,000 troops for purposes of guarding this frontier from 1993 to 2004, yet it remained relatively porous. All throughout this time thousands of Tajik refugees were easily able to cross into Afghanistan as well as opposition fighters from the other direction, to say nothing of a very active cross-border drug trade – amounting to several billion dollars per year – specializing in Afghan heroin destined for Europe. I personally travelled along this border over some 600 kilometres in the spring of 2017 (and again in 2018), and was amazed to see that it is now essentially unguarded apart from occasional mini-patrols of bored young Tajik conscripts. The Panj River (which becomes the Amu Darya further downstream) is in places no more than a few metres wide, and one could easily wade across – though locals informed me that there would be no point in this, since it was easy enough to smuggle things through the official border crossings (See fig. Ex. 1).

Against the backdrop of ongoing hostilities and UN-brokered peace efforts, Rahmonov called for elections in November 1994. After ballots were cast the sitting president claimed a 60 per cent victory over his Khujandi rival and former prime minister, Abdumalik Abdullojonov, while Helsinki Watch characterized the proceedings as having been 'conducted in a climate of fear and flagrant fraud'.[9]

Sporadic anti-government attacks continued for the next two years. With the capture of Kabul by the Taliban in 1996, Russia and other regional actors felt renewed pressure for a resolution to the Tajik conflict. Talks were held in Afghanistan in December 1996 between the Tajik government and the UTO, mediated by the Afghan Tajik leaders Aḥmad Shāh Masʿūd and Burhānuddīn Rabbānī. The resulting peace agreement, signed on 27 June 1997, won broad support across all levels of Tajikistan's battle-weary population. All told

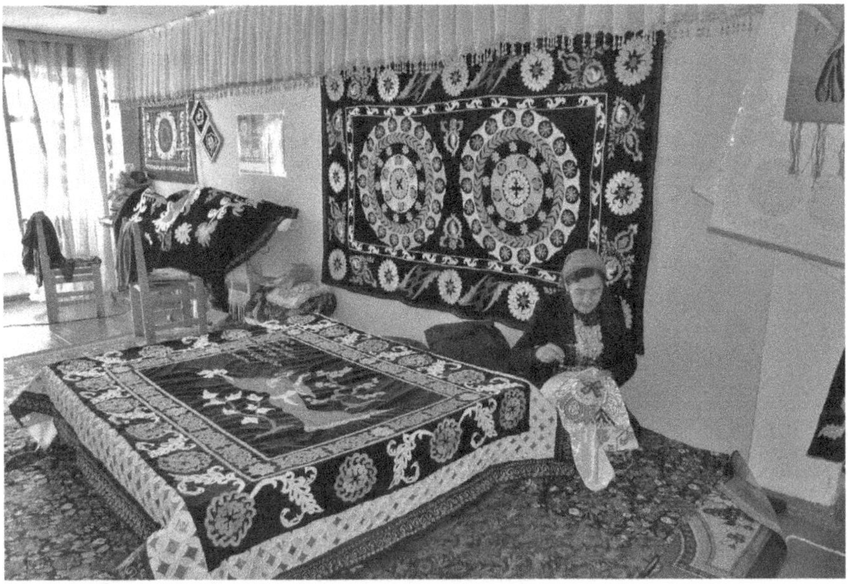

Figure 6.2 Traditional Tajik embroidery. Istaravshon, Tajikistan.

the war took between 50,000 and 100,000 lives. A further 500,000 became internally displaced refugees, many of whom fled the cities to their native villages where they were supported by traditional *mahalla* networks and survived on backyard produce. Factories were abandoned due to the fighting and fell into ruins, exacerbating unemployment and decimating the country's economy.

The overall outcome of the civil war was a confirmation and entrenchment of the neo-Soviet model. The major beneficiaries were President Rahmonov – who, notwithstanding a failed assassination attempt in April, no longer faced any serious rival for power – and the Kulobi and Qurghonteppa cliques that had supported him. These regional factions and their militias now worked their way into the government and security services, bringing their organized criminal networks with them. Other parties in the 1997 so-called 'power-sharing' arrangement – notably the UTO and more generally the Gharmis and Pamiris – were theoretically to have been accorded 30 per cent of all government posts, but in the years since the agreement was signed practice has fallen considerably short of this principle.

Changes were made to Tajikistan's constitution allowing Rahmonov to run for a seven-year term in 1997, an election he won with a claimed 97 per cent of the votes. (During the same year he de-Russified his surname, shortening it to 'Rahmon'.) Halfway through his second term President Rahmon sponsored an amendment which would allow him to run for two further terms, which he went on to win in 2006 and again in 2013. Two years later the Tajik parliament granted him lifelong immunity from legal prosecution, as well as the power to veto any legislation of which he disapproved. He was also given the right to address parliament at any time and to be present at any government meeting he chooses.[10]

Further legislation in May 2016, approved by a nationwide referendum, removed presidential term limits altogether, allowing Rahmon to remain 'president for life'. Also, claiming an increased threat of Islamic terrorism, Rahmon finally instituted a ban on religious parties. This formally ended twenty-five years of political participation by the IRPT, which had been designated as a 'terrorist organization' following a failed coup attempt in September 2015 in which they were accused of participating. By this point any traces of the 1997 power-sharing agreement seemed to have vanished once and for all.

The IRPT – which had been the only Islamic political party legally operating in any former Soviet country – survived as long as it did because from the very beginning it had downplayed any ambitions to forming an Islamic state, focusing instead on the more nationalistic goal of restoring Islam to its traditional place as a component of Tajik identity. This emphasis on associating Islam with Tajikness enabled the IRPT to participate in a marriage of convenience with secular nationalists for many years.

Akbar Turajonzoda, an influential former religious judge who strategically avoided becoming an official member of the IRPT, expressed the view on several occasions that the Tajiks' ignorance regarding Islam made any project of building an Islamic state in the short term impossible. As he put it in a 2006 interview, 'How can we think about the creation of an Islamic state when 90 per cent or more of Tajiks are without knowledge of their faith?' He suggested instead that 'We do not need an Islamic state, we need an Islamic nation'.[11]

Nevertheless, as President Rahmon sought to reinforce his own power by eliminating any form of opposition, political Islam increasingly came to be seen as the major obstacle to his aims. The radical and often-violent international Islamist organization Ḥizb-i Taḥrīr ('Liberation Party'), originally founded by Palestinians in 1953, became active throughout Central Asia, including Tajikistan, where, despite being outlawed and subject to official repression, it attracted several thousand supporters. The discovery of two Tajik citizens amongst the jihadis captured in Afghanistan by the United States and sent to Guantanamo prison in 2002 was taken as justification by Rahmon to shut down eight mosques in the northeastern town of Isfara. Today, being convicted of membership in Ḥizb-i Taḥrīr carries a fifteen- to twenty-year sentence.

Islamic organizations in the country are required by law to report to the semi-governmental Islamic Centre of Tajikistan to maintain official recognition, and any form of religious education or publication requires government approval. All of Tajikistan's nineteen madrasas were closed down by official decree on 3 August 2015, and students who travel abroad in search of formal religious education are blacklisted from finding legal employment when they return to the country.

Building a national identity

The regional divisions so apparent during the Tajik civil war served to highlight the fact that the Soviet system had failed to instil in the population any kind of strong unifying national identity as Tajiks. Moreover, during the years immediately before and after independence, Tajik intellectuals in both Tajikistan and Uzbekistan were focused largely on the question of re-attaching Samarkand and Bukhara to Tajikistan. This dream did not come to fruition, a setback that may have owed something to Uzbekistan's intervention in the Tajik civil war.[12]

Ironically, the Uzbeks and particularly their late president, Islom Karimov, were instrumental in consolidating the power of Tajik president Emomali Rahmon as the 'saviour of the nation' and the 'bringer of peace' – although, in reality, this peace owed more to mediation by the UN, Russia and Iran and to the concessions made by the United Tajik Opposition. Yet since that time, Rahmon has most often portrayed the Uzbek state as an enemy standing in the way of Tajik national integrity, which requires a repossession of the 'occupied' cities of Samarkand and Bukhara.

Nationalist discourse in all the former Soviet republics of Central Asia has preserved to a large extent the forms developed during the Soviet period, which included what John Heathershaw and Kirill Nourzhanov refer to as a 'personalistically authoritarian' component that post-Soviet dictators have used to legitimize their rule.[13] The construction and propagation of Tajik identity undertaken by Emomali Rahmon – relying heavily on the Soviet-era interpretations of Bobojon Ghafurov, Rahim Masov, Numon Negmatov, Yusufsho Yakubov and other nationalist historians – has sought to portray the Samanid Empire of the ninth and tenth centuries as the original 'Tajik' state, with Ismoil Somonī as its founding figure. It should be conceded that this claim, however occasionally exaggerated or distorted, stands up far better to historical scrutiny than the parallel project taking place in neighbouring Uzbekistan, wherein Amir Timur (Tamerlane) is touted as the 'Father of the Uzbek Nation' – an attribution that has required considerable manipulation of the historical sources.

As in most of the other former Soviet republics, Tajikistan's nation-building initiative has entailed frequent government-sponsored celebrations of historical periods and figures presented as essential to Tajik identity. To that end President Rahmon declared 1999 to be the '1,100th Anniversary of the Samanid Empire'. To mark the occasion, a massive statue of Ismoil Somonī was erected in Dushanbe's Lenin Square – now renamed Ismoil Somonī Square – where it stands today. By identifying itself so closely with the Samanids, the Tajik government has implicitly affirmed its claims to all the territories occupied by the Samanid state, including its capital cities Bukhara and Samarkand.

Stretching Tajik claims back even further, Rahmon – disregarding scholarly debates on the time and homeland of Zarathushtra – designated 2003 as the '3,000th Year of Zoroastrian Culture', an initiative that gained the approval and support of UNESCO. Tajikistan's claim to Zoroastrian heritage had earlier been expressed in 1991 when the 'First Avesta World Conference' was held in Dushanbe. The eruption of civil war did little to dampen the interest of Tajik intellectuals in Zoroastrianism as a nationalist symbol, and a second Avesta World Conference was organized in 1996. In 2001 a third conference was held, celebrating ten years of Tajik independence. On the occasion of this third gathering several Tajik scholars and their families underwent the *sidra-pushī* initiation ritual in order to become Zoroastrians.

Rahmon makes frequent mention of Zoroastrianism in his (ghostwritten) book *Tajiks in the Mirror of History*. 'My thoughts go back to Zarathustra,' the President wistfully recalls, 'who created the immortal Avesta, the first prophet of the Tajiks whose trace on earth has not been erased by the dust of millennia and the ashes left by countless bloody wars.'[14] Rahmon asserts that Zoroastrian ethics have influenced him throughout his life:

> From history books and from old Tajik-Persian literature I had already obtained certain knowledge about Zarathustra. Not infrequently in those hard times I recited in my mind his call for 'goodness in thoughts, words and deeds'. During the authoritarian regime [i.e., the Soviet period] when it became common practice that all the works in a collective farm – be it livestock breeding, sowing, harvesting or renovation of the premises – were ordered by the commanding voice of the chairman, the wisdom of Zarathustra's precept[s] quite often saved me from acting in a manner which otherwise I would have afterwards deeply regretted. At other moments when I was about to lose my temper and let some rude word escape my lips, the precepts of Zarathustra and of some other famous sons of the nation would always help me to regain my composure. More than anything in the Zoroastrian religion, I remember the deep reverence for the earth and water and a great respect for farming and cultivation of the land. Later on, when studying *The Tajiks* by B. Gafurov, especially the chapters of the book devoted to ancient historical events, I was repeatedly impressed by the humanistic essence and wisdom of Zarathustra's teaching.[15]

In a related effort to appropriate the past, Rahmon promoted the Persian New Year, Nawrūz, which was banned under the Soviets until the 1960s, as an 'indigenous' Tajik holiday.[16] His government constructed a massive Nawrūz assembly field (Nawrūzgoh) in the centre of Dushanbe, where the celebrations seem to get bigger every year – Nawrūz is now a week-long national holiday. The Tajik flag bears an arc of seven stars which some say are meant to represent the seven Amesha Spentas; the government online news agency is called Avesto (named for the Zoroastrian holy text), as is a major Dushanbe hotel and a stadium in Darvoz.

In the northern part of the country, the Sughd Museum nestled within the partially reconstructed fortress of Khujand features a 'Hall of Aryan Civilization', with a large banner over the entrance bearing the image of a *fravahr* (a bearded figure standing inside a winged disk, the most prominent Zoroastrian religious symbol); an inlaid inscription on the adjacent wall reads in Tojikī '*Pindori nek, Guftori nek, Kirdori nek*', – the Zoroastrian moral code of 'Good thoughts, good words, good deeds'. In the nearby city of Istaravshon, the late Paris-based Iranian Zoroastrian philanthropist Abtīn Sāsānfar subsidized the conversion of a building in the main government square into an 'Aryan Cultural Centre' (Farhangsaroyi Oriyoī). Here, local director Rano Zohirdukht runs weekend classes on Persian literature and culture for small numbers of rural children living in the area. Because her work emphasizes Iran's ancient heritage, she has received numerous threats from local Islamists and is considering giving up her work.[17]

In the final analysis, any enthusiasm for pre-Islamic culture among today's Tajiks seems limited to a tiny handful amongst the educated elite. Moreover, such feeling is entirely overwhelmed by the renewed interest which a majority of Tajiks, especially the younger generation, have found for Sunni Islam.

Islam, not Zoroastrianism

Ever since the fall of the USSR large numbers of Tajiks have been turning (or returning) to Islam as a source of identity. Attendance at Friday prayers jumped from 13 per cent in the 1990s to 52 per cent by 2010, and those reporting that they prayed five times a day went from 1 per cent to 63 per cent during the same period.[18]

Tajikistan today offers few opportunities for young people starting out in life, even those with university educations. For those who have only completed high school the prospects are even worse. In the words of a young middle-class man who left school at age sixteen, 'In Tajikistan nowadays there are no choices. If you want to go to university, you have to bribe teachers to get a place. If you have a diploma and want to get a job, again, you need to pay corrupt officials. Corruption is everywhere.'[19]

Facing such despairing conditions, many are seduced by the promises and sense of purpose and belonging offered by radical Islamic organizations such as Ḥizb-i Taḥrīr or even the al-Qaeda-affiliated Islamic Movement of Uzbekistan (IMU). Over 1,000 young Tajik men who joined the so-called 'Islamic State' in Syria and Iraq from 2014 to 2017 are said to have left Tajikistan mainly in search of better employment opportunities, rather than for specifically idealistic reasons.[20]

Bands of former UTO members launched raids into Tajik territory from Afghanistan in 2009–10. These were not successful, however, and only served to provide Raḥmon's government with a pretext for increased repression of perceived Islamism. In 2009 'Salafism' – a puritanical interpretation of Islam that has been materially promoted by Wahhabist states such as Saudi Arabia and Qatar for the past several decades – was officially banned by the Tajik parliament, which went on to formally label it an 'extremist movement' in 2014. Following the outlawing of the Islamic Renaissance Party in 2015 fourteen IRPT leaders were jailed, two of them given life terms. IRPT chairman Muhiddin Kabirī, now living in exile, predicted that the government crackdown on Islamism 'will play into the hands of radicals and more and more youths, having lost all trust in the government, will join the ranks of extremist groups'.[21]

Tajik men became subject to a 'de facto beard ban' (beards being perceived as a symbol of Islamist sympathies), with reports of police beating bearded men and some individuals being taken off to be forcibly shaven.[22] The government also began pressuring women not to wear *ḥijāb*, clamping down on *ḥalāl* restaurants for 'violating the rights of alcohol-drinkers' and banning Islamic components of personal names such as *hoji, shaykh* and *mullo* on the basis that they create 'class discrimination'.[23]

Recognizing that the attempt to win over the population to a pre-Islamic identity had largely failed and fearing the spread of Islamic activism, the Tajik government adopted the strategy of promoting an 'acceptable' version of Islam based on the Ḥanafī legal tradition. Accordingly, 2009 was declared the Year of 'Imomi Azam' (Abū Ḥanīfa, founder of the world's most widely practised school of Islamic jurisprudence), whom at the time President Rahmon called 'the noblest representative of the Tajik nation'. The following year Dushanbe was declared a 'Capital of Islamic Culture'.

Concomitant with this effort to fold Islam into the nationalist project, the Tajik government began to exercise more control over religious discourse through the appointment of officially sanctioned religious leaders. 'Tolerated' Islam became increasingly restricted to that operating within state-approved institutions such as the Department of Religious Affairs and the Islamic Centre (*Markazi Islomī*) with its High Council of Ulema (*Shuroi Olii Ulamo*), established in 1996 to replace the Qoziyyot (the Islamic Directorate, which in Soviet times many Tajiks had considered to be an extension of the KGB) as the country's most important official Islamic institution.

All this represents a clear effort on the part of the Tajik government to co-opt Islam away from the opposition and from extremist groups such as Ḥizb-i Taḥrīr. The promotion of traditional Ḥanafī Islam – as opposed to the interpretations of HT and other radical groups – as integral to 'authentic' Tajik national identity has been prominent in the work of Islamic scholar-turned-politician Akbar Turajonzoda, notably in his 2007 book *Shariat va Jomea* ('Sharia and Society').[24]

'Gigantomania' and the personality cult of the President

Erecting monumental structures has been another aspect of Tajikistan's national identity–building project. What was for several years the world's tallest flagpole looms above central Dushanbe, not far from the new National Library – the largest in Central Asia – a massive structure in the form of an open book facing the statue of Ismoil Somonī in Freedom Square. The library was opened in 2011, but its collections were initially quite meagre and had to be enhanced by forcing academics to donate their personal libraries. When I stopped in to offer a copy of one of my own published titles, a puzzled cataloguer asked me why I was donating 'only one' book.

What is promised to be 'Central Asia's largest mosque' is currently being built in Dushanbe, with Qatari money. (Qatari real estate firms have also invested heavily in building palatial residential complexes all across the capital, dramatically changing the face of the city.) Designed to accommodate 115,000 worshippers at a time, the mosque complex has an estimated price tag of $100 million. President Rahmon initiated the construction on 5 October 2011 – his own birthday – by ceremoniously donning a hardhat and taking over the controls of a bulldozer at the building site.

But since long before this mosque initiative was first announced in 2009, the most symbolically significant national building project has been the construction of the Rogun Dam on the upper Vakhsh River east of Dushanbe. Originally conceived during the Soviet period for the dual purposes of irrigation and hydroelectricity, this grandiose endeavour has been plagued by delays for more than five decades. If it is ever completed, the Rogun Dam will reach a height of 335 metres, making it the tallest dam in the world.[25]

The Rogun project has been riddled with controversy, however, its critics claiming that it is financially impractical and technologically obsolete. It has moreover been a source of political tension with downstream Uzbekistan, which fears the vulnerability of its own precious water resources. (The Vakhsh is a major tributary to the Amu Darya.) When the Tajik government sought to raise funds for the project by making an IPO in 2010, citizens were made into obligatory shareholders through payroll deductions and students had to show proof of owning shares before being allowed to take their exams.[26]

In recent years, efforts to develop a personality cult around the president have accelerated. In May 2017 it was decreed that all Tajik media must henceforth refer to the President in every instance as 'The Founder of Peace and Unity, Leader of the Nation, President of the Republic of Tajikistan, His Excellency Emomali Rahmon' (*Asosguzori sulhu vahdati milli, Peshvo'i millat, Prezidenti Jumhurii Tojikiston, Muhtaram Emomali Rahmon*), an epithet that television news presenters complain takes no less than nineteen seconds of air time to say each time. All over the country, massive portraits of the Tajik leader can be seen covering the exterior walls of every building and on huge billboards beside every stretch of road and in every town square (see Figure 6.3). The overwhelming proliferation of these public images, with their accompanying slogans enjoining peace, unity and reconciliation, surpasses even what could be seen during the Soviet period. Artistically speaking they are quite tacky, and the slogans and platitudes ('Language is the Wellspring of the Nation', 'Unity is the Basis of Well-Being', etc.), all signed by the president, hardly seem profound or inspirational. Yet, seen against the backdrop of the threat of renewed civil war they are perhaps having the desired effect, at least among schoolchildren who are perhaps their principal intended audience.

In 2017 the cult of Rahmon received a new boost with the publication of a play entitled 'The Chosen One', in which the Tajik president is portrayed as a divinely selected saviour figure. In a key scene, an angel appears to him and says, 'God doesn't choose just anybody to be a *Podishoh* (Emperor).' Tajik state

Figure 6.3 Emomali Rahmon: Give Thanks for Independence, Thanks to This Government!

radio has lent its services as well, producing audio-book versions of Rahmon's many (ghost-)written works for public broadcast.[27]

From bad to worse: Tajikistan's economic decline

Since the breakup of the Soviet Union Tajikistan has been one of the few countries in the world to see a steady decline in its standard of living. Given that it was already the poorest republic in the USSR this trend is deeply discouraging. While most Tajiks no longer face the absolute destitution they endured during the civil war years, the inequality gap between the governing elite and the rest of the population has continued to worsen and ordinary citizens struggle daily to make ends meet.

Whatever industry the republic possessed in Soviet times was severely crippled by the civil war following independence (during which it logged a negative GDP, with industrial production dropping by 80 per cent[28]), and apart from hydropower and cotton, Tajikistan produces little on its own that can be exported. Aluminium smelted at the Tajik Aluminium Company (Talco) factory outside the western city of Tursunzoda, which currently accounts for 60 per cent of Tajikistan's exports, has to be imported from other countries since it is not mined domestically. This single government-owned operation consumes no less than 40 per cent of the total national supply of electricity, even as power cuts and energy rationing remain a frequent fact of life for the general population.[29]

The agricultural sector, where two-thirds of Tajikistan's remaining workers are employed, has not recovered from the disappearance of Soviet-era subsidies or the ravages of the civil war. Collective farms were nominally 'privatized' into workers' cooperatives (*Khojagiyi dehqonī*) by 1999, but any structural changes were superficial. Machinery, seeds and water access fell under the control of monopolists with government connections, while border issues with Uzbekistan and Kyrgyzstan have restricted Tajik farmers' ability to export their produce to foreign markets.[30] The mass migration of working-age men to Russia has left a labour shortage in rural parts of Tajikistan, where women are left to fill the gap. Since deeds to land parcels are generally in the name of the male 'head of household', women whose husbands are working abroad are often left legally vulnerable.[31]

Cotton continues to provide the major source of agricultural revenue to the state, with apples a distant second. Even so, cotton yields in Tajikistan are less than half what they were during the late Soviet period.[32] Being an extremely water-intensive crop, cotton production uses up the lion's share of the country's water resources, as was the case during the Soviet period. The irrigation system – vital in Tajikistan's arid climate – has been subject to damage from earthquakes, and pumps have been underused because they are run on petroleum which is expensive and has to be imported. The cotton monoculture limits the availability of land, water and labour resources from being used for food production.

In 1995 the International Monetary Fund insisted that Tajikistan cease the state funding of agriculture as a condition for receiving IMF loans. It took thirteen years for the IMF to realize that the Tajik government had continued covertly to fund the cotton industry, which had nevertheless somehow managed to accrue a debt of half a billion US dollars. Yet, according to one analyst, 'The farm debt is mostly fictitious. State power has been systematically used to dominate the farms. Their nominal privatization has provided a convenient cover for exploitation of the rural population to benefit a small elite, creating a case study of post-Soviet crony capitalism.'[33]

Perhaps not surprisingly, in recent years the Tajik economy has become heavily dependent on China, a country with which it shares a border. China's massive 'Belt and Road' development initiative focuses heavily on Central Asia, and China now accounts for two-thirds of Tajikistan's foreign investment.[34] As of 2018 Tajikistan's total external debt was US$2.9 billion, of which $1.2 was owed to China's Exim Bank.[35] Tajik bazaars are full of cheap Chinese goods and most of the traffic slogging along the decrepit Pamir Highway consists of Chinese trucks. Belying much-trumpeted claims as part of its 'Belt and Road' propaganda to respect the interests of its partners, China has exploited Tajikistan's dependency by forcing the country to concede some 1,000 km^2 of territory along their disputed border, and even to hand over a gold mine to the Chinese. Of US$310 million received from China by Tajikistan in 2018, $230 million was spent on the construction of a new parliament building in Dushanbe, apparently a more pressing need than roads, factories, hospitals or schools.

Corruption and the drug trade

In the years following the civil war Tajikistan came to be considered something of a narco-state. The UN Office on Drugs and Crime estimated that about a third of Afghanistan's opium production – some ninety tonnes per year – was transiting through Tajikistan, enriching Tajik criminal gangs as well as numerous corrupt government officials. By the early years of the new millennium drug trafficking was believed to make up anywhere from one-third to one-half of the country's annual GNP.

The state appeared to be directly involved in protecting and facilitating the transit of drugs through the country, while Western governments and NGOs, not wishing to jeopardize their alliance with the Tajik government in 'combatting Islamists', turned a blind eye. Noting the surprisingly large numbers of luxury vehicles seen on the streets of the capital, one European aid worker remarked to *The Economist*, 'We give them cars, and they use them to transit drugs.'[36] Numerous high-ranking government figures, including diplomats and even drug-enforcement officials, have been involved in the drug trade. It would seem that in the context of post-Soviet Central Asia, as Madeleine Reeves wryly observed in regard to Kyrgyz politician Bayaman Erkinbaev, 'the wrestler-turned-drugs baron who becomes a law-writing state deputy is less a paradoxical figure than an emblematic one'.[37]

Most of the smuggling is believed to take place across legal border crossings from Afghanistan, making use of roads and bridges built with millions of dollars in US assistance since 2002. With drug seizures steadily declining every year, Western-devised sting operations tend to focus on small-time operators, thus inadvertently removing the minor-leaguers from competing with major traffickers.[38] Ironically, this has helped to reduce drug-related violence and ensure stability in Tajikistan, in contrast to the chaotic situations found in many other narco-states.

Although most Afghan heroin passing through Tajikistan is destined for Russia and the West, local consumption has also risen dramatically and the country now counts tens of thousands of addicts. Apart from exacerbating the problem of widespread criminality, the proliferation of drug abuse has led to an epidemic of HIV among intravenous users.

Still, the attitude of many Tajiks towards the reality of drug trafficking in their country is somewhat resigned. Given their proximity to the sources of opium production in lawless Afghanistan, combined with their own economic and social connections to Russia which constitutes such a huge market for illicit drugs, some Tajiks are inclined to see their government's participation in trafficking as a kind of 'tax' on an activity that is going to continue whether they like it or not. The drug trade has also been connected to an ongoing construction boom, especially in the capital, since large building projects are a convenient way of laundering ill-gotten gains.[39]

More recently the national elites – principally the president and his family and close associates – have ensured their personal fortunes by taking control of the country's large banks, local concessions of foreign corporations and other sectors of the economy. While this has perhaps reduced the need to rely on skimming off profits from the drug trade, it has only served to worsen perceptions of elite corruption in the minds of ordinary Tajiks.

Sadly, the culture of bribes and kickbacks remains endemic at all levels of Tajik society, whether in the form of no-bid government contracts, or the daily nuisance of petty extortion perpetrated by traffic police waving drivers over to the side of the road with their familiar red batons. Victims are allowed to proceed along their way for as little as one somonī, though with the constant stream of traffic throughout the day this form of salary supplement can be quite substantial. Annoyingly for drivers, such interruptions can take place as frequently as every few hundred metres, adding significant delays to travel times.

Tajiks' inevitable cynicism – a last line of defence for disempowered people everywhere – is well expressed through popular humour, as in a popular joke about a Tajik engineer who is invited to participate in a professional conference in the United States. His American host takes him out to an expensive restaurant, and the Tajik asks him how he can afford such a posh outing on an engineer's salary. Their table has a river view, and the American says, 'See that bridge over there? My company built it, and well, let's just say we did rather well on the deal.' A few months later the American visits Tajikistan where his new friend returns the favour by taking him out to a restaurant where the view is even more breathtaking, unspoiled by any human construction. Impressed, the American asks the same question, where does he get the money to dine out at this magnificent establishment? 'Well,' the Tajik replies, 'you see that river where there is no bridge? It was our company that was supposed to build one.'

The regression of women's rights

The immediate post-Soviet period saw a regression in the status of women, at least in parts of Tajikistan. Women were rarely present at daily neighbourhood teahouse gatherings, an informal tradition presided over by a male elder (*rais* or *aksakal*) where men discussed and resolved issues affecting their local community (*mahalla*). Polygynous marriages, banned under Soviet rule but occasionally practised in secret, became more visible even as they remained officially unregistered, preventing the state from enforcing the legal rights of unrecognized wives.

The civil war left an estimated 25,000 Tajik women widowed, and in the years since that time the emigration of Tajik men to Russia in search of work has greatly reduced the pool of available husbands. Religious leaders, making what some would consider to be unwarranted assumptions about single women, told their male followers that 'if you have the financial means, you should take second or third wives to reduce prostitution'.[40] By 2011 it was estimated that one in ten Tajik men had plural wives, leading women to joke that 'If a man has money, he will either buy a car or take another wife.'[41]

In fact, many village women were unaware they had rights at all, and there were numerous incidents of female suicide through self-immolation. As part of the peace process between rival regional factions following the civil war, many Gharmi families gave their daughters in marriage to powerful Kulobis as a way of securing protection, and Kulobi officials began to take second wives from these and other subjugated groups. Kamol Abdullaev observes that 'One may call this hostage taking, while others may see in it an important conflict-mitigation means and creating bonds between conflicting communities'.[42]

Even in urban environments traditional norms continue to carry substantial weight. It is still expected that girls will marry before they are 20, including those who intend to pursue higher education. It is not uncommon for young Tajik women to give birth while still at university, trusting that their mothers or other female relatives will assist in child-rearing while they complete their studies. A girl who chooses to postpone marriage may be suspected of having lost her virginity, and therefore unfit to be a wife.[43]

Women in traditional Tajik society are still seen as the guardians of family honour (*nomus*), in the sense that any behaviour on their part that could be construed as unchaste or even simply immodest – labelled broadly as *ayb*, literally 'defect' – risks destroying their family's reputation. This includes their choice of dress, which explains the strong preference among Tajik women for wearing traditional, rather than Western, clothing. For the sake of *nomus* women in contemporary Tajikistan are subjected on a daily basis to social controls from those around them, whether in the form of shaming from other women or domestic violence from their husbands, fathers or brothers.

Most marriages in Tajikistan are still arranged by their families. The young couple typically live with the groom's parents, sometimes for the duration of their lives. Within the extended household the daughter-in-law (*kelin*, a

Turkic word that literally means 'incomer') typically holds the lowest status. She spends her life as a sort of slave to her husband's mother, carrying out the bulk of the family chores. For this reason the groom's mother usually takes the initiative in choosing the bride, since it is in her interest to find one who will be appropriately subservient. The groom's first loyalty remains to his mother, so a young married woman may be without support in her new family until she manages to produce sons of her own who will look out for her.

University-educated girls are suspect since they are less likely to accept the submissive role that is required of them as wives and daughters-in-law. Accordingly, girls who have left school early tend to fetch a higher bride price. A new bride is generally expected to get pregnant as quickly as possible; failure to do so within a year can be used as a pretext for returning her to her family. Many young Tajik women would like to break out of this cycle but have few alternative options available to them.

Culture and the arts

As with Iranian peoples worldwide, for Tajiks 'culture' is often conceived of primarily in terms of literature, specifically poetry. The classical Persian poets continue to be taught in Tajik schools and most children can recite couplets of their works from memory. On-and-off cultural exchanges with the Islamic Republic of Iran – subject to vacillating political relations between the two countries – have facilitated the transliteration of many Persian works into Cyrillic. This situation may be favourably contrasted with that during the Soviet period, when Russian literature was emphasized at the expense of Persian and Tajik poets in the service of the government could survive only by promoting Soviet ideology and values. The work of figures such as Loiq Sheralī and Abulqosim Lohutī has been mentioned in the previous chapter.

Among the late Soviet-era poets who made the transition after independence none is better known than Mūʼmin Qanoat (1932–2018). Winner of the Lenin and Rudaki prizes, his elegy to the resistance fighters at the Battle of Stalingrad, 'Surudi Stalingrad', is still recited on memorial occasions in that Russian city. Qanoat was among the first Tajik intellectuals to openly envision an independent state prior to the fall of the Soviet Union, and to express in his verse hopes for how Tajik national identity might be rediscovered. He has been among those advocating for a return to the Persian script, though he admits such a transition will not happen overnight.[44]

The Pamiri poet Hussain Mir Sayid Mirshakar (1912–93), whose work emphasized such themes as peace and wisdom, can be credited with formalizing the genre of children's literature in Tojikī during the late Soviet period. Both Mirshakar and Qanoat continued to write after independence, modifying the content of their work to include more nationalist themes – and with the subsequent trauma of civil war, those of peace and reconciliation as well.

With the advent of independence and the eruption of infighting these motifs were taken up by the next generation of Tajik poets, including Bozor Sobir (1928–2018), Nizom Qosim (b. 1958) and Ato Mirkhujai Neru (b. 1963), who added their voices to the calls for peace, unity and nation-building. Among contemporary women poets one can mention Gulrukhsor Safieva (b. 1947), named Poet of the Tajik People in 1999 and winner of the Rudaki Prize in 2003, and Farzona Khujandī (b. 1964), who is known and read across the Persian-speaking world and beyond. Farzona often evokes images reflecting a common Iranian identity, as in the following verse:

Rohi bozor kujost?
Man base mekhoham az chashme mehrubonī bikharam.
Man base mekhoham pirohane doshta boshad
Ruham az hariri shodī.
Tojire hast ki az shahri tamannohoyam meorad
Rangi muniri shodī
Lek hayhot dar in bozor, bozori Khujand
Chihraho turshu sukhanho tundand,
Qandi Tabriz dilam mekhohad.

Where is the way to the bazaar?
I so want to buy an eyeful of kindness.
I so want to dress my soul in happiness.
There's a merchant from the city of my desires
who brings me great colours of joy.
But here at the bazaar of Khujand,

faces are sour, talk is harsh;
I long for the sweets of Tabriz.

(from '*Nainavoz*', 'The Flute Player'[45])

While poetry continues to maintain its privileged position as the most highly regarded forms of literature among Tajiks, fiction writing began to take shape during the Soviet period and has assumed new forms since independence. Once again, the most prominent figures were and remain government employees whose work is carried out in the service of the state, though this does not necessarily mean avoiding controversial subjects or social criticism.

As with poetry, Tajik fiction writing in the post-Soviet period has often dealt with the traumas and soul-searching provoked by the civil war. Karomatullo Mirzo (b. 1942) has chronicled the tragedies of this conflict in works such as *Sitorahoi pasi abr*, 2005 ('*The Stars behind the Clouds*') and *Margi Begunoh* ('*Death of an Innocent*'). His book *Dar orzui padar*, 1989 ('*Wishing for a Father*') was made into a popular televised series.

Due to censorship writers tend to avoid treating contemporary social issues, preferring instead to address them by projecting them into historical fiction. The works of Bahmanyor (b. 1954), including several short story collections and *Shohinsho*, 2010 ('the novel *King of Kings*'), employ themes from traditional folk tales and traditional village life in modern settings. Urun Kuhzod (b. 1937) is considered by many to be Tajikistan's greatest living novelist; his monumental three-volume work *Hayjo*, 2007 ('*Battleground*') recounts the successive traumas and challenges faced by Tajik society throughout the twentieth century.

The Tajik film industry, which had already gone into decline during the late Soviet period due to an inability to compete with production from other republics, essentially ceased to function with the onset of the civil war. Director Bakhtiyor Khudoinazarov (1965–2015) somehow managed to film his dark love story *Qosh ba Qosh*, 1993 ('*Odds and Evens*') against the real-life backdrop of the Tajik civil war; it was awarded the Silver Lion at the 1993 Venice Film Festival. He moved to Berlin the same year and continued to live there until his untimely death; though backed by European financing he returned briefly to Tajikistan in 1999 where he made his most successful film, *Luna Papa*, a comedic road movie about a young woman whose family takes her on a search for the man who impregnated her.

Most other prominent figures of Tajik cinema – including Davlat Khudonazarov after his failed transition to politics – went into exile during the civil war period. The Tajik film industry has not recovered from this mass emigration, despite the unsuccessful efforts of Iranian filmmaker Moḥsen Ma<u>kh</u>malbāf to revive it during the late 1990s and early 2000s when he shot several films of his own in Tajikistan. With the collapse of Soviet-era support for the arts the expense of making a film became prohibitive. An additional limitation arose from a 2004 law stating that a film can be considered 'Tajik' only 'if its content and theme reflects the most important principles of development of Tajik culture, its national characteristics, and traditions' and if the producers, directors, writers, composers and so on are Tajik citizens.[46]

In the wake of Khudoinazarov's triumph at Venice in 1993 several other Tajik filmmakers have received international attention over the past two decades. Jamshed Usmonov's black comedy *Farishtaii Kifti Rost*, 2002 ('*An Angel on the Right Shoulder*') – about a small-time thug lured back to his home village where he owes everyone money – was screened at Cannes. Nosir Saidov's absurdist *Qiyomi ruz*, 2009 ('*True Noon*'), focusing on a village divided by the Tajik–Uzbek border, was selected for festivals in Rotterdam and Marrakesh, and Rumi Shoazimov's grown-up fairy-tale, *Khobi Hamduna*, 2016 ('*The Dream of the Ape*'), at Qingdao. Such works can hardly be considered representative of the Tajik film industry, however, since they are invariably European co-productions and sometimes even use European actors and crew. Rather, as Epkenhans notes, they 'belong to the genre of *films d'auteur*, critically acclaimed at international festivals but without an audience in Tajikistan'.[47]

The field of popular music would seem to be the area in which young Tajiks today are most closely connected with their fellow Persian-speakers in Iran and Afghanistan – a community facilitated by the near-universal availability of music videos accessed via satellite dishes. Iranian singers, mostly based in Los Angeles, are popular throughout the Persian-speaking world, and some Tajik and Afghan singers are known to Iranians as well. The Tajik performer Jonibek Murodov (b.1986) – son of a highly respected classical musician based in Khujand, Jurabek Murodov (b. 1942) – has worked in LA and elsewhere with Iranian celebrities such as Andy, Mansur and others. Daler Nazarov (b. 1959), a Pamiri who often sings in Shughni (and is son of a former Minister of Culture), is also quite popular, sounding a bit like a Central Asian Chris De Burgh – who, incidentally, is quite beloved by Tajiks as well. Nazarov also wrote the scores for several of the films mentioned above.

7

Tajiks in Uzbekistan

Az on ki tu namurdaī, man niz zindaam
Dar qabzai hijoi tu ovardaam panoh
Ore, faqat tu budaī dar hifzi joni man
Alhaq, faqat tu budaī manro panohgoh

As long as you are not dead, I too am alive
I have taken refuge in the grip of your syllables
Yes, it is only you who have sheltered my soul
Truly, it is only you who have provided me refuge

Tūkhtamysh Tūkhtaev, aka 'Paymon', 'Mother Tongue'

As noted in Chapter 5, the politically driven fabrication of new national identities during the early years of the USSR in the 1920s was massively damaging to the historical status of the Persian language and its speakers living in the Soviet Union. The Persian-speaking cities of Samarkand and Bukhara, which were the main centres of Tajik culture and identity, were allocated to the newly formed Uzbek Soviet Socialist Republic (UzSSR), along with large chunks of Tajik-majority territories stretching from the Afghan border in the south to the Ferghana Valley in the east. The Tajik SSR was tardily carved out of the UzSSR in 1929 from mountainous regions that lacked any major urban centres or historical importance, a process Tajik intellectuals have described as 'a deliberate decapitation of the Tajik nation'. The Bolsheviks saw the Tajiks as the custodians – with Persian as the linguistic vehicle – of the long-established traditions and institutions of Islamic Central Asia, which the revolution aimed to render obsolete. A freshly re-imagined 'Uzbek' – that is to say, Turkic – identity served as a blank page upon which the Soviets hoped to design the new Central Asian. Moreover, the requirement that citizens choose a national identity by which to be known in their internal passports created an artificial bifurcation among the urban populations, known as Sarts, that had been functionally bilingual in Persian and Turki for over a thousand years. Moreover, this division was purely linguistic, since the two resulting nations of Uzbeks and Tajiks were culturally identical in every other respect, as well as being genetically indistinguishable.[1]

Notwithstanding the political imbalances arising from these new territorial realities, throughout the Soviet period all national identities enjoyed official respect, and their rights were guaranteed regardless of where in the USSR they lived. Thus, Tajiks, like other minorities in the Uzbek SSR, had access to Tojikī-language schools, media, and literary publishing. After the fall of the Soviet Union, however, these rights were rapidly taken away. Embracing a Turkic national identity, the government of newly independent Uzbekistan sought to put down the surge of Tajik nationalism that had arisen by the late 1980s, removing Tajiks from important positions and placing some Tajik leaders under house arrest. The outbreak of civil war in Tajikistan in 1992 provided the government with an additional incentive to discourage the expression of Tajik identity in Uzbekistan. Uzbek President Islom Karimov enforced these anti-Tajik policies with an iron fist, a situation that persisted up until the dictator's death in 2016.

The five-year civil war in Tajikistan reduced life to a matter of bare survival for people living in that country, but the economic and political crises of the 1990s made it a difficult decade all across the former Soviet Union, Uzbekistan included. Central Asia's traditionally Tojikī-speaking Jewish communities, broadly referred to as 'Bukharan Jews', who had lived in the region for over two thousand years, took advantage of opportunities to migrate to Israel and the United States, and they have now become almost completely extinguished in Uzbekistan. Many of these 'Bukharan Jews' were quite wealthy, but pressed to leave the country as quickly as possible they sold off their palatial mansions, antique carpets and other prized possessions to their neighbours at bargain prices during the 1990s. A number of former Jewish mansions in Bukhara and Samarkand have since been converted into hotels or restaurants.

Despite what appeared to be a concerted effort on the part of the Karimov regime to eliminate the Tajik language and identity altogether, Tojikī dialects have nevertheless continued to be spoken as the mother tongue of a considerable proportion of Uzbekistan's citizens. Although the official Uzbek census has consistently put the share of Tojikī-speakers at less than five per cent, the true figure may be anywhere from three to ten times that.

While political factors continue to make any kind of accurate accounting impossible, it is likely that the number of native speakers of Tojikī dialects in Uzbekistan today exceeds that of Tajikistan by a large margin, and may even approach that of Afghanistan. Some Tajik nationalists go so far as to claim that Tojikī speakers constitute no less than half of Uzbekistan's total population, based on an extrapolation of censuses conducted prior to the Soviet period. This more generous estimate, derived through a methodology that fails to account for linguistic Uzbekification and out-migration of Tajiks over the past century, is no doubt excessive, but a more conservative figure of eight to twelve million Tojikī speakers in Uzbekistan today is perhaps not unrealistic.

From marginalization to active suppression

With the advent of independence in 1991 Uzbekistan, like all the former Soviet republics, embarked on a reinvigorated campaign to construct its national identity. The entire historical and cultural legacy of Central Asia was claimed for the Uzbeks, such that Tamerlane (who had in fact been a member of a rival tribe that despised the Uzbeks of the time) was christened as the 'Founder of the Uzbek nation'. His astronomer grandson, Ulugh Bek, was dubbed an 'Uzbek' scientist, and the poet Alisher Navo'i (who spent his life in Herat) became the 'Father of Uzbek literature'. Even Babur, the Timurid prince forced out of the region precisely by the Uzbeks during the early 16th century before going on to establish the Mughal Empire in India, was retroactively claimed as an 'Uzbek' hero.

Obviously, this all-encompassing policy of Uzbekification left no room for Tajik demands for recognition within the nation-state of Uzbekistan. In the years following independence many of the most outspoken Tajik leaders in Samarkand, Bukhara and elsewhere were arrested, beaten, and imprisoned by the Uzbek authorities. A new Tajik-language pedagogical institute opened in 1992 was shut down by the government within a year. Some found this repression ironic given that the country's president, Islom Karimov, was a Samarkandi of Tajik origin.

Figure 7.1 Modern statue of Tamerlane, claimed by the Uzbek government as 'founder of the Uzbek nation'; Samarkand.

While living in Samarkand as a graduate student in 1995 I was approached by Jamol Mirsaidov of an underground organization called the National Cultural Centre of Tajiks and Tajik-Speaking Peoples (Kanuni milli-farhangii Tojikon va mardumi Tojik-zabon). He handed me a copy of a letter he had sent on behalf of his group to then UN Secretary-General Boutros Boutros-Ghali, parts of which I reproduce here:

> Dear Mr. Secretary-General,
>
> In the Year of Indigenous and Small Nationalities, as the year 1993 was proclaimed by the UN decision, we, representatives of the Tajiks living in Uzbekistan, plead to you that the UN examine and verify the observation of civil rights and freedoms by the state and the presence

> of necessary conditions for the national-cultural development of this ancient ethnic group on the territory of the contemporary sovereign Republic of Uzbekistan . . . Today the Tajiks, the largest ethnic minority of Uzbekistan, are still discriminated [against], which threatens the stability of the whole area . . . Uzbekistani authorities used force to unlawfully forbid the Uzbek delegation to attend the World Congress of Tajiks, helped between Sept. 9 and 16, 1992 in Dushanbe . . . During the 2nd World Congress of Tajiks, which took place last [month] . . . unlawful restrictions were again imposed by the police and the national security services on the freedom of travel of Uzbekistani Tajik leaders . . . Secretary of the Samarkand Cultural Association Uktam Bekmuhammadov was convicted on false evidence in June 1991. After [an] amnesty, he was unlawfully detained again together with Abumannob Pulatov and another human rights activist by Uzbek security services in Bishkek [Kyrgyzstan] right after the International Human Rights conference held there . . . [Also] in June 1991, [Samarkand State University professor] Jamol Mirsaidov [was fired] . . . on July 8, 1993 Aziza Yusupova, senior intern of the Samarkand State University Faculty of Tajik Philology, [and the following month an administrator for Tajik-speaking schools] Amina Sharafiddinova [were fired, all three] for their human rights activities . . .[2]

Tajik irredentist claims to Samarkand and Bukhara have played a central role in ongoing tensions between the governments of Tajikistan and Uzbekistan. Tajik president Emomali Rahmon has referred to the Uzbek rulers of these Tajik-majority cities as 'enemies of the Tajik nation,' and on two occasions he actually got into fistfights with the late Uzbek president Islom Karimov. 'Once I was with Karimov in Samarkand,' Rahmon recalled in an interview. 'I asked a man standing next to us: "Who are you by nationality?" He looked at Karimov, but I saw his fear and he answered: "I am from Samarkand." This is today's situation with Tajiks there.'[3] Many Tajiks in Uzbekistan took to calling themselves *Eronī* (Iranians), as way of asserting their distinct identity within Uzbek society without raising the ire of the authorities,[4] although technically the term refers to people who immigrated from Iran prior to the Soviet period and are mostly Shiʿites.

At the same time, it should not be imagined that all of Uzbekistan's Tajiks feel they are living under the thumb of cultural oppression. Just as many bilingual Central Asians at the dawn of the Soviet period, faced with the necessity to 'choose' an ethnic identity, decided that Uzbek nationality was preferable to Tajik, in Uzbekistan today many whose first language is Tojikī, or who have mixed parentage, have no qualms about calling themselves Uzbeks. (The situation is mirrored in Tajikistan, where ethnic Uzbeks have increasingly chosen to register as Tajiks.) Tashkent-based literary historian Aftandil Erkinov offers the following personal testimony, which is taken from the introduction to his forthcoming book on Tajik-Uzbek bilingualism:

> Despite the fact that my passport identifies me as an Uzbek, at the same time I feel myself a Tajik as well. In fact, my father is a Tajik and my mother is an Uzbek. My spouse is an Uzbek, while her paternal grandmother was a Tajik. What share of these nationalities will express itself through my children, I do not know. But this question does not worry me. Even if identity could be established in terms of a percentage, what would we gain by that? These two Central Asian nations have become so assimilated and intermingled over the centuries that culturally speaking the Uzbeks became virtually identical with the Tajiks – an Iranian people – rather than with the Turkic peoples with whom they share their linguistic roots. There are many like me in Uzbekistan, who, while identifying themselves as Uzbeks, also have Tajik ancestry and an inherited Persianate culture. How is it that our hybrid past can now so easily be forgotten? Across the border in Tajikistan there are many in a similar situation, but whose passports identify them as Tajiks.[5]

During the last years of Islom Karimov's presidency the government of Uzbekistan stepped up its attempts to quash the use of Tojikī by closing Tajik-medium schools and media outlets. Under Karimov's successor, Shavkat Mirziyoyev, however, the situation began to show signs of improvement.[6] On 27 January 2018 the Tajik cultural centre Oriyono held the First General Conference of Tajiks of Uzbekistan at the government-run International Cultural Centre of the Republic of Uzbekistan in Tashkent, something that would have been unthinkable even a few months previous. As reported by the Persian-language Radio Zamaneh, Tajiks from Ferghana, Surxondaryo, Qashqadaryo, Tashkent, Samarkand, Bukhara, Navoiy, and Jizzakh, who, 'according to unofficial statistics may make up half the population of the country,' were able for the first time to openly gather to recite Persian poetry and 'speak together of their need and wishes'.[7] Around the same time, ten long-closed border crossings between Uzbekistan and Tajikistan were re-opened and visa restrictions for citizens of the two countries lifted, allowing thousands of Tajiks on both side of the border to rediscover each other and their respective territories. In a particularly remarkable development, the Uzbekistan Ministry of Foreign Affairs added a Tajik-language page to its official website, allowing some to dream that Tojikī might even one day be accorded recognized status alongside Uzbek.

Severed from the literary tradition

The standardized literary forms of Persian, Darī and Tojikī are close enough that they should rightly be considered dialects of the same language – *fārsī* – originally the language of the Fars (Pars) region in southwestern Iran. Darī and Tojikī are somewhat more conservative in this respect, preserving many words and expressions that have fallen out of use in modern Persian. Nevertheless, a speaker of Tehrani Persian, who might understand little of the Zoroastrian dialect of Yazd or the Lurī of Khurramabad, will have no problem communicating with educated residents of Kabul or Dushanbe.

The situation in Uzbekistan is rather different. As a result of the anti-Tajik policies that were implemented after the fall of the Soviet Union, Tojikī education and written media went into a steep decline. Consequently, the influence of a standard written language to balance the natural divergence of local spoken dialects of Tojikī was largely extinguished. Thus, while in Afghanistan and Tajikistan an educated person will be able to converse in a more or less universal form of standard literary Persian even though his or her native dialect may be very different, the same is not true for Tojikī speakers in Uzbekistan, most of whom have been educated in Uzbek and have rarely if ever read anything in Tojikī. Moreover, the fact that Uzbekistan has abandoned the Cyrillic alphabet in favour of Latin means that many younger Tajiks in Uzbekistan are actually unable to read Tojikī, which still uses Cyrillic. In contrast to Afghanistan, where many illiterate peasants are still able to quote classical Persian poets from memory, few Tajiks in Uzbekistan who have been educated since independence are able to do so.

Of course, in Uzbekistan there are some Tajiks who still champion their ethnic language and literature, and who make the effort to read the classical poets whose works – whether in Arabic or Cyrillic script – must be brought in from abroad (and on an individual basis, since there is no commercial importation at present), but they are relatively few in number. The readers of Tojikī media appear to be mainly of a generation raised during the Soviet period, when national identity politics were more subdued.

The number of Tojikī-medium schools operating across the country has decreased from over five hundred at the time of independence in 1991 to less than half that number today – 241 as of 2022. Ironically, this has been due not to pressure from the government, but rather from parents who see Uzbek-language education as offering more opportunities for their children's advancement. This is notably true of university admissions, since the entrance exams are in Uzbek and students from Tojikī-language schools have traditionally done poorly when taking them. Textbooks used for teaching the history of Uzbekistan in public schools make not a single mention of the very existence of Tajiks, although they discuss other national minorities such as the Kazakhs, Kyrgyz, Turkmen and Karakalpaks. 'How can our young people have any pride in their identity,' laments educator Amina Sharafuddinova, 'when they feel they have been erased from the nation's history?'[8]

Local dialects in search of a standard

In Samarkand, Bukhara, and certain other regions of Uzbekistan the dominant spoken language is clearly Tojikī, but a Persian-speaker hoping to communicate with the average person on the street or in the marketplace will likely run up against some frustration, as will be the local interlocutor who will often try switching to Russian (the default 'speak foreign' idiom) or even English. Although I am fluent in Persian and have spent enough time in Tajikistan to adapt my speech to the norms of vocabulary, pronunciation and expressions there (*khojjatkhona* for *dastshū'ī*, 'washroom'; *bubakhshed* for *bebakhshīd*, 'excuse me'; *salomat boshed* for *khoda hāfez*, 'goodbye'; etc.), I was somewhat flummoxed while trying to get a haircut in Bukhara when the stylist, a chic, twenty-something male with a poster of New York's Empire State building on his wall, shook his head at my instructions and asked me in a patronizing tone, 'What language are you trying to speak?' 'Um . . . Tojikī?' I volunteered, my confidence slipping by the second. 'That's not Tojikī,' he replied with a smirk, 'That's Fārsī.'

In fact, while Tajiks in Uzbekistan today most definitely speak a language derived from Persian, mutual comprehensibility can be extremely low. One can recognize many verbs and the occasional noun – though not necessarily having the same meaning as in Persian – but Uzbekistani Persian is well on its way to becoming a different language, heavily permeated by Turkic syntax and both Uzbek and Russian vocabulary.[9] The standard greeting, '*Shumo naghz mi*?', has only the first term, 'you', in common with standard Persian. The suffix '*mi*' is the Turkic question marker, while the adjective '*naghz*' is in fact an ancient survival from Sogdian, the eastern Iranian language of the region in pre-Islamic times. On the other hand, the pronunciation of the word for 'camel' – '*shotor*' in standard Persian – is '*üshtür*' in Bukharan Tojikī, which is actually closer to the ancient Avestan form, '*ushtra* ' (cf. Zarathushtra, 'owner of [many] camels').[10]

Who is a Tajik?

In contrast to the early and late Soviet periods when territorial irredentism – focused primarily on Samarkand and Bukhara, but also on Surkhondaryo and parts of the Ferghana Valley – was high, especially among Tajik intellectuals, in Uzbekistan today most Tojikī-speakers seem to have little problem identifying as Uzbeks,[11] seeing themselves as full members of the formal nation who just happen to also speak Tojikī at home or among friends. In what sense then, can they or should they be considered as members of a national minority?

Identities are multi-layered and fluid, and Tajik identity in Uzbekistan is no exception. Since Shavkat Mirziyoyev came to power as Uzbekistan's president in 2016 there seems to be less pressure now on Tajiks to identify as Uzbeks than there was under the Karimov regime, and activities promoting the Tajik language and culture – principally poetry readings – are no longer explicitly forbidden. Mirziyoyev's attention has been mainly focused on the economy, and he has shown little of his predecessor's paranoia regarding the supposed dangers of Tajik nationalism. Yet while a certain class of intellectuals and nationalists continue strongly to promote their Tajik identity, most citizens of Uzbekistan who could be considered Tajiks are concerned mainly with ensuring the best opportunities for themselves and their children. This would explain why the ongoing conversion of Tajik-medium schools to teaching in Uzbek is being brought about not by pressures from above, but rather by parents who see Uzbek instruction as more vital to their children's future.

The question remains of how many or what percentage of Uzbekistan's population – estimated at over 35 million in 2022 – could be considered ethnic Tajiks. Official figures have not changed: Tajiks are said to constitute no more than 4.9 per cent of Uzbekistan's total population; that is to say, about 1.7 million individuals (Uzbekistan State Statistics Committee, 2021). And yet major cities such as Samarkand and Bukhara, as well as significant portions of the southern province of Surkhondaryo (which borders Afghanistan) and other regions including Qashqadaryo, the mountainous areas outside of Navoiy and Jizzakh, as well as the Ferghana Valley, are home to large numbers of Tajiks. The latter region notably includes the troubled exclave of Sokh (Uz.: So'x, Toj.: Сух) which is entirely surrounded by Kyrgyzstan and whose population of over 80,000 is one hundred per cent Tajik (see concluding chapter).

But when the vast majority of 'potential' Tajiks in Uzbekistan continue to list themselves as Uzbeks on their identity cards as they have done since the 1920s, how can one hope to measure their actual presence in the country with any degree of accuracy? What, in the end, defines one as being Tajik, beyond the deliberate obfuscation of the official statistics? As a Samarkandi acquaintance said to me of his native city, 'Everyone speaks Tojikī, except the Uzbeks.' Should speaking Tojikī then be used as a benchmark to determine who is a Tajik? If that is the case, then it would seem that Samarkand is still an overwhelmingly Tajik city, and Bukhara perhaps even more so. It should be acknowledged, of course, that in predominantly Tajik contexts some Uzbeks do in fact acquire competence in Tojikī; moreover, intermarriages mean that many people claim both identities.[12] At the same time, conversations among Tajiks in Uzbekistan characteristically mix up Tojikī, Uzbek and Russian, such that any kind of 'pure' Tojikī is unlikely to be heard. Almaty-based Tajik scholar Safar Abdullo, a native of Panjakent on the border with Uzbekistan some sixty-two kilometres from Samarkand, considers that 'In Uzbekistan today the [Tojikī] language has become very sloppy and low class.'[13]

While the mostly Tajik character of Samarkand and Bukhara is widely acknowledged, in fact there are Tojikī-speaking communities in every district (*viloyat*) of Uzbekistan. There are many Tajiks living in Tashkent, and numerous Tajik villages can be found in the mountainous regions outside the capital. One of the best known is Nanai – presumably a memory of the Sogdian goddess of that name, and which local legend claims was founded by Alexander the Great. The Tojikī dialect of Nanai has preserved a number of Sogdian words. Previously there was another Tajik village called Nanai in the Ferghana Valley, which has now become Uzbekified. Other Tajik villages in the Tashkent region include Burjimullah, Boghiston, Khojakent, Buka, and Parken.

In the Ferghana Valley, apart from the Sokh enclave mentioned above, the towns of Rishton, Marghilon and Chust are primarily Tojikī-speaking. In the south, the Surkhondaryo region perhaps half the population are native speakers of Tojikī, not surprisingly since it borders both Tajikistan and Afghanistan. The Qashqadaryo region, with its capital Qarshi (known in Sogdian times as Nakhshab, also as Nasaf after the Arab conquest), hosts many Tojikī-speakers, as do the mountain villages outside of Jizzakh and Navoiy in the ancient Sogdian heartland of the Zarafshan Valley.

Poetry: the keystone of Tajik-Persian identity

Like their linguistic cousins in Iran, Afghanistan and elsewhere, a love for poetry would seem to be the number one feature by which educated Tajiks express pride in their identity, since most Tajiks in Uzbekistan will readily admit that apart from language they do not differ culturally from Uzbeks. It comes as little surprise, then, that the principal activity of Tajik cultural centres, which have existed in most parts of the country since the late 1980s, is organizing poetry readings. A national centre, the Markazi Millīi Farhangīi Tojikoni Uzbekiston, was established in Tashkent in 2008. Their events, which also include Nawrūz and other national celebrations, typically draw several dozens of attendees.

Figure 7.2 Uzbek Tajik poet Tūkhtamysh Tūkhtaev, aka 'Paymon'. Photo courtesy of Wikimedia Commons.

Many Tajik intellectuals in Uzbekistan write poetry in Tojikī, and some even manage to get their work published in Iran.[14] In Uzbekistan, however, almost no books in Tojikī are put out by established publishing houses, and self-publishing – what in the West would be called 'vanity publishing' – is the norm (although this is actually the case throughout most of the former Soviet Union). As Tashkent-based Tajik journalist Tojiboy Ikromov explains, 'The author pays the publication costs and then gives ten copies to each of his friends to sell.'[15] A rare exception is when a member of the official state-run Writer's Union manages to publish a book in Tojikī, as was the case when Tūkhtamysh Tūkhtaev, aka 'Paymon' (b. 1955), published a *dīvān* of original poetry in 2022.

A Tojikī branch of the Uzbekistan Writer's Union was launched in Samarkand in June 2021, offering the hope of more officially sanctioned publications by Tajik writers, but so far that has not happened. On 5 May 2022 the Uzbekistan Writer's Union in Tashkent hosted a literary event sponsored by the Embassy of Tajikistan at which several Uzbekistani Tajik writers were inducted into the Writer's Union of Tajikistan, although it is not clear how this honour can benefit their careers in Uzbekistan.

Despite a few such promising signs, at present books in Tojikī are largely absent from Uzbekistan's bookstores, which are dominated by Uzbek, Russian, and even English titles. We asked a street bookseller in Tashkent if he carried any books in Tojikī. He said no, adding that whenever he does come across any he offers them to Tajik customers, only to have them reply that while they speak Tojikī they cannot read it. Lack of literacy in Tojikī is the norm in Uzbekistan, such that even Tajik scholars and other educated people frequently make spelling mistakes when texting their friends in Tojikī, which is about the only occasion they ever have to write the language.

Kitob Olami (Book World), located in Samarkand's city center, appears to be the only bookstore in Uzbekistan with a section formally devoted to Tojikī books, six shelves hidden away near the rear of the establishment holding about fifty titles (less than the space allocated to works purportedly penned by the Uzbek president, an entire wall of which confronts the customer upon entering the store). About two-thirds are books of poetry by Uzbekistani Tajiks. A few are collections of short stories and essays. There are also books of advice, some children's books and primary school texts. Almost all date to within the past two years. Most are published by Turon-Iqbol and Yog'dusi, both located in Tashkent, but several titles are from Samarkand-based publishers such as Mahorat – though one should recall that these publications are all author-funded. The production quality is quite low, and about half of these 'books' are really little more than flimsy pamphlets.

What is especially striking is the total absence of any publications from Tajikistan. Apparently it is still forbidden to import books from a country that is only forty kilometres away, although this interdiction falls under the category of 'laws that are generally known but not publicly written,' as a friend put it to me. But the government's aversion to reading is not limited to Tajiks: in recent years bookstores all across the country have been shut down, and in Samarkand even readers of Uzbek and Russian currently have a choice of only a tiny handful of poorly stocked bookshops, in a city of nearly a million inhabitants.

Tojikī in higher education

There are about a half dozen universities in Uzbekistan with Tojikī language programs. The most active is the Department of Tajik Philology at Samarkand State University, which was created after absorbing the Samarkand Tajik Pedagogical Institute in 1980. The university now has no less than ten faculties where courses are taught in Tojikī, and the Tajik Language and Literature department has an enrolment of over 170 students.

Elsewhere in the country higher education in Tojikī is quite limited. Tashkent Regional Pedagogical College in Chirchik has a Tajik Language and Literature Department, geared to training teachers for the ever-diminishing number of Tojikī-medium schools. There are departments of Tajik Language and Literature at Termiz, Ferghana, and Bukhara State universities, but their enrolments are very low. In Bukhara the department currently has only 16 students. The main obstacle to growing these programs would seem to be that in Uzbekistan today, a degree in Tajik Language and Literature offers few job prospects.

Tajik media – for those that want it

The government-run newspaper *Ovozi Tojik* (The Tajik Herald), founded in 1924 by the renowned Tajik intellectual Sadriddin Ainī (1878–1954), will soon celebrate its centennial of publishing. It currently has a national circulation of only 5,000 – down from 50,000 at the end of the Soviet period. It is also available on the internet in an electronic version, however, which may get as many readers as the print edition or even more. Circulation figures for regional newspapers such as *Ovozi Samarqand* and *Sadoi Sux* (The Voice of Sokh) are also relatively low, as they are for the privately-owned *Xovar* (The Orient) published in the southern city of Termiz on the border with Afghanistan. Some Uzbek newspapers offer a regular page in Tojikī.

In March 2022 a quarterly magazine devoted to the literature and culture of Uzbekistan's Tajiks, *Durdonai šarq* (The Faraway East), was launched in Samarkand with an initial printing of fifty copies. Asadullo Shukurov, *Ovozi Samarqand*'s chief editor and head of the Samarkand branch of the Uzbekistan

Writer's Union, optimistically hailed the event as heralding 'a new era of life and productivity in Uzbekistan.'[16]

National Uzbek television offers a bi-weekly 20-minute program called *Rangin Kamon* ('Colourful Rainbow'), although it used to run for a full hour. Similarly infrequent Tojikī-language broadcasts can be seen on local television channels in Samarkand, Bukhara, Ferghana, Surkhondaryo and Syrdaryo provinces. Such programs are mostly devoted to the relatively harmless cultural expressions of music videos or the making of handicrafts. As award-winning Tajik writer Adash Istad caustically remarks, 'These programs are a joke. What can you do in twenty minutes?'[17] Numerous Tojikī radio shows are likewise available throughout the country, but only in half-hour slots several days per week. Some Tajiks in Uzbekistan watch channels from Tajikistan using satellite dishes.

All of this may be growing increasingly irrelevant, since – as seems to be the case around the world – the younger generation in Central Asia get most of their information from social media. The *Sadoi Tojik* group on Telegram (the platform of choice throughout the post-Soviet world) counts 4,712 members, nearly rivaling the print circulation of the venerable *Ovozi Tojik*.

The youth are the future

The Tojikī-speaking youth in today's Uzbekistan, in contrast to earlier generations of nationalists and language-activists, do not seem particularly concerned with issues of identity. They appear rather to be perfectly content to identify themselves as Uzbeks, who also happen to speak Tojikī. When asked which language they feel more comfortable with, they invariably reply 'both'. Like millennials everywhere they mostly have little interest in reading anything longer than a social media post, which distances them from the arguably central feature of Persianate identity – namely, a love for poetry. Their tastes in popular music include some artists who sing in Persian, including those from Iran, Afghanistan, Tajikistan, and even a few from Uzbekistan. But Persian-language pop music has quite a broad reach, and is listened to by many throughout the world who don't know Persian. The so-called 'Shash Maqom' style of classical music is still featured in concerts and taught in conservatories, but it is considered today as much an expression of Uzbek culture as Tajik – indeed, traditional music is one of the many cultural elements that unite rather than divide the two peoples.

'Our youth think that Uzbekistan belongs to the Uzbeks,' admits Sharofat Ermatova, director of the Tojikī-language television program *Rangin Kamon*. 'They haven't studied history or geography.'[18] Again, the same could probably be said for the younger generation in most parts of the world, but this lack of attachment to the immense importance of Persian language and culture in world history, to which today's Tajik youth are mostly unwitting heirs, is striking. Speaking Tojikī is not the source of shame it once was, but it is not a source of pride either. And while it is no longer the cause for exclusion from educational and professional activities that it was under the former regime, the recent loosening of repression has not been accompanied by any substantial new opportunities for Tojikī-speakers.

Public life in Uzbekistan is conducted in Uzbek, with Tojikī still restricted to the private, personal sphere. It is telling that nowhere in the country does one see anything written in Tojikī: signs are in Uzbek, then to a lesser extent in Russian. English is increasingly visible. Never by just looking around would one suspect that millions of Uzbek citizens are speaking Tojikī amongst themselves on a daily basis, even in predominantly Tajik areas. In such an environment, even if speaking Tojikī no longer represents a danger to one's security, it seems that nothing is to be gained by advocating it. Young Tajiks in Uzbekistan are perfectly comfortable speaking Uzbek when the situation calls for it, which is most of the time, so why insist?

Conclusion

Questions regarding the survival of Tajik language and identity in present-day Uzbekistan remain difficult to answer with any certainty. The Persian language, in its various Tojikī dialects spoken by communities spread throughout the country, remains alive and may in some isolated cases even be said to be thriving. Most Tajiks in Uzbekistan continue to consider their mother tongue an important part of their identity, although usually not in a way that excludes having an Uzbek identity as well. Highly educated Tajiks remain strongly attached to the Persian literary tradition, particularly classical poetry, and are able to converse comfortably with Persian-speakers from other countries, but they are a small minority. Visiting Iranologists should be wary of allowing the ready availability of informants from among this educated class to skew their assessment of the importance of Persian in contemporary Uzbekistan in a way that is excessively favourable. In fact, literacy in standard Tojikī among Uzbekistan's Tajiks is extremely low, and mutual comprehensibility among the country's regional dialects is not a given. The Bukhara dialect, in particular, is universally acknowledged to be quite distinct and difficult for outsiders to understand. At the other end of the scale, Tajiks in Samarkand tend to have a higher sense of membership in what could be called a universal Persianate culture, making their city the country's most vibrant centre of Tajik national identity and cultural production, relatively speaking.

While an attachment to the Tojikī language and Persian literature remains evident among a small proportion of Uzbekistan's citizens who could be considered Tajiks, the vast majority today are equally comfortable functioning in Uzbek and see themselves as 'Uzbeks whose first language is Tojikī'. In fact, cultural differences between the two language communities are all but non-existent – a legacy of the bilingual urban culture of the Sarts in pre-Soviet times. Tellingly, in Tajik-majority areas such as Bukhara and Samarkand where there are significant numbers of *Eronī*, whose ancestors migrated from Iran during the 19th and 20th centuries, Tajiks see themselves as being culturally closer to Uzbeks than to their Iranian linguistic cousins. They tend to be more willing to intermarry with their fellow Sunni Uzbeks than with Shiʿite Eronīs, for example, religion rather than language being the operative identifier.[19]

Given the legacy of linguistic and cultural marginalization to which Tajiks in Uzbekistan have been subjected for the past one hundred years, it is surprising that Tojikī has persisted as the mother tongue of a substantial minority of the population of Uzbekistan, despite an entire generation having grown up under a regime that appeared bent on eliminating it completely. Contrary to the views of the late Richard Frye, who used to bemoan what he saw as the inevitable eclipse of Persian in the fabled cities of Bukhara and Samarkand which gave it new life during the 'New Persian Renaissance' of the 10th century CE, spoken Tojikī in Uzbekistan seems to be in no imminent danger of disappearing. Rather, it seems more likely that without a strong, normative literary culture, the Tojikī dialects of Uzbekistan will continue to diverge both from standard Persian and from each other, tending increasingly towards mutual incomprehensibility as they are reduced to regional patois.

If a culture of teaching and spreading literary Persian were to be revived, as a small handful of Tajik intellectuals are hoping, the sheer numbers of Tojikī-speakers existing in Uzbekistan could provide a basis for the return of Persian as a cultural medium, uniting them once again with Persian-speakers across the broader Iranian world. However, in the absence of thriving educational institutions, media and publishing, not to say the apparent lack of interest on the part of most of those concerned, such a development appears – for now at least – unlikely to occur.

Excursus: Afghanistan at a Stone's Throw

As an historian of Iranian civilization I have long wished to visit Afghanistan, that ancient and deeply troubled land. Much of Iranian history unfolded in places that are now part of Afghan territory: until the establishment of Afghanistan in 1747 by the Pashtun tribal leader Aḥmad Durranī, himself a former general in the Persian army, the country was merely part of eastern Iran. Hence, my reading of this history over the years has been illustrated throughout with mental images of stories, sites and peoples now claimed as part of the Afghan legacy, from the Silk Road caravans plying the route between Herat and Balkh to the heroic tales of Rustam, fearless champion of the 60,000-line Persian national epic, the *Shāh-nāma* or Book of Kings. How could I not wish to bring these legendary visions to life by seeing the country with my own eyes?

These days it takes an admittedly peculiar kind of traveller to see Afghanistan as a dream destination, and whether actually seeking to turn this dream into reality is a sign of being intrepid, foolish or merely suicidal is a matter of opinion. The country has been in a state of war for the past forty years, and hardly a week goes by without news of yet another round of civilian casualties through bombings or other atrocities. Foreign journalists and aid workers have been kidnapped for ransom or killed in crossfire. Sixteen years of NATO 'peace-keeping' presence has utterly failed to keep the peace. The conflict shows no signs of abating, and indeed often seems to be getting worse if such a thing were possible. While life somehow goes on for Afghans, this banal fact tends to be obscured by the endless gruesome images and reports of violence and suffering that have been the mainstay of Afghanistan's depiction in the mass media since the late 1970s.

Amazingly for anyone conditioned by this enduring portrayal of a nation ruined beyond hope, Afghanistan is nevertheless visited by dozens, if not hundreds, of tourists every year. Most emerge unscathed from the experience, and many go on to post blogs or publish articles extolling Afghan hospitality, the country's stunning landscapes, its breathtaking historical monuments. Others, more self-focused perhaps, boast of surviving life-threatening encounters or close brushes with terrorists, land mines, bad roads and corrupt officials. Despite having now been surpassed by such challenging locales as Syria, Yemen and Somalia, Afghanistan remains a major draw for 'adventure travellers'. The fact that the rare visitor – no less than the average Afghan – is more likely than not to survive to see another day does not mean that Afghanistan is a safe place to be.

Amongst the regrets of my youth none looms larger than an opportunity – like so many in life, never to be repeated – which I passed up as a naïve seventeen-year-old in the summer of 1978. Hitchhiking south on France's Autoroute du Soleil outside of Paris, I was picked up by a pair of heavily bearded hippies driving a clunky Citroen 2cv. Asked by them where I was headed, I said the Cote d'Azur. 'We're going to Afghanistan,' they replied. 'Would you like to join us?' My horizons at that time being limited to the image of a Mediterranean I was about to see for the first time, I declined this invitation. In doing so I unwittingly and permanently forfeited any chance to experience pre-invasion Afghanistan, as well as the pre-revolution Iran I would later spend decades hearing about from friends, colleagues and family. The thought gnaws away at me, even now.

In my capacity as an academic, my idea of area studies has always been that books alone are not enough to study a culture. Information absorbed through reading needs to be illuminated through lived personal experience, which can be achieved only by subjective immersion in the target environment. How many times as a student did I hear my Western professors muse over the 'unsolved problems' and 'conundrums' plaguing their field of study, which, when later shared with my Iranian wife, she proved easily able to explain through the intuitive knowledge common to anyone having been raised in her culture. Imagine my private shame, then, when I once accepted an invitation to speak on Afghanistan at no less prestigious a venue than the Smithsonian Institution in Washington, DC. Feeling like a complete charlatan, I spent the entire evening dreading questions from the audience that would force me to admit I'd never actually been there – an exposure from which, in the event, I was blessedly spared.

My lack of first-hand Afghanistan experience would rise to haunt me again in 2016 when I signed a contract to write this book on the history of the Tajiks. Since as much as half or more of the world's Tajiks live in Afghanistan, where anywhere from 35 to 50 per cent of the population is classified as 'Tajik', I felt discomfort at not having personally experienced such a significant aspect of my subject. I had lived in the Tajik-majority city of Samarkand, Uzbekistan, as a graduate student in the 1990s, and had spent time in Tajikistan in 2012 (and would again in 2017 and 2018), but the Tajik population of Afghanistan likely equals or even exceeds that of those two countries combined. How could I claim to know the Tajiks without having seen Kabul, the world's easternmost Persian-speaking city, or gazed up at the towering Jām minaret in Ghur Province, legacy of a twelfth-century Tajik dynasty that briefly ruled India?

I resolved to visit the country at last, dangers be damned. Combing through successive internet posts by recent travellers to Afghanistan, I convinced myself that statistically speaking I would be putting myself at no more risk than by visiting, say, Chicago, and in this frame of mind I confidently sent off my visa application to the Embassy of Afghanistan in Ottawa. According to their website I needed only submit the duly filled form along with my passport and a money order for the processing fee.

A few days later I was surprised to receive a phone call from a young man working at the embassy, who informed me that my application was 'incomplete'. I needed a written invitation from someone inside Afghanistan, he told me. When I protested that this requirement was not listed on their website, he replied that the relevant page was 'being updated'. Annoyed, I contacted an old friend from university, Masood, an Afghan journalist now working for the Voice of America in Washington. He managed to secure a letter of invitation from a relative within less than twenty-four hours, which I promptly passed on to the embassy. The following day I received another call from their young employee saying that in fact a letter from an individual would not suffice; it had to be from a registered tourist agency recognized by the Afghan government. At this point I was about to depart for Tajikistan and could not spend any further time chasing receding goalposts, so I reluctantly renounced my attempt to secure an Afghan visa.

I did, however, indulge myself in the luxury of writing an angry e-mail directly to the Afghan ambassador, with Masood's name in the cc line, in which I complained that they appeared to be making up requirements as they went along. I further ventured the opinion that if the embassy were a business, taking fees without respecting their own published conditions might be considered to constitute a kind of fraud. For this insolence I was rewarded with a full refund of my visa fee by overnight courier. Masood commented that while he was saddened I would not be able to visit his country, I should take solace in surely being the first person in the history of diplomacy to receive a refund on a visa application fee.

This dubious honour notwithstanding, it was with a sense of bitterness and failure that I boarded the plane to Dushanbe, Tajikistan, in April 2017 for a research trip that would not include my getting to know Afghanistan's Tajiks. My book would still cover their history, but without the benefit of the kind of first-hand, intuitive knowledge I had always preached as being a necessary part of scholarly expertise. At least I had tried.

As it turned out, my travels in Tajikistan would bring me closer to this elusive goal than I had imagined – indeed, quite literally as close as possible without actually reaching it. A lover of maps since childhood, I had practically memorized the geography of Central Asia. I knew that the border between Tajikistan and Afghanistan was demarcated by the tortuous meanderings of the Panj River, which becomes the mighty Amu Darya (the Oxus to the ancient Greeks) at the confluence of the Vakhsh near the city of Shahrituz in southwestern Tajikistan. Further to the east this border runs nearly the full length of the Wakhan Corridor, a nineteenth-century geopolitical curiosity resulting from an agreement between tsarist Russia and the British Raj to recognize this thin sliver of Afghanistan as a neutral buffer zone between their two expanding empires. Isolated between the soaring Pamir and Hindu Kush mountain ranges and connected to the outside world only via the often-narrow canyon carved out by the Panj, the Wakhan holds the romance of being one of the world's most inaccessible and least-visited regions. It was also, very nearly up to the time of my first visit there in 2017, the only part of Afghanistan considered to be safe.

The only way in or out is via the Pamir Highway, a modern fragment of the fabled Silk Road which has become legendary for its cliff-hanging curves and often poor condition. Officially known as the M41, the route begins in Tirmiz, Uzbekistan, on the banks of the Amu Darya. It winds north to Dushanbe, the Tajik capital, before bending southeastwards through Kulob to rejoin the Afghan border at Khirmanjoi. From there, the road hugs the right bank of the Panj – the Tajik side – for the next 353 kilometres as far as Khorugh, the Shangri-La-like capital of Tajikistan's Gorno-Badakhshan Autonomous Region or GBAO. At Khorugh the path splits, the M41 proper cutting across the Pamiri highlands to the eastern settlement of Murghab and thence northward to the Kyrgyz border and ultimately to the city of Osh in the Ferghana Valley, where it formally ends. A branch route, meanwhile, continues south from Khorugh a further hundred slow, bumpy kilometres as far as the village of Ishkashim at the bend in the Panj, which it follows from there across the suddenly expansive Wakhan Valley spreading out towards the east.

Although I had seen photos of this dramatic route, no printed image could ever capture the utter immensity of the Badakhshan landscapes, starkly marked out by some of the tallest mountains and deepest valleys in the world. Although I have stood in the mists beneath the falls at Iguassu and watched the glaciers calving in Greenland, never have I felt so dwarfed by nature as when following the diligent Panj along the narrow path it has carved over millions of years between these rocky screes that stretch upwards as far as the eye can see.

What amazed me even more than the sheer scale of these spectacular gorges was the fact that the Panj itself is so *small*. How could a river that is rarely more than ten metres wide, and often as narrow as two, have created such a deep, plunging rift, driving apart 5,000-metre peaks immediately to either side? And moreover, where were the border guards? This looked less like an international frontier than any place I had ever seen. Was there anything to stop one merely wading across to set foot in Afghanistan?

My Tajik travel companions stared at me with incomprehension. 'Why would anyone want to do that?' they asked me. 'I don't know,' I answered defensively. 'For smuggling?' My friends looked at me like one would an idiot child. 'If you want to smuggle, you just use the bridge,' they explained, pointing out the obvious.

Not ready to give up, I spelled out my true intended meaning. 'What if I just wade across, put my foot on Afghan soil, then wade back?' I suggested. That would be a bad idea, they said. Why? They might shoot you. Which 'they'? There is nobody to be seen on the other side of the river except burqa-clad women hanging up laundry beside their mud huts, farmers tilling tiny terraced plots of grain or packing hay onto the backs of donkeys, and kids kicking a ball across a dusty makeshift soccer field. Look, they're waving at us. They're less likely to shoot me than invite me to tea.

A chorus of reproachful stares from my friends finally persuaded me to back down and return to the car. But the longer we lurched and bumped along our way towards Khorugh, the temptation to leap this tiny, artificially imposed divide only grew worse. Look at those two boulders in the middle of the river! One could make it across in a couple of hops!

At Khorugh there is an official border crossing over the bridge to Afghanistan, for those who have visas. Visaless, my hopes had been piqued by reading about a Saturday market at Ishkashim, the next and last border crossing a hundred kilometres to the south, held on an island in the river that was technically considered Afghan territory. Apparently the Tajik border guards would allow foreigners on single-entry Tajik visas to cross over to the island for the market just for the day, meaning that one could then legitimately claim to have been in Afghanistan. Upon arriving in Khorugh in May 2017, however, I was told that due to Taliban presence on the Afghan side of the river the Saturday market had been closed for over a year.

An online travel club of which I am a member has an ongoing debate about what constitutes a visit to a country. Some wonder whether airport transit counts, or observing the passing countryside from an automobile or train without getting out. What about cruising a country's coastline by boat, or low flyovers in a private plane? I tend to side with those who feel that at the very least setting foot on a nation's soil should be a basic requirement for a 'visit', but having at this point in my life travelled some 640 kilometres along the Panj River – much of it thrice – gazing eagerly across all the while to count the Afghan villages, admire their rustic architecture, and marvel at the endurance of age-old farming techniques, I have to confess that I feel I have seen more of Afghanistan than I have of numerous other countries for which my passport bears stamps. Still, nothing would ever possess me to claim that I had 'been' there. Hence the unrelenting temptation to cast all caution to the winds, roll up my jeans and wade, wade …

I am able to feel only slightly less embarrassed to admit this silly, but inescapable, obsession thanks to an acquaintance I made on my second trip to Badakhshan in May 2018, a young environmental scientist from British Columbia by the name of Chris. We met thanks to invitations from the University of Central Asia (UCA) – a brilliantly conceived new tri-country English-medium institution established by the Aga Khan – to visit their Tajikistan campus in Khorugh. Chris, along with three of his Vancouver-based colleagues, had come to serve as a consultant for UCA's new science curriculum, while I, in exchange for providing a few lectures, was benefitting from the university's unparalleled hospitality as I conducted research for my book. From the vantage point offered by the campus's spectacular eagle's nest setting Khorugh lay spread out below like a mountain paradise, a green oasis of tall poplars snuggled in between the impossibly high bare rock walls reaching up to the sky, with the snowy basin of Afghanistan's Shughnani peaks forming a dramatic backdrop to the west. I e-mailed my mother a photo of the view from the living room window of my faculty apartment, accompanied by the caption 'Those mountains are in Afghanistan!' 'It is beautiful,' she wrote back, 'but *please* don't go there!'

As it turned out the scientists were travelling to the Wakhan Valley on exactly the day I intended to make the same trip. There was extra space in their Land Rover, so they invited me along. It was an excellent opportunity for me to learn from them something of the local geology, flora and fauna, as well as the ecological implications of certain traditional farming and grazing techniques still practised in the region. My new travel companions flattered me that what their expedition had really been missing up to that point was a historian.

These fellow Canadians were as amazed as I had been to see how little the modest Panj River resembled an international border, and how few obstacles it seemingly placed in the way of transgression. Our own 8,891-kilometre frontier with the United States, sometimes referred to as the 'longest unguarded border in the world', seems positively forbidding by comparison. As our vehicle lumbered along, Afghanistan appeared at times to be so close you could reach out and touch it. Chris made the same observation I had done the year before: namely, that the river seemed to be literally *urging* one to wade across.

We stopped and got out of the Land Rover. Frustrated, Chris picked up a rock and flung it across to the Afghan side where it crashed loudly against a boulder. A stone's throw away, literally. Assuming the wise role of the more experienced, I repeated to Chris the admonitions that had been made to me by my Tajik friends during the course of my previous visit. But secretly, having sensed a kindred spirit, I was already scanning the river for places the two of us might eventually attempt a crossing, perhaps under cover of night.

Over the next two days as we explored the Wakhan Valley, hiking its tributary gorges and visiting man-made sites that included Sufi shrines, medieval fortresses, a cliffside spring overseen by an ancient fertility goddess, a Buddhist stupa and Bronze Age petroglyphs (the group did need a historian after all!), the river remained ever in sight, stubbornly provoking us, daring us, mocking us with its apparent passivity. The opportunity to organize a crossing with Chris never presented itself, however, and at Langar, where the Wakhan forks into two distinct valleys heading always higher towards the impassable borders with China and Pakistan, I parted ways with my scientist friends and hired a jeep to take me to Murghab.

After Langar the road becomes little more than a track, climbing its winding way up to the barren plateau of central Badakhshan. Even the river, meandering in narrow streams across a stony alluvial bed, can support little vegetation at such an altitude. The notion that this patchwork of pleasantly gurgling streams could possibly constitute the only division between Tajikistan and one of the most dangerous countries in the world seems increasingly preposterous. Shepherds manoeuvre their flocks here and there amongst the various effluents (Figure Ex.1).

I ask my driver, what do the shepherds do if one of their sheep wanders across to the Afghan side? Don't they just wade over and retrieve it? 'No!' he emphatically replies. 'The border guards are extremely strict around here! No one would ever do that!' Which border guards? Again, I scan the banks for any signs of armed presence. Apart from a band of colourfully tribal-looking individuals on horseback plodding along single file in the distance, nothing. 'So what do they do?' I ask. My driver gives me an impatient look. 'They go to the nearest border post,' he says, not without a hint of condescension, 'and ask the Tajik guards to radio those on the Afghan side to go and bring

Figure Ex.1 Tajik–Afghan border, Upper Panj River.

the sheep back.' This seems unlikely: the nearest border post is a hundred kilometres away! But, daunted by my driver's serious tone, and with one last longing look at a 'river' that is no more than an arm's length wide and ankle-deep, I give up. It was my easiest chance, and my last. Is it for the best? Who can say.

Conclusion: Differing Contexts, Manifold Challenges

Although Tajiks have had an independent nation to call their own since 1991, only about a quarter of those who identify as Tajiks actually live there – between six and seven million individuals. More than double that figure live in Afghanistan, where they are the country's second largest ethnic group, slightly outnumbered by Pushtuns. And as noted in chapter 7, while an accurate

Map 3. The Tajiks Today

estimate of Tajiks in Uzbekistan is currently impossible, they are at least as numerous there as in Tajikistan and possibly far more so. The Tajik diaspora must also be taken into consideration, including at least one million guest workers living in the Russian Federation. Each of these groups has faced its own challenges, and never more so than over the past few years.

Tajiks in Afghanistan

As in Tajikistan, Soviet hegemony in Afghanistan was replaced not by a new sense of nationhood, but rather by a degeneration into civil war. As Barfield has observed, 'Unfortunately the successful resistance strategy of making the country ungovernable for the Soviet occupier also ended up making Afghanistan ungovernable for the Afghans themselves.'[1]

The various Mujaheddin resistance groups spread throughout Afghanistan had been united by only one thing: the desire to expel the Soviets from their country. Once this was accomplished there was no arrangement for power sharing among the diverse faction leaders that could be agreed upon, and none had a support base that extended beyond their own regional or political group. Moreover, most of these leaders – including the Tajik Burḥānuddīn Rabbānī, head of the Jami'at-i Islāmī rebel group, who was named President in 1992 through a UN-brokered arrangement that ultimately failed – had spent the worst years of the conflict outside the country's borders, calling the shots from the sidelines in Peshawar, Pakistan. The Tajik military strategist Aḥmad Shāh Mas'ūd was an exception to this, remaining ensconced in Afghanistan's Panjshir Valley north of Kabul throughout the conflict. He and his militia were the first to occupy Kabul once the communist regime collapsed, but he allowed Rabbānī – his colleague of convenience – to take over the reins of government whilst accepting the post of defence minister for himself. In the western part of the country the regional Jami'at-i Islāmī leader, a Tajik by the name of Ismā'īl Khan, held control.

Meanwhile, the Pushtun head of the Ḥizb-i Islāmī faction, Gulbuddīn Ḥikmatyār, as well as the Junbish militia under the Uzbek warlord Abdul Rashīd Dostum and a number of other groups including the Hazara Ḥizb-i Waḥdat, refused to recognize the new Tajik-led government. They spent the next four years (1992–96) attacking Kabul, which, having escaped the worst of the fighting against the Soviets, was now reduced to rubble. Under these conditions Rabbānī's regime could barely exercise power within the capital, much less elsewhere in the country which more closely resembled an amalgamation of feudal fiefdoms than anything like a modern state.

During this period the Tajik populations of Kabul and the Shamali region to the north, as well as those in and around Herat in the west and Badakhshan in the northeast, were at least nominally governed by Rabbānī's Jami'at-i Islāmī with which they had long been connected and could identify. Those in the north of the country, however, including the mostly Tajik city of Mazar-i Sharif, were under the rule of Dostum's Uzbek forces. The Twelver Shī'ite Hazaras controlled their own territory around the central region of Bamiyan, and the south and east were held by Pushtun groups.

The rise of the radically 'traditionalist' Taliban movement among exiled Pushtuns beginning in 1994 brought a new dimension to Afghanistan's civil war. Led by Muslim clerics trained in Pakistan's reactionary Deobandi madrasas and bred amongst the squalor and despair of that country's Afghan refugee camps, the Taliban – literally, 'religion students' – erupted on the scene with the promise of bringing an end to Afghanistan's political crisis through a revival of traditional Islamic values and institutions that had been marginalized by modernity.

Aided by Pakistan's notorious spy agency, the Directorate for Inter-Services Intelligence (ISI), the Taliban first seized control of the largely Pushtun city of Kandahar in the south. Next they took over the southern Helmand province, where opium production would become a major source of their income. Many ordinary Pushtuns initially welcomed them, placing hope in the Taliban's promise to restore order and security while overlooking their extremist social program. Local military commanders were often bought off by the Taliban with cash bribes and offered little resistance.

During the first months of 1995, inspired by the fire-and-brimstone sermons of their mysterious one-eyed master Mullah Omar the Taliban began a push to the north. But, despite an alliance of convenience with the 'heretic' Hazaras, they were successfully held off at Kabul by Aḥmad Shāh Mas'ūd's Tajik forces. Ismā'īl Khān then attacked the Taliban's rear flank from Herat, but rather than assisting in this effort President Rabbānī sought instead to weaken his Tajik counterpart in the west, perceiving him at the time as a greater threat than the

Taliban. Deprived of reinforcements Ismāʿīl Khān's militia was unable to hold off Mullah Omar's highly-motivated fighters who took Herat in September 1995.

Now in control of all southern Afghanistan, the Taliban turned their attention once again to Kabul. Masʿūd retreated from the capital rather than engage them and established a front just north of the city. Over the next two years the Taliban extended their control from Herat to Mazar-i Sharif in the northwest, as well as to the central region inhabited by the Hazaras. The latter group, considered as Shīʿite heretics, were subjected to brutal massacres. The northeastern part of the country was the only part of Afghanistan to avoid falling to the Taliban, thanks to Masʿūd's Tajiks and their allies.

The Taliban's extraordinarily harsh policies – which featured public whippings, mutilations and executions for a wide range of offenses – soon alienated them from most Afghans, even those who had initially supported them. They likewise made the country a pariah on the international stage, not least by hosting and protecting a plethora of so-called *jihādī* groups. These included not only al-Qaeda but also revolutionary militants and separatists from Chechnya, Kashmir, and elsewhere. Apart from their ally Pakistan the Taliban regime was surrounded by enemies, from Iran to Tajikistan, who, along with Russian and Indian help, actively sought their overthrow by funneling weapons to Masʿūd's Northern Alliance.

The assassination of Masʿūd by a Tunisian suicide bomber on 9 September 2001 would have appeared to remove the single greatest threat to the Taliban's hold on power. However, the infamous attacks on New York and Washington, DC two days later, orchestrated by their al-Qaeda guests, brought about a swift military response by the US that spelled an end to the Taliban regime. Within two months the Tajik-led Northern Alliance had retaken Kabul and other major cities, with US support.

After the fall of the Taliban by December 2001 many Afghans hoped that the US would disarm the various regional militias – who had already been severely weakened by years of fighting against the Taliban and had discredited themselves amongst the population by their violence and corruption – and replace them with an international peacekeeping force. Instead, the Americans supported the militias in the misguided hope that they would cooperate with each other and provide a bulwark against the remnants of the Taliban and al-Qaeda. The result was a lapse into feudalism that persists to the present day. Since that time Afghans have joked that their society has three components:

'al-Qaeda' – that is, terrorists and those who enable them – 'al-Faeda', literally, 'the Beneficiaries' – corrupt politicians and their patronage networks – and 'al-Gaeda', 'the Fucked', meaning everyone else.[2]

Although Tajiks are Afghanistan's second largest group they are in some ways the most coherent, identifying themselves primarily by language, culture, and region rather than in terms of tribal affiliation as is the case of other Afghans. They have rarely held political power, and then only for short periods of time. And yet, the elite culture in which nearly all Afghans take pride – particularly the Persian literary tradition, but also music, the arts, formal social interaction, and even food – is Tajik. Darī Persian has the status of official language throughout the country, and in Afghanistan's multi-ethnic interactions which are a fact of daily life it is Darī, and not Pashto, that serves as the nation's lingua franca. Three of Afghanistan's most important cities, along with a number of smaller ones, are predominantly Persian-speaking. The national media, public discourse, and most of higher education (notably the universities of Kabul, Herat, and Mazar-i Sharif) are largely conducted in that language as well.

Perhaps Afghanistan's most highly-respected living literary figure is poet and essayist Partaw Nāderī (b. 1953). Born in the remote northern province of Badakhshan, Nāderī trained as a teacher in Kabul then studied science at university. During the 1980s, like many intellectuals he was imprisoned by Afghanistan's communist regime. After the Taliban takeover he fled to Pakistan in 1997 and began to work for the BBC's broadcasts in Darī. He returned to Kabul in 2002; since then he has worked for the Afghan Civil Society Forum and for the Afghan branch of the international writers' association PEN.

Much of Nāderī's poetry was composed under the Taliban and reflects the brutality of their rule. The following excerpt from his poem 'The Bloody Epitaph' (*Katība-yi khūnīn*) provides an example:

Īn nakhl-rā havā-yi bahārān namānda'st
Īn nakhl-rā tamāmī andām
Bashikufta az shigūfa-yi sad zakhm
Zakhm-i hazār fāj'a dar rūz
Zakhm-i hazār hādisa dar shab
Khūnīn katība'ī-st
Dar chārsū-yi qarn

Figure C.1 Tajik Afghan poet Partaw Naderi. Photo courtesy of Partaw Naderi.

This palm tree has no hope of spring
This palm tree blossoms with a hundred wounds
The daily wounds of a thousand tragedies
The nightly wounds of a thousand calamities
This palm tree is a bloody epitaph
At the crossroads of the century.[3]

Taliban 2.0

During the summer of 2021 much of the world looked on in dismay as Afghanistan, having struggled for two decades to build a semblance of democracy and modern institutions, once again fell under Taliban control following the withdrawal of US-led Western military forces from the country.

As the Afghan government fell on 15 August 2021, pilots of the Afghan air force flew their planes (about eighty, representing half the country's government-owned aircraft) across the border into Tajikistan and Uzbekistan, where they have remained ever since. This became an ongoing regional diplomatic problem, with the Taliban demanding they be returned. Yet despite the Tajikistan government's ostensibly hostile attitude towards Taliban, whom it accuses of harbouring terrorist camps in the north of the country,[4] it signed a $69m agreement with them in December 2021 to supply Afghanistan with 1.5 billion kilowatt hours of hydro-electricity for 2022.[5]

Although the Taliban have been publicly emphatic about not taking their fight across international borders, their return to power was seen as a threatening portent in Tajikistan where the state has struggled for decades against an Islamist insurgency. Tajikistan has not recognized the Taliban government, and has made such recognition conditional on Afghanistan's government giving an important role to ethnic Tajiks (something that seems highly unlikely to happen).[6] The Tajikistan military, which continues the Soviet practice of annual 'round-ups' (*oblava*) of conscripts, has been accused of press-ganging thousands of unwilling young Tajik men by kidnapping them off the streets and sending them to guard the border with Afghanistan. Such conscripts live in miserable conditions and are paid a salary equivalent to around two dollars per month. Wealthy families generally spare their sons from this experience by paying bribes. The poor state of the Tajikistan military has led for calls to shift to a professional army.[7]

Meanwhile, the Afghanistan-based Islamic State in Khurasan Province (ISKP) has begun to court non-Pushtun communities throughout the country, hoping to muster support for themselves as an alternative to the Taliban. They have also launched a campaign to recruit citizens of Tajikistan fed up with President Emomali Rahmon's notoriously corrupt regime, using social media channels to criticize the Tajik dictator and provide guidance on traveling to Afghanistan to join ISKP.[8] In March 2022 the group published a book in Cyrillic Tojiki entitled *Why Jihad is Obligatory*.[9] ISKP's aims, unlike those of the Taliban, are explicitly transnational. They claim to have launched rockets into Uzbekistan and Tajikistan from their bases in northern

Afghanistan, an indication of the potential security threat they pose to both countries.

Tajik migrant workers: a fluid diaspora

Prior to the breakup of the Soviet Union the Tajik SSR was more dependent on economic transfers from the centre than any other union republic – as much as 45 per cent of its total annual budget. The disappearance of these important subsidies created a severe financial crisis for independent Tajikistan, which certainly played some part in the political crisis that led to the civil war from 1992–97. It bears repeating that while at the level of the elites the war was largely a competition for power, for most ordinary participants on the ground it was about such basic issues as securing food for one's extended family.

In the postwar years external subsidies took on a new form as up to one million Tajiks per year – mostly men – began taking up seasonal work abroad, mainly in Russia and Kazakhstan, as a way of supporting their families back in Tajikistan. The Tajik economy is more dependent on labour migration than any country in the world,[10] another sad superlative for this impoverished nation. Remittances from abroad now account for more than half of Tajikistan's GNP[11] – essentially replacing one form of economic dependence on Russia with another. Combining this figure with that generated by the drug trade, it becomes apparent that the legitimate economic output of Tajikistan today is negligible indeed, and one wonders how its people could survive if these two unbecoming sources were not keeping the nation's economy afloat.

Tajik migrant workers in Russia fill the lowest professional niches: stall vendors, waiters, stevedores, car wash attendants, and construction workers. In 2016 a reporter for *The Guardian* interviewed a former medical doctor now working as a bathroom attendant, earning far more than he did as a physician practicing in Tajikistan.[12] Russian visa restrictions have been tightened, forcing Tajik laborers to leave the country every three months to have them renewed. Police harassment is a way of life.

One effect of so many Tajik men moving to Russia in search of work is that, whether or not they have wives back home, they often develop intimate relationships with Russian women. Freed from the pressures they would typically experience from their families in Tajikistan, migrant workers living abroad are more likely to enter into liaisons that are based on love and shared interests. They may even start new families, becoming in some cases more attached to them than to those they have left behind. Needless to say, this kind of situation can cause a whole range of problems for all concerned. Usually, however, the worker's wife and children in Tajikistan are dependent on him for financial support, so their capacity to control or sanction his behaviour is limited.

Conversely, in Russia Tajik men may be at the mercy of their Russian female partners – in order to obtain legal residence, for example – in ways that force them to relinquish some aspects of their familiar gender roles. They may learn to share in household chores, for example, and they are unlikely to be able to dictate their Russian partner's movements and social behaviour the way they would in the case of a Tajik woman. When visiting their families back in Tajikistan, however, these men typically revert to their traditional norms when dealing with the Tajik wife they have left there.[13]

Young women in Tajikistan, meanwhile, are left with a dearth of prospective husbands. Some reluctantly agree to become second wives to men who can afford them, an option they see as preferable to remaining unmarried. When marriages can be arranged with migrant workers living abroad, they are sometimes conducted via Skype.[14] Similarly, the appearance of 'SMS divorces,' whereby distant husbands sought to rid themselves of unwanted financial responsibilities simply by sending the text message '*taloq, taloq, taloq*,' (divorce, divorce, divorce) prompted Tajik religious authorities to issue fatwas condemning the practice.[15] Since many Tajik marriages are performed only Islamically and remain officially unregistered, divorcées in this situation can find no protection under Tajik law. An estimated 95 per cent of divorces are initiated by the husband, and many Tajik women are unaware that they are legally entitled to support. Even for those that do know their rights, migrant laborers living abroad often have no fixed address so it can be difficult for their wives to track them down. With shrinking prospects abroad and few or none at home, the outlook today for young Tajik men and the families that depend on them seems grim.

A record over three million Tajik residents in Russia registered in 2021, nearly one-third the population of Tajikistan. Many are getting citizenship

– 103,681 in 2021.[16] These migrants include not just manual laborers, but increasingly trained professionals such as doctors, teachers and engineers. During the COVID crisis in 2020–21 the Tajik government announced a shortage of 6,000 doctors.

With remittances from Tajik workers in Russia accounting for as much as half or more of Tajikistan's GDP, declines in the ruble, due mainly to sanctions imposed in response to Russia's annexation of Crimea in 2014 and again in 2022 following Russia's invasion of Ukraine, have had a devastating impact on Tajikistan's economy. Between 2013 and 2016, US-led sanctions cut Tajik remittances by 50 per cent,[17] and beginning in 2020 the COVID pandemic followed by a second round of sanctions in 2022 reduced these even further.

In addition, the fall of the ruble has meant that staples such as flour, sugar and vegetable oil have seen price hikes of 50 per cent or more, while rising petrol and LNG (liquid natural gas) prices have put many taxi drivers out of work. Zafar Abdullaev, former owner of the Avesta news agency who is now in exile, predicted that as a result of these developments 'There will be few vitamins in people's diet, less meat, less fruit, less medicine, and so on. Surviving, just surviving. This is going to be survival, not life.'[18] A Tajik economist, equally pessimistic, opined in an interview with the independent news outlet Asia-Plus that 'In general, the whole strategy of dependence on migration and remittances from Russia will become completely unviable for Tajikistan when the Russian economy collapses.'[19]

Given the country's relatively minor economic importance, many analysts were bemused when on 28 June 2022 Russian President Vladimir Putin chose Tajikistan as the destination of his first trip abroad following his country's invasion of Ukraine four months earlier. The aim of his visit was reportedly to discuss with his Tajik counterpart Emomali Rahmon 'issues related to military cooperation and Tajik migrant workers in Russia.'[20] Some observers, however, speculated that the agenda likely included the ongoing civil unrest within Tajikistan's borders and the process for eventually handing over power to Rahmon's son, along with proposals for helping Tajikistan cope with Western sanctions against Russia and facing up to the reality of Taliban control in Afghanistan.[21] At the time Russia had some 7,000 troops stationed in Tajikistan – its largest contingent outside of Russia – ostensibly to guard the border with Afghanistan.

In this respect Russia is not without competition from the US, however. Just one week prior to Putin's unexpected visit, US Army General Michael

Kurilla, head of the US Central Command (CENTCOM), visited Tajikistan with promises to provide 'the training, equipment, and infrastructure to defend the [Afghan] border.'[22] In fact CENTCOM had already provided the Tajik border services with 4,800 radios and more than 400 patrol vehicles, and was slated to oversee the construction of a new border post near Shahrituz in the southwestern part of the country. Clearly, the US was not yet prepared to completely cede Tajikistan to the Russian sphere of influence, and its policy of encouraging the Tajik government to withhold recognition of the Taliban puts it at clear odds with Russia which seems to be pushing for it.

Border disputes around Tajik enclaves in Kyrgyzstan

Soviet-era borders between republics were often somewhat haphazard, and since independence the Central Asian states have been plagued by the problem of delineations. This lack of clarity has led to repeated disputes over water and pastureland. Competition over water resources has been exacerbated by decreasing rainfall due to climate change, and by outdated and inefficient irrigation infrastructures which were built without regard to borders between the republics. After the fall of USSR Kyrgyz rented out some pastures situated on their side of the border to Tajiks but with the subsequent privatization of these lands this practice ceased, depriving many Tajik shepherds of vital grazing areas for their livestock.

The COVID crisis brought about an increase in cross-border criminality, principally the smuggling of drugs, cigarettes, toilet paper, and cooking oil but also the rustling of livestock. The pandemic restrictions also meant that migrant workers of both countries were unable to travel to Russia, causing economic pressures that were compounded by rising food prices.[23]

Major clashes along the Tajik-Kyrgyz border began in January 2014 following the installation of surveillance cameras by Tajik border guards in Vorukh enclave, where Kyrgyz were accused of stealing water by 'upgrading' irrigation canals. Further violence erupted in May 2020. A subsequent outbreak of fighting between Tajik and Kyrgyz residents on 28–29 April 2021 was joined by security forces on both sides, resulting in death of 36 Kyrgyz and 183 wounded, with an estimated 50,000 leaving the area.[24] There were yet more clashes in January and

March of 2022, and shootouts between Kyrgyz and Tajik border guards over the next two months resulted in several more deaths and many wounded.

The Uzbek-controlled Sokh enclave some 40km to the east – whose inhabitants are Tajiks – has likewise been plagued by violence between the neighbouring Tajik and Kyrgyz communities. The conflict first erupted in January 2013 after Kyrgyz border guards attempted to install electrical poles on Sokh territory. In response, the Kyrgyz government closed the 80km road linking Sokh to Uzbekistan through Kyrgyz land, ostensibly because Kyrgyzstan is a member of the Eurasian Economic Union (EEU) and Uzbekistan is not. Kyrgyz politicians stated that Sokh is 'overpopulated,' and that its residents should be moved to mainland Uzbekistan.[25]

Sokh saw renewed fighting in May 2020 over access to water. In an attempt to resolve the ongoing disputes, in March 2021 Kyrgyz President Sadyr Japarov signed agreement in Tashkent with Uzbek President Shavkat Mirziyoyev delimiting the enclave's border and re-opening road to Sokh. Construction of a new airport was completed in October 2021 and flights linking Sokh to Ferghana using single engine An-2 propeller planes began on 12 December, for the first time since the Soviet period.

Preparing a dynastic succession

For a number of years Tajikistan President Emomali Rahmon has been taking steps to ensure that his son Rustam Emomali will eventually succeed him as leader of the country. Born in 1987, Emomali holds a degree in International Economic Relations but came to prominence as a football player, co-founding Dushanbe's Istiklol club in 2007 and playing as striker and team captain. From 2011 Istiklol won five consecutive national championships, a feat some attributed to favourable refereeing.[26] During the same period Emomali was appointed to a number of important diplomatic and government positions, including being made head of Tajikistan's Customs Service in 2013, mayor of Dushanbe in 2017, and Chairman of the national parliament in 2020. A 2016 referendum amended the country's constitution to reduce the minimum age for the presidency from 35 years of age to 30, apparently a contingency in the event that Emomali should be immediately required to succeed his father.

Emomali has sought to portray himself as an advocate of the people, receiving direct petitions and making high-profile interventions to settle problems. These have included such issues as improving internet service, preserving the house-museum of the celebrated writer Sadruddin Aini which had been slated for destruction, and pressuring the judiciary to convict a powerful businessman, Parviz Davlyatov, and his wife for the murder of his mistress. While there are no signs that a change in leadership would lead Tajikistan to be more democratic, in the words of one Tajik politician, 'people see in Rustam at least the illusion that something might change under his stewardship.'[27]

Restiveness in Gorno-Badakhshan

Unfortunately, if recent tensions in Tajikistan's Gorno-Badakhshan Autonomous Oblast (GBAO) are any indication, any hope of the country moving in a more democratic direction would seem to be misplaced. Covering 45 per cent of Tajikistan's territory the GBAO is home to only three per cent of its population, known collectively as Pamiris and speaking their own regional languages. Most follow the Aga Khan's Ismāʿīlī Shiʿism, considered heretical by the country's Sunni majority. Fearing separatism, the Tajik government has attempted to control the region though the appointment of governors loyal to the ruling regime.

Tensions between representatives of the central government and local community leaders – dismissively referred to by the former as 'warlords' – led to outbreaks of violence in 2012 and again in 2018, centered mainly in the district capital, Khorugh. Hostilities erupted once again in November 2021 after a young Pamiri activist, Gulbiddin Ziyobekov, was murdered while in police custody. This event provoked massive protests, during which two protesters were killed and a number wounded as police fired into the crowd. There was no serious investigation to these deaths, leaving locals feeling that justice had not been served. Significantly, more than half the protestors were women, belying government claims that they were merely made up of criminal gangs. The Tajik government sought to quell further protest by cutting off all communication networks as well as travel in and out of the region, with the internet ban being lifted only four months later.

The protests reignited in May 2022 after Tajik authorities, on what were widely viewed as trumped up charges, tried and convicted two well-known Pamiri figures who had been living in Russia and forcibly brought to Tajikistan. Mixed Martial Arts (MMA) fighter Chorshanbe Chorshanbiev, who had been deported by the Russian authorities at Tajikistan's request, was sentenced to eight and a half years in prison, while Pamiri diaspora leader Amriddin Alovashoev, who had been kidnapped in Moscow by Tajik agents, received an eighteen-year term. Following these convictions, on 16 May Pamiri leaders organized a fresh protest, at which 29-year-old activist Zamir Nazrishoev was shot to death by riot police. Two days later at least twenty-five more civilians were killed when police fired into the crowd – including from helicopters – in what the Tajik government referred to as an 'anti-terrorist operation.'[28] With the crisis showing no signs of abating, the Tajik government reinstated the internet ban.[29] By early summer 2022 at least 50 Pamiri locals were reported killed by police and security forces, with hundreds more injured, and virtually all of the Pamiri community leaders had been arrested and imprisoned.

Some Tajiks saw their government's iron-fisted crackdown in GBAO as portending a more widespread repression to come. As one observer told RFE/RL, 'Badakhshan is only the first step, a kind of testing ground for a complete crackdown on civil society and the eradication of all kinds of potential dissidents.' A series of arrests and attacks on journalists in Dushanbe, including four members of RFE/RL's Tajik service and two popular bloggers, appeared to lend weight to this prediction.[30]

As Central Asia specialist Bruce Pannier observed, 'The [Tajik] government has always had at best a tenuous hold over this region, based on informal agreements with informal leaders, whom they are now going after all at once, calling them "criminals" and "terrorists" and forcing people to go on television to denounce them.'[31] Pannier also noted that previous crackdowns had largely attempted to control the local informal economy, whereas on this occasion the aims appeared to be more political. Meanwhile, the Aga Khan Development Network (AKDN) was described in the Russian media as an 'instrument of the West,' suggesting an orchestrated propaganda campaign presumably aimed at providing an opportunity for Dushanbe to reassert its authority over the Pamir region with the support of Moscow and Beijing.

While Russia clearly continues to have a strong influence in Tajikistan's internal affairs, it faces growing competition from the Chinese. China has recently built a new military base at the Tajik-Afghan border town of Ishkashim, from which it is constructing a road link leading across the entire length of the Wakhan Corridor to a new border crossing with China at the eastern end. China's presence has also become an added cause for tension between the Pamiris and the Tajik government. As an 'autonomous region' the GBAO is theoretically entitled to tax goods coming in from China, but since these goods are destined for companies owned by President Rahmon's family and friends the regional government is prevented from collecting those taxes.

China's Pamiri 'Tajiks'

Since the 1860s the eastern edge of the Pamirs – specifically the eastern slope of the Sarikol mountain range – has been under Chinese control. In recognition of the region's distinct ethnic and linguistic character, in 1954 the Chinese government established the Tashkurgan Tajik Autonomous County within the predominantly Uighur (Turkic-speaking) province of Xinjiang. Named for the district's largest town, this administrative unit gave recognition to the 'Tajiks' as an official nationality within the Chinese state.

Here I use quotes, because the Chinese 'Tajiks' are in fact Ismāʿīlī Pamiris, speakers of the eastern Iranian Sarikoli and Wakhi languages, whose cousins across the border in Tajikistan to the west tend rather to consider themselves as ethnically *distinct from* the Tajik majority of their country. Thus, in accordance with contemporary usage, the second group should perhaps more properly be referred to as 'Tajikistanis' than 'Tajiks' (see Fig. C.2). In the Chinese case, use of the term 'Tajik' harkens back to its original sense of a thousand years previous, denoting Iranian-speakers in contradistinction to their Turkic-speaking Uighur and Kyrgyz neighbours.

Covering an area of 52,400 square kilometres and with a population of around 40,000, the Tashkurgan Tajik Autonomous County holds significant political importance both as a border region with Tajikistan and because the Karakorum Highway, which links western China across the length of Pakistan all the way to the Arabian Sea, passes through it. All land traffic between

Islamabad and Kashgar – and by extension Karachi and Beijing – transits through Tashkurgan.

By way of contrast, the East-West border crossing over the Kulma Pass into Tajikistan (which I crossed on foot in 2018, to the bemusement of the border guards on both sides) has been open only since 2004, and sees far less traffic. There is little contact between the communities on adjacent sides of the border despite their shared languages and Ismāʿīlī religion. The Chinese government allows only one mosque to operate in the Tashkurgan region, and children under 18 are prohibited from attending it. The Aga Khan Development Network (AKDN) – which financially supports projects in Ismāʿīlī communities throughout the world – is not authorized to offer aid to the Tashkurgan Ismāʿīlīs, and foreign Ismāʿīlī religious leaders are not allowed to preach in Chinese territory.[32] The Aga Khan himself, however, has been allowed to personally visit the district on two occasions.

Since 2000 the Chinese government has made substantial investment in its border regions as a way of bringing them more directly under the centre's control.[33] This has consisted largely of building roads to facilitate commerce as

Figure C.2 Sarikoli Tajiks in Tashkurgan, China.

well as schools and hospitals, but has also included bringing in Han settlers. Recently the economic situation for Pamiri 'Tajiks' in China has been much better than for those across the border. This fact is highlighted through 'special economic zones' where visitors from Tajikistan on daytrips can witness the successes of the Chinese economic miracle.[34] Whether this translates into a preference on the part of Tashkurgan's residents to remain under Chinese rule is difficult to assess, however, since their contacts with outsiders are tightly controlled. As of 2018 Chinese security forces, apparently lumping Tajiks along with the restive Turkic-speaking Uighurs as a threat to national security, were severely clamping down on any form of interaction between residents of the Tashkurgan region and the outside world. I witnessed first-hand this climate of fear during a visit to the region in May 2018 when contacts I had been given refused to speak with me, including the brother of a colleague living in London. The police presence was everywhere and the sense of living under occupation palpable. As of this writing an estimated one million Chinese Muslims have been sent to re-education camps,[35] and this includes many Tajiks.

And yet, officially, the Chinese government promotes the Tajik identity as a unique and valuable component of Chinese society, proudly describing Tajiks in official statements as 'China's only Caucasian ethnic minority'. Their long presence on the territory they inhabit is implicitly recognized through recent (and to our mind, spurious) claims by Chinese archaeologists to have discovered 'the world's oldest Zoroastrian site' outside of Tashkurgan, which they have dated to around 500 BCE.[36] Labelled as a cemetery due to the presence of thirty-nine human burials, it appears to have served more importantly as a kind of solar calendar with parallel lines of alternating black and white stones indicating the solstices, the equinoxes, and other key moments in the annual cycle. Some of the graves include small fire altars, but these are not in and of themselves evidence of 'Zoroastrianism' since fire cults were extremely widespread in ancient times. In the absence of further evidence specifically linking the site to known Zoroastrian rituals, what we may in fact have here is some kind of Saka equivalent to Stonehenge.

What future for the Tajiks?

Notwithstanding the cheery tone of the Tajik government's public propaganda, there are few signs that would allow an outside observer to be optimistic about the country's future. Tajikistan is plagued by a whole array of problems, not the least of which are the old bugbears of poverty, unemployment, and corruption. Those privileged with decision-making power have failed to provide the younger generation with either hope for a rewarding career or a sense of national belonging, and many Tajiks are turning to radical Islam for an alternative sense of purpose in life.

The paternalistic Tajik government seems intent on maintaining the population in an infantile state of dependence rather than equipping them with the means to become thinking, empowered global citizens. A 2018 report issued by the US-base Freedom House classified Tajikistan as a 'consolidated authoritarian regime,' with a democracy score of 6.79 (down from 6.64 the previous year and 6.25 in 2009), on a scale where 7 is 'least democratic.' The same report gave Tajikistan a solid 7 rating for corruption, 'due to evidence of pervasive nepotism and continued state capture by members of the political elite.' Tajikistan is a 'nepotocracy,' the report concluded, where 'politics and business are dominated by relatives of the president's family.'[37]

Tajiks are heirs to one of the world's great civilizations, but the government's efforts to muster this national pride have largely backfired. The fact that the entire Iranian world, from the Islamic Republic of Iran to Afghanistan and Uzbekistan, continues to chafe under corrupt, authoritarian leadership does little to foster a sense of unity or participation in a broad Iranian heritage among the world's Persian-speakers. Quite the contrary, it serves to keep them in separateness and isolation, both from each other and from the global community as a whole.

Two decades after suffering the destructive effects of a catastrophic civil war, Tajikistan's economy shows few signs of recovery or improvement. Its industries are mismanaged and cannot compete internationally. Merely completing another large hydroelectric dam – even if this elusive goal is one day achieved – will not be sufficient to remedy the country's massive economic problems. Tajiks by and large were far better off under the Soviet system, but nostalgia for that ever more distant past will not help them now. Worse, newly global standards of comparison, fed through the mass media, have raised Tajiks' expectations to levels that their present circumstances can never meet, as images from around the world purport to show them everything they are missing.

On the other hand, as an ancient people the Tajiks have shown an impressive historical resilience. They have faced far worse times than what they are living through now, and survived. The late Uzbek President Islom Karimov (that turncoat Tajik!), referring to his own adopted Uzbek identity, used to like to say that 'a nation possessing a great past will also have a great future'. Perhaps the Tajiks, whose historical legacy can stand proud against any the world has to offer, have that to look forward to.

They just may have to wait a while.

Notes

Preface to the Second Edition

1 'The Tajiks of Uzbekistan,' *Central Asian Survey* 15/2 (1996): 213–216 and 'Uzbekistan's Tajiks: A Case of Repressed Identity?' *Central Asia Monitor* no. 6 (1996): 17–19.

A Note on Transliteration

1 Richard N. Frye, *The History of Bukhara*, Cambridge, MA, 1954, p. 3.
2 Elton Daniel, *The Political and Social History of Khurasan under Abbasid Rule 747–820*, Minneapolis, 1979, p. 8.
3 Richard N. Frye, *The Heritage of Central Asia: From Antiquity to the Turkish Expansion*, Princeton, 1996, p. 3.

Introduction

1 Soviet-era Tajik academician B.G. (Bobojon) Ghafurov's seminal two-volume Russian work, *Tadzhiki*, completed in 1970, was published in an English translation in Dushanbe in 2011, ostensibly in commemoration of twenty years of Tajik independence; it is almost impossible it to find outside of Tajikistan. Previously an English translation of a work ghostwritten by Yusufsho Yakubov on behalf of Tajikistan's long-time president, Emomali Rahmon, appeared in 1997 under the title *Tajiks in the Mirror of History* (original title: *Tojikon dar oinai ta'rikh*); unfortunately, the book is so badly written and disorganized as to be essentially unreadable. An earlier 'official' history, edited by Ghafurov and B.A. Litvinskii, was published in Russian as a five-volume *Istoriia tadzhikskogo naroda* in 1963–65. A later six-volume work, also titled *Istoriia tadzhikskogo naroda*, was compiled during the 1980s at the end of the Soviet period and has been published serially beginning in 1998. The recent work

by Kirill Nourzhanov and Christian Bleuer, *Tajikistan: A Political and Social History*, Canberra, 2013, while very useful for the modern and contemporary periods, is quite thin on pre-modern Tajik history and has little to say about Tajik culture.

2 Abū Ja'far Muḥammad Ṭabarī, *Tarjome-ye tafsīr-e Ṭabarī*, Habīb Yāḡmā'ī, (ed), 7 vols., Tehran, 1339–44 [1960–65], vol. 1, p. 5.

3 Moḥammad Reẓa Shafi'ī-Kadkanī, 'Borbad's *Khusravanis* – First Iranian Songs', in Iraj Bashiri (tr and ed), *From the Hymns of Zarathustra to the Songs of Borbad*, Dushanbe, 2003, p. 135.

4 Shafi'ī-Kadkanī, 'Borbad's *Khusravanis*', p. 136.

5 Abū Bakr Muhammad b. Ja'far Narshakhī, *The History of Bukhara*, Richard N. Frye, (tr), Cambridge, MA, 1954, p. 48.

6 Frye, *History of Bukhara*, p. 135, note 183.

7 English translations of the Mt. Mugh documents, along with many other Sogdian texts, have been included in a recent edition of V.A. Livshits's *Sogdian Epigraphy of Central Asia and Semirech'e*, Corpus Inscriptionum Iranicarum Part II, vol. III, London, 2015.

8 'Izz al-dīn ibn Athīr, *Chronicon quod perfectissimum inscribitur (Al-Kāmil fī al-tārīkh)*, C.J. Tornberg, (ed), Leiden, 1853–67, vol. 6, p. 366.

9 Abū Ishaq Ibrahīm b. Muhammad al-Fārisī al-Istakhrī, *Kitāb al-Masālik wa'l-Mamālik*, in M.J. de Goeje, (ed), *Bibliotheca Geographorum Arabicorum*, vol. 1, 1870, p. 314.

10 Muhammad Ibn Hawkal, *Kitāb Sūrat al-ard*, J.H. Kramers and G. Wiet, (trs), *Ibn Hauqal, Configuration de la Terre*, Paris, 2001 [1965], vol. 2, p. 469.

11 Richard N. Frye, *Bukhara: The Medieval Achievement*, Costa Mesa, CA, 1996 [Norman, 1965], p. 44.

12 Frye, *Bukhara: The Medieval Achievement*, pp. 62–63.

13 See Gilbert Lazard, 'Darī', *Encyclopaedia Iranica* online.

14 Narshakhī, *History of Bukhara*, p. 48. The two commands are somewhat incorrectly transcribed in the Perso-Arabic text: The standard Sogdian forms are *nk'npt' nk'np* and *nkwnt' nkwn*. We should recall that Qubavī's redaction dates to four centuries after the events it describes, and that he himself is unlikely to have known Sogdian.

15 See John R. Perry, 'Tajik', *Encyclopaedia Iranica* online.

16 Dariush Rajabian, 'Goftogū bā Ṣafar 'Abdullah, dānešmand-e Tājīk', *BBC Persian Service*, 6 September 2014.

17 Kamoludin Abdullaev, 'Conflict Resolution in Tajikistan', in Hans-Jorg Albrecht et al. (eds), *Conflicts and Conflict Resolution in Middle Eastern Societies – Between Tradition and Modernity*, Berlin, 2006, p. 308.

18 Bert Fragner, 'The Nationalization of the Uzbeks and Tajiks', in Andreas Kappeler and Edward Allworth (ed), *Muslim Communities Reemerge: Historical Perspectives on Nationality, Politics, and Opposition in the Former Soviet Union and Yugoslavia*, Durham, 1994, p. 15.

19 Personal conversation, 5 February 2018.

20 See Thomas Loy, *Bukharan Jews in the Soviet Union: Autobiographical Narrations of Mobility, Continuity and Change*, Wiesbaden, 2016.

21 One may cite Arne Haugen, *The Establishment of National Republics in Soviet Central Asia*, London, 2003, among many other works.

22 It bears noting in this regard that outside the urban centres, the villages of the plains were predominantly Turkic-speaking, while the inhabitants of mountain villages more often spoke Iranian dialects.

23 See Rahim Masov, *Istoriia topornogo razdeleniia*, Iraj Bashiri, (tr), *The History of a National Catastrophe*, www.angelfire.com/rnb/bashiri/Masov/MasovHistoryNationalCatastrophe.pdf.

24 I am grateful to Pavel Lurje for reminding me of this important historical fact.

25 Richard Foltz, 'Uzbekistan's Tajiks: A Case of Repressed Identity?' *Central Asia Monitor* no. 6 (1996): pp. 17–19; and Richard Foltz, 'The Tajiks of Uzbekistan', *Central Asian Survey* 15/2 (1996): pp. 213–16.

26 Frye, *Bukhara: The Medieval Achievement*, p. ix.

27 Richard Foltz, *Iran in World History*, New York, 2016.

Chapter 1

1 Use of the term 'Farsi' in English is incorrect, not to say somewhat pompous; it is like calling French 'français' or German 'deutsch'. The correct English term for the language is 'Persian'.

2 A good general reference work is J.P. Mallory and D.Q. Adams, *The Oxford Introduction to Proto-Indo-European and the Proto-Indo-European World*, Oxford, 2006.

3 For an excellent and exhaustive treatment see Elena E. Kuz'mina, *The Origin of the Indo-Iranians*, Leiden, 2007.

4 Alan K. Outram et al., 'The Earliest Horse Harnessing and Milking', *Science*, 6 March 2009, pp. 1332–35. But see also Erin Blakemore, 'Ancient DNA Study

Pokes Holes in Horse Domestication Theory', *National Geographic* online, 9 May 2018, https://news.nationalgeographic.com/2018/05/horse-domestication-dna-indo-european-science/#close.

5 David Anthony, *The Horse, The Wheel and Language: How Bronze Age Riders from the Eurasian Steppes Shaped the Modern World*, Princeton, 2007.

6 Christoph Baumer, *The History of Central Asia, vol. 1: The Age of the Steppe Warriors*, London, 2012, p. 143.

7 Calvert Watkins, *How to Kill a Dragon: Aspects of Indo-European Poetics*, New York, 1995. The various literatures which emerged from this heroic poetic tradition are discussed at length in Christopher I. Beckwith, *Empires of the Silk Road: A History of Central Eurasia from the Bronze Age to the Present*, Princeton, 2009.

8 The Indo-European caste system was most notably schematized by the French scholar Georges Dumézil during the mid-twentieth century. On the reception of Dumézil's theory, see Wouter W. Belier, *Decayed Gods: Origin and Development of Georges Dumézil' s 'idéologie tripartie'*, Leiden, 1991.

9 Manya Saadi-Nejad, 'Arəduuī Sūrā Anāhitā: An Indo-European River Goddess', *Analytica Iranica* 4–5 (2013), pp. 253–74.

10 Christine Keyser et al., 'Ancient DNA Provides New Insights into the History of South Siberian Kurgan People', *Human Genetics* 126 (2009), pp. 395–410.

11 V. Sarianidi, 'Excavations at Southern Gonur', *Iran* 31 (1993), pp. 25–37.

12 See B.A. Zheleznyakov, *Tamgaly: The Rock Art Site, Nature, Vicinities, Reserve-Museum*, Almaty, 2016.

13 Henri-Paul Francfort, 'La Civilisation de l'Oxus et les Indo-Iraniens et Indo-Aryens en Asie Centrale', in Gerard Fussman, Jean Kellens, Henri-Paul Francfort, and Xavier Tremblay (eds), *Āryas, Aryens et Iraniens en Asie Centrale*, Paris, 2005, p. 282.

14 Gian Luca Bonora, 'Evolution of Early Urban Societies in Prehistory', in Michele Bernardini, Gian Luca Bonora, and Giusto Traina (eds), *Turkmenistan: Histories of a Country, Cities and a Desert*, Torino, 2016, pp. 22–31.

15 Bertille Lyonnet, 'Another Possible Interpretation of the Bactro-Margiana Culture (BMAC) of Central Asia: The Tin Trade', in Catherine Jarrig and Vincent Lefèvre (eds), *South Asian Archaeology 2001, Vol. 1: Prehistory*, Paris, 2005, pp. 191–200.

16 A. Askarov and T. Shirinov, 'The "Palace," Temple, and Necropolis of Jarkutan', *Bulletin of the Asia Institute* 8 (1994), pp. 13–25.

17 Saadi-nejad, 'Anāhitā'.

18 For a concise overview of these influences, see Anders Hultgård, 'Zoroastrian Influence on Judaism, Christianity, and Islam', in Michael Stausberg (ed), *Zarathustra and Zoroastrianism*, London, 2008, pp. 101–12.

19 Jean Kellens, 'Considérations sur l'histoire de l'Avesta', *Journal Asiatique* 286/2 (1998), pp. 451–519.

20 Kellens suggests that the Young Avestan rites may have been imported from Arachosia (southeastern Afghanistan) during the time of Darius I, within the context of rivalry among several priestly groups at the Persian court (Kellens, 'Considérations', p. 514).

21 The argument for this is spelt out in Michael Witzel, 'Linguistic Evidence for Cultural Exchange in Prehistoric Western Central Asia', *Sino-Platonic Papers* 129 (2003), pp. 1–70.

22 H.-P. Francfort, 'Animals in Reality, Art and Myths in the Oxus Civilization (BMAC): Bison, Deer', in *Near the Sources of Civilizations*, Moscow, 2004, p. 183.

23 Herodotus, *The Histories: The Complete Translation, Backgrounds, Commentaries*, IV, Walter Blanco, (tr), New York, 2013, p. 59.

24 Witzel, 'Linguistic Evidence', p. 37.

Chapter 2

1 Strabo, *Geography*, Horace Leonard Jones, (tr), Cambridge, MA, 2014, 15.2.8.

2 Nicholas Sims-Williams, Frantz Grenet, and Aleksandr Podushkin, 'Les plus anciens monuments de la langue sogdienne: Les inscriptions de Kultobe au Kazakhstan', in *Comptes rendus des séances de l'Académie des Inscriptions et Belles-Lettres*, Paris, 2007, pp. 1005–34.

3 '*Bitīm asaŋhąmca šōiϑranąmca vahištəm frāϑβərəsəm azəm yō ahurō mazdå gāum yim* ***suγδō*** *šaiianəm*', *Vidēvdāt* (*Vendidad*): 1.4 (Titus Avestan Corpus).

4 First suggested by Émile Benveniste, pointed out to me by Pavel Lurje.

5 Herodotus, *The Histories*, I, p. 214.

6 Judith Lerner, 'Some So-called Achaemenid Objects from Pazyryk', *Source: Notes in the History of Art* 10/4 (1991), p. 12.

7 In Firdawsi's *Book of Kings* Bessos and Barsaentes are referred to as Jānūspār and Māhyār, which are likely closer to their actual Bactrian names than the Greek versions.

8 Rachel Mairs, *The Hellenistic Far East: Archaeology, Language, and Identity in Greek Central Asia*, Berkeley, 2014, pp. 1, 74; Greek original on p. 189.

9 Reports from the excavations, which took place from 1964 to 1978, have been published in successive volumes under the title *Fouilles d'Aï Khanoum*, by the Délégation Archéologique Française en Afghanistan (DAFA). For an overview of the DAFA's work since its establishment in 1923 see Mairs, *The Hellenistic Far East*, pp. 16–25. Sadly the excavations were bulldozed by the Taliban in 2000.

10 I was prevented from visiting this site in May 2018 by Taliban taking potshots from across the river in Afghanistan; Tajik border guards would not allow us to approach the ruins.

11 Mairs, *The Hellenistic Far East*, p. 33.

12 Craig Benjamin, *The Yuezhi: Origin, Migration and the Conquest of Northern Bactria*, Turnhout, 2007.

13 Sima Qian, *Records of the Grand Historian*, Burton Watson, (tr), rev. ed., New York, 1993, p. 245.

14 Valerie Hansen, *The Silk Road: A New History*, New York, 2012, p. 17.

15 B.Ja. Staviskij, *La Bactriane Sous les Kushans: Problèmes d'histoire et de culture*, Paris, 1986, pp. 196–200.

16 Staviskij, *La Bactriane Sous les Kushans*, p. 223.

17 Richard Foltz, *Religions of the Silk Road: Premodern Patterns of Globalization*, 2nd ed., New York, 2010.

18 Frantz Grenet, 'Crise et sortie de crise en Bactriane-Sogdiane aux ive-ve s. de n. è.: de l'héritage antique à l'adoption de modèles sassanides', in *La Persia e l'Asia Centrale da Alessandro al X secolo*, Roma, 1996, pp. 367–90.

19 Xuanzang, *The Great Tang Dynasty Record of the Western Regions*, Li Rongxi, (tr), Berkeley, 1996, p. 27.

20 Étienne de la Vaissière, *Sogdian Traders: A History*, James Ward, (tr), Leiden, 2005, p. 72.

21 de la Vaissière, *Sogdian Traders*, p. 76.

22 Nicholas Sims-Williams, 'Ancient Letters', *Encyclopaedia Iranica* online; also de la Vaissière, *Sogdian Traders*, pp. 43–70.

23 Nicholas Sims-Williams, *Sogdian and Other Iranian Inscriptions of the Upper Indus*, 2 vols., London, 1989 and 1992.

24 Nar<u>sh</u>a<u>kh</u>ī, *History of Bukhara*, p. 17.

25 Ibid., p. 23; cf. Abu Rayhan Biruni, *Kitāb al-ā<u>th</u>ār al-bāqiya 'an al-qurūn al-<u>kh</u>āliya*, C. Edward Sachau, (tr), *The Chronology of Ancient Nations*, London, 1879, p. 222.

26 Yusufshah Yaqubshah, 'The Image of Funerary Dances on Sughdian Ossuaries', in Iraj Bashiri (tr and ed), *From the Hymns of Zarathustra to the Songs of Borbad*, Dushanbe, 2003, pp. 177–78.

27 Christoph Baumer, *The History of Central Asia*, vol. 2, *The Age of the Silk Roads*, London, 2014, p. 142.

28 Xuanzang, *Great Tang Dynasty Record*, p. 27.

29 de la Vaissière, *Sogdian Traders*, pp. 228–32.

30 Ibid., pp. 242–49.

31 Edward H. Schafer, *The Golden Peaches of Samarkand*, Berkeley, 1963, p. 55. The last line consists of sexual metaphors, no doubt reflecting that these dancers were often also prostitutes.

32 Quoted in Baumer, *History of Central Asia*, vol. 2, p. 190.

33 Matteo Compareti, *Samarkand the Center of the World: Proposals for the Identification of the Afrasyab Paintings*, Costa Mesa, 2016.

34 Boris I. Marshak, *Legends, Tales and Fables in the Art of Sogdiana*, New York, 2002, p. 5.

35 Xuanzang, *Great Tang Dynasty Record*, p. 34.

36 Ibid., p. 44.

37 de la Vaissière, *Sogdian Traders*, p. 274.

38 Abū Jaʿfar Muḥammad Ṭabarī, *Tarjome-ye tafsīr-e Ṭabarī*, Ḥabīb Yāḡmāʾī, (ed), 7 vols., Tehran, 1339–44 [1960–65], vol. 22, pp. 165–66.

39 Seemingly a variant of the ancient Central Asian title *Tarkhan* (the linguistic origins of which are disputed) rather than a personal name.

40 Narshakhī, *History of Bukhara*, p. 48. This incident is discussed further in the Introduction.

41 Livshits, *Sogdian Epigraphy*, p. 67, lines 21 and 22, with commentary on pp. 72–73.

42 See footnote 2 in the Introduction.

43 They utilized some symbolic elements later associated with Shīʿism, but to call them 'Shīʿites' would be both overstretched and anachronistic.

44 Modern Yaghnobi appears to have descended from one of what must have been diverse regional spoken dialects of Sogdian, and not the literary language known from surviving texts. See Antonio Panaino, 'The Yaghnobis and Their Valley: Towards a New Historical Perspective', in Antonio Panaino, Andrea Gariboldi, and Paolo Ognibene (eds), *Yaghnobi Studies I: Papers from the Italian missions in Tajikistan*, Milano, 2013, pp. 20–1.

45 Narshakhī, *History of Bukhara*, p. 67.

Chapter 3

1 D.G. Tor, 'The Islamization of Central Asia in the Sāmānid Era and the Reshaping of the Muslim World', *Bulletin of the School of Oriental and African Studies* 72/2 (2009), p. 285.
2 Luke Treadwell, 'The Samanids: The First Islamic Dynasty of Central Asia', in Edmund Herzig and Sarah Stewart (eds), *Early Islamic Iran, The Idea of Iran, vol.* 5, London, 2011, p. 6.
3 Niẓām ul-Mulk, *The Book of Government or Rules for Kings: The Siyar al-Muluk or Siyasat-nama of Nizam al-Mulk*, Hubert Darke, (tr), New Haven, 1960, p. 156.
4 Quoted in Frye, *Bukhara: The Medieval Achievement*, p. 59.
5 Ibn Hawqal, *Configuration de la Terre*, pp. 469–70.
6 Ibid., p. 454.
7 Ibid., p. 472.
8 'Alā al-dīn 'Atā Malik Juvaīnī, *The History of the World Conqueror*, J.A. Boyle, (tr), Cambridge, MA, 1958, vol. 1, pp. 95–6.
9 Quoted in S.M. Stern, 'Ya'qub the Coppersmith and Persian National Sentiment', in C.E. Bosworth (ed), *Iran and Islam: In Memory of the Late Vladimir Minorsky*, Edinburgh, 1971, pp. 541–42.
10 Askarali Rajabov, 'Historical Traditions of the Time of Rudaki', in Iraj Bashiri (tr and ed), *From the Hymns of Zarathustra to the Songs of Borbad*, Dushanbe, 2003, pp. 155–56.
11 The poem was likely sung in a form known as *laskavī*, attributed to the Sasanian court musician Borbad (Rajabov, 'Historical Traditions', p. 154).
12 Sa'īd Nafīsī, *Moḥīṭ-e zendagī va aḥvāl o aš'ār-e Rūdakī*, 3rd ed., Tehran, 2357 [1978], pp. 394–404.
13 These have been collected and translated into French in Gilbert Lazard, *Les premiers poètes persans (ix – xe siècles): Fragments rassemblés*, 2 vols., Paris, 1964.
14 See Introduction, note 2.
15 Frye, *Bukhara: The Medieval Achievement*, p. 93.

Chapter 4

1 '(The Turkic chieftain Küli Chor) fought with Tāzīk and subdued them'; from the runic inscription on a stele at the Küli Chor memorial complex, Kazakhstan.

(*Türik Bitig*, Language Committee of the Ministry of Culture and Information of the Republic of Kazakhstan, n.d., http://bitig.org/?lang=e&mod=1&tid=1&oid=18&m=1).

2 B. Martínez-Cruz et al., 'In the Heartland of Eurasia: The Multilocus Genetic Landscape of Central Asian Populations', *European Journal of Human Genetics* 19/2 (2011), pp. 216–23.

3 Cited in Peter B. Golden, 'Turks and Iranians: An Historical Sketch', in Lars Johanson and Christiane Bulut (eds), *Turkic-Iranian Contact Areas: Historical and Linguistic Aspects*, Wiesbaden, 2006, p. 17, with some modifications to Golden's English translation.

4 Maḥmūd al-Kāshgarī, *Compendium of the Turkic Dialects (Dīwān lughāt al-turk)*, R. Dankoff and J. Kelly, (trs), Cambridge, MA, 1982, vol. 1, p. 84.

5 Ibn Battuta, *The Travels of Ibn Baṭṭūṭa, A.D. 1325–1354*, H.A.R. Gibb, (tr), 5 vols., Cambridge, 1958–2000, vol. 3, p. 567.

6 Bobojon Ghafurov, *Tajiks: Pre-ancient, Ancient and Medieval History*, P. Jamshedov, (tr), Dushanbe, 2011, vol. 2, p. 350. Jamshedov goes so far as to mistranslate *g͟harībī* as 'motherland'.

7 Jo-Ann Gross and Asom Urunbaev, *The Letters of Khwāja 'Ubayd Allāh Aḥrār and His Associates*, Leiden, 2002, p. 1.

8 On the importance of these pious endowments in the Central Asian context, see Robert D. McChesney, *Waqf in Central Asia: Four Hundred Years in the History of a Muslim Shrine, 1480–1889*, Princeton, 1991 and Maria Subtelny, *Timurids in Transition: Turko-Persian Politics and Acculturation in Medieval Iran*, Leiden, 2007, esp. pp. 148–90.

9 Gross and Urunbaev, *Letters*, p. 1.

10 'Abd al-Razzāq Samarqandī, *Maṭla'-i sa'dayn*, p. 1062; quoted in Gross and Urunbaev, *Letters*, p. 13.

11 Aftandil Erkinov, 'Les Timourides, modèles de légitimité et les recueils poétiques de Kokand', in F. Richard and M. Szuppe (eds), *Écrit et culture en Asie centrale et dans le monde turko-iranien, XIVe-XIXe siècles*, Paris, 2009, p. 294.

12 The Mughals' unprecedented wealth was due in large part to the influx of European silver and gold from the New World, since European traders could offer few goods of interest to the Mughals and had to pay cash for Indian spices and other commodities.

13 Scott C. Levi, *The Indian Diaspora in Central Asia and Its Trade, 1550–1900*, Leiden, 2002.

14 Richard Foltz, *Mughal India and Central Asia*, Karachi, 1998, p. 74.

15 Foltz, *Mughal India and Central Asia*, p. xxviii.

16 Ibid., pp. 93–105.

17 Mutribi Samarqandi, *Conversations with Emperor Jahangir*, p. 87.

18 Thomas T. Allsen, 'Sharing out the Empire: Apportioned Lands under the Mongols', in Anatoly M. Kazanov et André Wink (eds), *Nomads in the Sedentary World*, London, 2001, pp. 172–90.

19 Muhammad 'Maliha' Samarqandi, *Muzakkir al-ashāb*, Tashkent, Oriental Manuscript Collection, MS Taj. 58/1.

20 Abdul-Ghani Mirzoyev, *Saĭido Nasafi i ego mesto v istorii tadzhikskoĭ literatury* (Sayido Nasafi and His Place in Tajik Literature), Stalinabad, 1954. I would like to thank Professor Kamoludin Abdullaev for suggesting this example as being representative of Saido's distinctive style.

21 Scott C. Levi, *The Rise and Fall of Khoqand, 1709–1876: Central Asia in the Global Age*, Pittsburgh, 2017, p. 34.

22 Levi, *The Rise and Fall of Khoqand*, pp. 82–83. Levi underemphasizes the distinct identity of these Pamiris, stating that they spoke 'highly localized Persian dialects nearly incomprehensible even to Tajik speakers from the plains' – in fact the Pamiri languages are not 'dialects of Persian', but separate tongues which would have been *entirely* incomprehensible to lowland Tajiks.

23 Peter Hopkirk, *The Great Game: The Struggle for Empire in Central Asia*, New York, 1992.

24 Thomas Barfield, *Afghanistan: A Cultural and Political History*, Princeton, 2012, p. 5.

25 L.A. Perepelitsyna, *Rol russkoi kultury v razvitii kultur narodov Srednei Azii*, Moskva, 1976, p. 8; quoted in Nourzhanov and Bleuer, *Tajikistan*, p. 20.

26 Aftandil Erkinov, 'Persian-Chaghatay Bilingualism in the Intellectual Circles of Central Asia during the 15th–18th Centuries (The case of poetical anthologies, *bayāz*)', *International Journal of Central Asian Studies* 12 (2008): pp. 57–82.

27 The Timurid poet Alisher Navoi in the fifteenth century refers to the Tajiks as the 'Sart nation' (*Sart ulusi*) and a few decades later Babur uses the term to refer to the Tajiks of Ferghana as well as to the residents of Kabul. The term likely derives from the Sanskrit *sarthavaha*, 'merchant' or 'caravan leader'; cf. the Chinese term for the head of the Sogdians, *sabao*.

28 Alexander Morrison, *Russian Rule in Samarkand 1868–1910: A Comparison with British India*, Oxford, 2008, p. 43, crediting Paul Bergne with the observation.

29 Sadriddin Aini, *The Sand of Oxus: Boyhood Reminiscences*, John R. Perry and Rachel Lehr, (trs), Costa Mesa, 1998, p. 111.

30 See Adeeb Khalid, *The Politics of Muslim Cultural Reform: Jadidism in Central Asia*, Berkeley, 1999.

Chapter 5

1 Joseph Stalin, 'Marxism and the National Question', in Bruce Franklin (ed), *The Essential Stalin: Major Theoretical Writings, 1905–1952*, London, 1973.

2 This despite the publication in 1925 of pre-revolutionary scholar Vassili Barthold's *Tadzhikistan: sbornik statiei* (Tajikistan: An Anthology of Articles), which connected the Tajiks with the general heritage of Iranian civilization.

3 'Paīkarai Loiq Sheralī', *Shkola informatsionnykh i telekommunikatsionnykh tekhnologiī* online, Dushanbe, 2008, www.cit.tj/index.php?menu=corpus&page=loiq_poem_13&poem=638&lange=tj.

4 See for example Qodiri Rustam, 'Tojikon va Zaboni Forsi', *Ozodagon* 13/517 (28 March 2018), p. 15.

5 Muhammadjon Shakurī, *Khuroson ast in jo: ma'naviyat, zabon va ihyoi millii Tojikon*, 2nd ed., Dushanbe, 2005, p. 194.

6 Rahim Masov, *Istoriia topornogo razdeleniia* (History of an Axe-like Dividing), Dushanbe, 1991, p. 103; also subsequent works published in 2003 and 2005.

7 Adeeb Khalid, *Making Uzbekistan: Nation, Empire, and Revolution in the Early USSR*, Ithaca, 2015, p. 292.

8 Muhammadjon Shakurī, *The Imperialist Revolution in Bukhara*, Anvar Shukurov and Bahriddin Alizoda, (trs), Dushanbe, 2013, p. 105.

9 Nourzhanov and Bleuer, *Tajikistan*, p. 39.

10 The irony is perhaps best explained by noting that at the dawn of the Soviet period the term 'Tajik' was generally used for mountain-dwellers.

11 The process is described in detail in Masov, *Istoriia topornogo razdeleniia*.

12 Nourzhanov and Bleuer, *Tajikistan*, p. 7.

13 Sergei P. Poliakov, *Everyday Islam: Religion and Tradition in Rural Central Asia*, London, 1992.

14 Saidbek Goziev, *Mahalla – Traditional Institution in Tajikistan and Civil Society in the West*, London, 2014, p. 53.

15 Otambek Mastibekov, *Leadership and Authority in Central Asia: The Ismaili Community in Tajikistan*, London, 2014, p. 83.

16 Mastibekov, *Leadership and Authority in Central Asia*, pp. 98–103.

17 An evocative description of the *tūyi khatna* from the boy's perspective can be found in Sadriddin Ainī's memoirs (*The Sand of Oxus*, pp. 38–42).
18 Colette Harris, *Control and Subversion: Gender Relations in Tajikistan*, London, 2004, p. 22.
19 Monica Whitlock, *Land beyond the River: The Untold Story of Central Asia*, New York, 2003, p. 68.
20 Goziev, *Mahalla*, p. 88.
21 See bibliography.
22 Isaac Scarborough, '(Over)determining Social Disorder: Tajikistan and the Economic Collapse of Perestroika', *Central Asian Survey* 35/3 (2016), p. 455.
23 Loiq includes this couplet in his introduction to Shakurī's book *Khuroson ast in jo*, p. 15.
24 Whitlock, *Land beyond the River*, p. 139.
25 Nourzhanov and Bleuer, *Tajikistan*, p. 185.
26 Stéphane Dudoignon, *Communal Solidarity and Social Conflicts in Late 20th Century Central Asia: The Case of the Tajik Civil War*, Tokyo, 1998, p. 18.
27 Dagikhudo Dagiev, *Regime Transition in Central Asia: Stateness, Nationalism and Political Change in Tajikistan and Uzbekistan*, London, 2014, p. 29.

Chapter 6

1 Martha Brill Olcott, 'Nation Building and Ethnicity in the Foreign Policies of the New Central Asian States', in Roman Szporluk (ed), *National Identity and Ethnicity in Russia and the New States of Eurasia*, Armonk, NY, 1994, p. 209.
2 Adeeb Khalid, *Islam after Communism: Religion and Politics in Central Asia*, 2nd ed., Berkeley, 2014, p. 149.
3 Tim Epkenhans, *The Origins of the Civil War in Tajikistan: Nationalism, Islamism, and Violent Conflict in Post-Soviet Space*, Lanham, 2016, p. 109.
4 'Interview with Davlat Khudonazarov', *Igrunov*, 16 April 2012, www.igrunov.ru/ukr/vchk-ukr-articles/articles/1103960023.html.
5 Muriel Atkin, *The Subtlest Battle: Islam in Soviet Tajikistan*, Philadelphia, 1989, p. 47.
6 Qurghonteppa was re-named Bokhtar in January 2018, reflecting the Tajik government's effort to claim to the heritage of ancient Bactria.
7 Olivier Roy, *The New Central Asia: Geopolitics and the Birth of Nations*, rev. ed., New York, 2007, p. 94.

8 Barnett Rubin, 'Russian Hegemony and State Breakdown in the Periphery', in B.R. Rubin and J. Snyder (eds), *Post-Soviet Political Order: Conflict and State Building*, New York, 1998, p. 155.
9 Helsinki Watch, *Tajik Presidential Election Conducted in a Climate of Fear and Fraud*, Helsinki, 1994.
10 'Teflon Rahmon: Tajik President Getting "Leader" Title, Lifelong Immunity', *Radio Free Europe Tajik Service*, 10 December 2015.
11 Mastibekov, *Leadership and Authority in Central Asia*, p. 115.
12 Dagiev, *Regime Transition in Central Asia*, p. 136.
13 John Heathershaw and Kirill Nourzhanov, 'Nation Building in Tajikistan: Soviet Legacy, Civil War and Authoritarian Politics', unpublished typescript.
14 Emomali Rahmon, *The Tajiks in the Mirror of History*, Dushanbe, 1997, p. 44.
15 Rahmon, *The Tajiks in the Mirror of History*, p. 43.
16 Alexander Sodiqov, 'Novruz and Nation-Building in Tajikistan', http://old.cacianalyst.org/?q=node/5753.
17 Personal conversation, 7 May 2017.
18 International Federation for Electoral Systems, *Public Opinion in Tajikistan 2010: Findings from an IFES Survey*, Washington, DC, 2010, cited in Kirill Nourzhanov, 'Nation-Building and Political Islam in Post-Soviet Tajikistan', in Mariya Y. Omelicheva (ed), *Nationalism and Identity Construction in Central Asia Dimensions, Dynamics, and Directions*, Lanham, MD, 2015, p. 84.
19 Khayrullo Fayz, 'Tajik Youth Turn to Radical Islam', *BBC News* online, 27 September 2010.
20 Avaz Yuldoshev, 'The Majority of Tajiks Fighting for ISIL in Iraq and Syria Salafists, Says Tajik Chief Prosecutor', *Asia-Plus* online, 3 March 2016, www.news.tj/en/news/tajikistan/security/20160303/majority-tajiks-fighting-isil-iraq-and-syria-salafists-says-tajik-chief-prosecutor.
21 'Tajikistan Human Rights Fears as Banned Party's Ex-leaders Jailed for Life', *The Guardian*, 2 June 2016.
22 Akbar Borisov, 'Devout Muslims Claim Crackdown in Tajikistan Amid Syria Fears', *Agence France Presse*, 23 April 2015.
23 Abdulfattoh Shafiev, 'Tajik Authorities Hunt the Hijab and Battle the Beard', *Global Voices* online, 15 April 2015.
24 Tim Epkenhans, 'Defining Normative Islam: Some Remarks on Contemporary Islamic Thought in Tajikistan – Hoji Akbar Turajonzoda's *Sharia and Society*', *Central Asian Survey* 30/1 (2011), pp. 81–96.

25 Filippo Menga, 'Building a Nation through a Dam: The Case of Rogun in Tajikistan', *Nationalities Papers* 43/3 (2015): pp. 479–94.

26 Menga, 'Building a Nation through a Dam', p. 486.

27 'Tajikistan: God's Chosen President Gets Play Treatment', *Eurasianet*, 28 November 2017, http://www.eurasianet.org/node/86221.

28 William C. Rowe, 'Agrarian Adaptations in Tajikistan: Land Reform, Water and Law', *Central Asian Survey* 29/2 (2010): pp. 189–90.

29 John Heathershaw, 'Tajikistan Amidst Globalization: State Failure or State Transformation?', *Central Asian Survey* 30/1 (2011): p. 157.

30 Anna Kellar, 'The Apples of Garm: Problems of Land Reform in Tajikistan', *Asian Affairs* 46/1 (2015): p. 119.

31 Kellar, 'The Apples of Garm', p. 120.

32 Don Van Atta, '"White Gold" or Fool's Gold? The Political Economy of Cotton in Tajikistan', *Problems of Post-Communism* 56/2 (2009): p. 18.

33 Van Atta, '"White Gold" or Fool's Gold?' p. 19.

34 Marlene Laruelle, 'Introduction', in Marlene Laruelle (ed), *Tajikistan on the Move: Statebuilding and Societal Transformations*, Lanham, 2018, p. xvi.

35 'Tajikistan: Chinese Company Gets Gold Mine in Return for Power Plant', *Eurasianet* online, 11 April 2018, www.eurasianet.org/tajikistan-chinese-company-gets-gold-mine-in-return-for-power-plant.

36 'Addicted: Drugs in Tajikistan', *The Economist*, 21 April 2012.

37 Madeleine Reeves, *Border Work: Spatial Lives of the State in Rural Central Asia*, Ithaca, 2014, p. 171.

38 Joshua Kucera, 'The Narcostate', *Politico* online, March/April 2014.

39 John Heathershaw, 'Why Is There So Much Construction in Central Asia's Capitals?', *Exeter Central Asian Studies Network*, Exeter, 2013, https://excas.net/2013/07/why-is-there-so-much-construction-in-central-asias-capitals.

40 Juliette Cleuziou, '"A Second Wife Is Not Really a Wife": Polygyny, Gender Relations and Economic Realities in Tajikistan', *Central Asian Survey* 35/1 (2016): p. 84.

41 Cleuziou, 'A Second Wife', p. 76.

42 Abdullaev, 'Conflict Resolution in Tajikistan', p. 316.

43 Harris, *Control and Subversion*, p. 86.

44 'Mumin Qanoat Believes Using Persian Alphabet in Tajikistan Possible but Needs Time', *Avesta News Agency* online service, 4 May 2015.

45 *Poetry Translation Centre*, adapted from the translation of Narguess Farzad, www.poetrytranslation.org/poems/flute-player.

46 Kamoludin Abdullaev, 'Cinema', in *Historical Dictionary of Tajikistan*, 3rd ed., Lanham, 2018, pp. 100–01.

47 Tim Epkenhans, 'Oblivion, Ambivalence, and Historical Erasure: Remembering the Civil War in Tajikistan', in Laruelle (ed), *Tajikistan on the Move*, p. 207.

Chapter 7

1 Martínez-Cruz et al., 'In the Heartland of Eurasia.'

2 Foltz, 'Uzbekistan's Tajiks: A Case of Repressed Identity?', p. 19.

3 Dagiev, *Regime Transition in Central Asia*, p. 30.

4 Slavomír Horák, 'In Search of the History of Tajikistan: What Are Tajik and Uzbek Historians Arguing About?' *Russian Politics and Law* 48/5 (2010), p. 75, n. 17.

5 Aftandil Erkinov, *From Persian Poetic Classicism to Reviving Timurid* adab*: Turkic-Persian bilingualism in the intellectual circles of Central Asia (1475–1900)*, Wiesbaden, forthcoming. My thanks to Dr. Erkinov for allowing me to reprint this passage prior to his book's publication.

6 Mir Mehrdad Mirsanjari, 'Negāh-e Tāškand be mellīgarī-ye Tājīkī dar Ozbakistān' (Tashkent's View of Tajik Nationalism in Uzbekistan), International Peace Studies Centre, 10 Mordād 1395 [31 July 2016].

7 'Avvalīn hamāyesh-e sarāsarī–ye Tājīkān-e Ozbakestān dar šahr-e Taškand' (First General Conference of Tajiks of Uzbekistan in Tashkent), *Rādiyo Zamāneh*, 9 Bahman 1396 [29 January 2018].

8 Personal conversation, 3 May 2022.

9 A. Sharifzadeh, 'The Persian Vernacular of Samarkand and Bukhara: A Primer,' 24 May 2019, <https://borderlessblogger.wordpress.com/2019/05/24/on-the-persian-vernacular-of-samarkand-and-bukhara>.

10 Michael Witzel believes that it is originally a non-Iranian loanword from the unknown language of the Bactria-Margiana people who predated the Sogdians (Witzel, 'Linguistic Evidence for Cultural Exchange in Prehistoric Western Central Asia,' pp. 23, 25, 29, and 35).

11 Peter Finke, *Variations on Uzbek Identity: Strategic Choices, Cognitive Schemas and Political Constraints in Identification Processes*, Oxford, 2014.

12 Peter Finke and Meltem Sancak, 'To Be an Uzbek or Not to Be a Tajik? Ethnicity and Locality in the Bukhara Oasis,' *Zeitschrift für Ethnologie*, 137/1 (2012), pp. 56–58.

13 Safar 'Abdullah, "Zabān-e fārsī dar Khorāsān-e bozorg" (The Persian Language in Greater Khorasan), Markaz-e dā're ol-ma'ārefat-e bozorg-e eslāmī, 4 Azar 1394 [25 November 2015].

14 Ja'far Kholmu'minov (Ja'far Muhammad Termizī), *Hanūz ešgh* (Still Love), Tehran, 1390 [2011]; Tūkhtamysh Tūkhtayev, aka Paymon, *Az Samarqandī čō qand* (From Samarkand Like Sugar), Tehran, 1384 [2005]; Idem, *Dānešnāme-ye zabān va adabiyāt-e fārsī-ye Ozbakestān* (Encyclopædia of the Persian Language and Literature of Uzbekistan), Tehran, 1385 [2005]; Idem, *Fārsīsarāyān-e Ozbakestān* (The Persian-speakers of Uzbekistan), Tehran, 2010.

15 Personal conversation, 18 April 2022.

16 A. Sarkhatzoda, 'Durdonai šarq: majallai adabī, ilmī va farhangii Tojikoni Uzbekiston' (The Faraway East: A literary, scientific and cultural journal of the Tajiks of Uzbekistan), *Ovozi Tojik*, 4 March 2022.

17 Personal conversation, 26 April 2022.

18 Personal conversation, 18 April 2022.

19 Finke and Sancak, 'To Be an Uzbek or Not to Be a Tajik?'

Conclusion

1 Barfield, *Afghanistan*, p. 6.

2 Masood Farivar, *Confessions of a Mullah Warrior*, New York, 2009, p. 290.

3 Text and translation (by Yama Yari and Sarah Maguire) from the Poetry Translation Centre online: <http://www.poetrytranslation.org/poems/the-bloody-epitaph>.

4 'Taliban, Tajikistan embroiled in battle of words, saber-rattling,' *Eurasianet*, 30 September 2021.

5 'Afghanistan signs electricity supply contract with Tajikistan amid power crisis,' *WION*, 28 December 2021.

6 'Tajikistan: President demands Tajik role in running Afghanistan,' *Eurasianet*, 25 August 2021.

7 Kamila Ibragimova, 'Tajikistan press-gangs an army to defend long Afghan border,' *Eurasianet*, 2 December 2021.

8 Lucas Webber, 'Islamic State uses Tajikistan's Dictator in Recruitment Drive,' *Eurasianet*, 2 June 2022.

9 Lucas Webber and Riccardo Valle, 'Islamic State in Afghanistan Seeks to Recruit Uzbeks, Tajiks, Kyrgyz,' *Eurasianet*, 17 March 2022.

10 Joe Schottenfeld, 'The Labour Train – Following the Migrant Workers of Tajikistan,' *The Guardian* (10 July 2016).
11 David Trilling, 'Tajikistan: Migrant Remittances Now Exceed Half of GDP,' *Eurasianet.org* (15 April 2014).
12 Schottenfeld, 'The Labour Train.'
13 Harris, *Control and Subversion*, pp. 128–29.
14 Farangis Najibullah and Ganjinai Ganj, 'The Skype Ceremony – The Young Tajiks Getting Married Online,' *Radio Free Europe/Radio Liberty* (23 July 2015).
15 Farangis Najibullah, '"SMS Divorces" Cut Tajik Migrants' Matrimonial Ties to Home,' *Radio Free Europe/Radio Liberty* (6 December 2009).
16 Farangis Najibullah, 'Doctor Drain: 'Exodus' Of Tajiks To Russia Seen As Migration Laws Eased,' *Radio Free Europe/Radio Liberty*, 12 February 2022.
17 Charu Sudan Kasturi, 'The Russia-Ukraine Crisis is Squeezing Central Asian Economies,' *Al Jazeera*, 16 February 2022.
18 Kamila Ibragimova, 'Tidal wave of austerity crashing against Tajikistan as Russian economy nears precipice,' *Eurasianet*, 14 March 2022.
19 Pairav Chorshanbiev, 'Skovannye odnoi tsep'iu: Kak sanktsii protiv Rossii otraziatsia na Tadzhikistane?' (Connected by One Chain: How will sanctions against Russia affect Tajikistan?), *Asia-Plus*, 9 March 2022.
20 'Putin Arrives In Tajikistan For First Stop On Trip To Central Asia,' *Radio Free Europe/Radio Liberty*, 28 June 2022.
21 'V Dushanbe soobschili porobnosti visita Putina. Sovetnik Zelenskogo predoctereg Tadzhikistan ot pomoschi RF v obkhode sanktsii' (Dushanbe Reprted the Details of Putin's Visit: Zelenesky's advisor warned Tajikistan against Russia's assistance in circumventing sanctions), *Radio Ozodi*, 28 June 2022.
22 'What was Putin Doing in Tajikistan?', *Eurasianet*, 29 June 2022.
23 'What drove the worst Kyrgyz-Tajik conflict in years?' *The Third Pole*, 28 May 2021.
24 Bruce Pannier, 'Kyrgyzstan, Tajikistan Withdraw Military Units From Border After Deadly Armed Clashes,' *Radio Free Europe/Radio Liberty*, 3 May 2021.
25 Farkhod Tolipov, 'Border Problems in Central Asia: Dividing Incidents, Uniting Solution,' *The Central Asia-Caucasus Analyst*, 16 July 2020.
26 Abdulmumin Sherkhanov, 'Tajik Football Club Sanctioned After Beating Team Founded by President's Son,' *Radio Free Europe/Radio Liberty*, 26 April 2012.
27 Kamila Ibragimova, 'President's son adopts growing role on center stage,' *Eurasianet*, 17 February 2022.
28 'Tajikistan: Tensions Escalating in Autonomous Region,' *Human Rights Watch*, 18 May 2022.

29 Lorenzo Tondo, 'Twenty-five Ethnic Pamiris Killed by Security Forces in Tajikistan Protests,' *The Guardian*, 19 May 2022.

30 'Fear and Outrage in Pamir: Tajikistan's Gorno-Badakhshan reeling from brutal state crackdown,' *Radio Free Europe/Radio Liberty*, 22 June 2022.

31 Muhammad Tahir and Bruce Pannier, 'What's Happening In Tajikistan's Gorno-Badakhshan?' *Radio Free Europe/Radio Liberty* podcast, 13 February 2022.

32 Igor Rotar, 'Xinjiang's Isma'ilis Cut Off from International Isma'ili Community,' *Forum 18 News Service* (23 September 2003).

33 Steven Parham, 'The Bridge that Divides: local perceptions of the connected state in the Kyrgyzstan–Tajikistan–China borderlands,' *Central Asian* Survey 35/3 (2016), p. 354.

34 Parham, 'The Bridge that Divides, p. 358.

35 'China Uighurs: One million held in political camps, UN told,' *BBC News* online, 10 August 2018.

36 'Zoroastrian Cemetery found in Xinjiang, Tashkurgan Tajik Autonomous County,' *Chinese Archaeology* (26 October 2013). I personally visited the site in May 2018 and could find nothing specifically Zoroastrian associated with it.

37 Edward Lemon, 'Tajikistan Country Profile,' *Nations in Transit*, 2018.

Bibliography

Abdullaev, Kamoludin, *A Historical Dictionary of Tajikistan*, 3rd ed., Lanham, 2018.

Abdullaev, Kamoludin, 'Conflict Resolution in Tajikistan', in Hans-Jorg Albrecht et al. (eds), *Conflicts and Conflict Resolution in Middle Eastern* Societies – *Between Tradition and Modernity*, Berlin, 2006, pp. 307–17.

'Addicted: Drugs in Tajikistan', *The Economist* (21 April 2012).

Aini, Sadriddin, *The Sand of Oxus: Boyhood Reminiscences*, John R. Perry and Rachel Lehr, (tr), Costa Mesa, 1998.

Allsen, Thomas T., 'Sharing Out the Empire: Apportioned Lands under the Mongols', in Anatoly M. Kazanov et André Wink (eds), *Nomads in the Sedentary World*, London, 2001, pp. 172–90.

Anon., 'Afghanistan signs electricity supply contract with Tajikistan amid power crisis,' *WION*, 28 December 2021.

Anon., 'Fear and Outrage in Pamir: Tajikistan's Gorno-Badakhshan reeling from brutal state crackdown,' *Radio Free Europe/Radio Liberty*, 22 June 2022.

Anon., 'Putin Arrives In Tajikistan For First Stop On Trip To Central Asia,' *Radio Free Europe/Radio Liberty*, 28 June 2022.

Anon., 'Tajikistan: President demands Tajik role in running Afghanistan,' *Eurasianet*, 25 August 2021.

Anon., 'Tajikistan: Tensions Escalating in Autonomous Region,' *Human Rights Watch*, 18 May 2022.

Anon., 'Taliban, Tajikistan embroiled in battle of words, saber-rattling,' *Eurasianet*, 30 September 2021.

Anon., 'V Dushanbe soobschili porobnosti visita Putina. Sovetnik Zelenskogo predoctereg Tadzhikistan ot pomoschi RF v obkhode sanktsii' (Dushanbe Reported the Details of Putin's Visit: Zelenesky's advisor warned Tajikistan against Russia's assistance in circumventing sanctions), *Radio Ozodi*, 28 June 2022.

Anon., 'What drove the worst Kyrgyz-Tajik conflict in years?' *The Third Pole*, 28 May 2021.

Anon., 'What was Putin Doing in Tajikistan?', *Eurasianet*, 29 June 2022.

Arrian, *The Campaigns of Alexander*, Aubrey de Sélincourt, (tr), New York, 1958.

Askarov, A. and T. Shirinov, 'The "Palace," Temple, and Necropolis of Jarkutan', *Bulletin of the Asia Institute* 8 (1994): pp. 13–25.

Atkin, Muriel, *The Subtlest Battle: Islam in Soviet Tajikistan*, Philadelphia, 1989.

'Avvalīn hamāyesh-e sarāsarī–ye Tājīkān-e Ozbakestān dar šahr-e Taškand' (First General Conference of Tajiks of Uzbekistan in Tashkent), *Rādiyo Zamāneh*, 9 Bahman 1396 [29 January 2018].

Barfield, Thomas, *Afghanistan: A Cultural and Political History*, Princeton, 2012.

Barthold, W., *Turkestan Down to the Mongol Invasion*, 3rd ed., London, 1987 [1928].

Bashiri, Iraj, (tr), *The History of a National Catastrophe*, www.angelfire.com/rnb/bashiri/Masov/MasovHistoryNationalCatastrophe.pdf.

Bashiri, Iraj, *Prominent Tajik Figures of the Twentieth Century*, Dushanbe, 2002.

Baumer, Christoph, *The History of Central Asia*, 4 vols., London, 2014–17.

Benjamin, Craig, *The Yuezhi: Origin, Migration and the Conquest of Northern Bactria*, Turnhout, 2007.

Bergne, Paul, *The Birth of Tajikistan: National Identity and the Origins of the Republic*, London, 2007.

Biruni, Abu Rayhan, *Āthār-al-baqiya*, C. Edward Sachau, (tr), *The Chronology of Ancient Nations*, London, 1879.

Bonora, Gian Luca, 'Evolution of Early Urban Societies in Prehistory', in Michele Bernardini, Gian Luca Bonora, and Giusto Traina (eds), *Turkmenistan: Histories of a Country, Cities and a Desert*, Torino, 2016, pp. 15–31.

Borisov, Akbar, 'Devout Muslims Claim Crackdown in Tajikistan Amid Syria Fears', *Agence France Presse* (23 April 2015).

'China Uighurs: One Million Held in Political Camps, UN Told', *BBC News* online, 10 August 2018, www.bbc.co.uk/news/world-asia-china-45147972.

Chorshanbiev, Pairav, 'Skovannye odnoi tsep'iu: Kak sanktsii protiv Rossii otraziatsia na Tadzhikistane?' *Asia-Plus*, 9 March 2022.

Cleuziou, Juliette, '"A Second Wife Is Not Really a Wife": Polygyny, Gender Relations and Economic Realities in Tajikistan', *Central Asian Survey* 35/1 (2016): pp. 76–90.

Compareti, Matteo, *Samarkand the Center of the World: Proposals for the Identification of the Afrasyab Paintings*, Costa Mesa, 2016.

Dagiev, Dagikhudo, *Regime Transition in Central Asia: Stateness, Nationalism and Political Change in Tajikistan and Uzbekistan*, London, 2014.

Daniel, Elton, *The Political and Social History of Khurasan under Abbasid Rule 747–820*, Minneapolis, 1979.

de la Vaissière, Étienne, *Sogdian Traders: A History*, James Ward, (tr), Leiden, 2005.

Delegation archeologique francaise en Afghanistan, *Fouilles d'Ai Khanoum*, 9 vols., Paris, 1973–2016.

Dixon, Robyn, 'The Opium Trail Has a New Stop', *Los Angeles Times* (25 July 2001).

Dudoignon, Stéphane, *Communal Solidarity and Social Conflicts in Late 20th Century Central Asia: The Case of the Tajik Civil War*, Tokyo, 1998.

Epkenhans, Tim, *The Origins of the Civil War in Tajikistan: Nationalism, Islamism, and Violent Conflict in Post-Soviet Space*, Lanham, 2016.

Epkenhans, Tim, 'Defining Normative Islam: Some Remarks on Contemporary Islamic Thought in Tajikistan – Hoji Akbar Turajonzoda's *Sharia and Society*', *Central Asian Survey* 30/1 (2011): pp. 81–96.

Erkinov, Aftandil, 'Les Timourides, modèles de légitimité et les recueils poétiques de Kokand', in F. Richard and M. Szuppe (eds), *Écrit et culture en Asie centrale et dans le monde turko-iranien, XIVe–XIXe siècles*, Paris, 2009, pp. 285–330.

Erkinov, Aftandil, 'Persian-Chaghatay Bilingualism in the Intellectual Circles of Central Asia during the 15th–18th Centuries (The Case of Poetical Anthologies, *bayāz*)', *International Journal of Central Asian Studies* 12 (2008): pp. 57–82.

Farivar, Masood, *Confessions of a Mullah Warrior*, New York, 2009.

Finke, Peter, *Variations on Uzbek Identity: Strategic Choices, Cognitive Schemas and Political Constraints in Identification Processes*, Oxford, 2014.

Finke, Peter and Meltem Sancak, 'To Be an Uzbek or Not to Be a Tajik? Ethnicity and Locality in the Bukhara Oasis,' *Zeitschrift für Ethnologie*, 137/1 (2012): pp. 47–70.

Foltz, Richard, 'Co-opting the Prophet: The Politics of Tajik and Kurdish Claims to Zarathustra and Zoroastrianism', in Alan Williams, Sarah Stewart, and Almut Hintze (eds), *The Zoroastrian Flame: Exploring Religion, History and Tradition*, London, 2016, pp. 325–41.

Foltz, Richard, *Iran in World History*, New York, 2016.

Foltz, Richard, *Religions of Iran: From Prehistory to the Present*, London, 2013.

Foltz, Richard, *Mughal India and Central Asia*, Karachi, 1998.

Foltz, Richard, 'The Tajiks of Uzbekistan', *Central Asian Survey* 15/2 (1996): pp. 213–16.

Foltz, Richard, 'Uzbekistan's Tajiks: A Case of Repressed Identity?' *Central Asia Monitor* no. 6 (1996): pp. 17–19.

Francfort, Henri-Paul, 'La Civilisation de l'Oxus et les Indo-Iraniens et Indo-Aryens en Asie Centrale', in Gerard Fussman, Jean Kellens, Henri-Paul Francfort, and Xavier Tremblay (eds), *Āryas, Aryens et Iraniens en Asie Centrale*, Paris, 2005, pp. 253–328.

Francfort, Henri-Paul, 'Animals in Reality, Art and Myths in the Oxus Civilization (BMAC): Bison, Deer', *Near the Sources of Civilizations*, Moscow, 2004, pp. 182–92.

Fragner, Bert, 'The Nationalization of the Uzbeks and Tajiks', in Andreas Kappeler and Edward Allworth (eds), *Muslim Communities Reemerge. Historical Perspectives on Nationality, Politics, and Opposition in the Former Soviet* Union *and Yugoslavia*, Durham, 1994, pp. 13–32.

Frye, Richard N., *Bukhara: The Medieval Achievement*, Costa Mesa, 1996 [Norman, 1965].

Frye, Richard N., *The Heritage of Central Asia: From Antiquity to the Turkish Expansion*, Princeton, 1996.

Frye, Richard N., 'Sughd and the Sogdians: A Comparison of Archaeological Discoveries with Arabic Sources', *Journal of the American Oriental Society* 43/1 (1943): pp. 14–16.

Ghafurov, B.G., *Tadzhiki: Drevneišaya, drevnyaya i srednevekovaya istoriya*, 2 vols., Dushanbe, 1989 [1970].

Ghafurov, B.G., *Tajiks: Pre-ancient, Ancient and Medieval History*, P. Jamshedov (tr), Dushanbe, 2011.

Ghafurov, B.G. and B.A. Litvinskii, (eds), *Istoriia tadzhikskogo naroda*, 3 vols., Moscow, 1964–65.

Golden, Peter B., 'Turks and Iranians: An Historical Sketch', in Lars Johanson and Christiane Bulut (eds), *Turkic-Iranian Contact Areas: Historical and Linguistic Aspects*, Wiesbaden, 2006, pp. 17–38.

Goziev, Saidbek, *Mahalla – Traditional Institution in Tajikistan and Civil Society in the West*, London, 2014.

Grenet, Frantz, 'Crise et sortie de crise en Bactriane-Sogdiane aux ive-ve s. de n. è.: de l'héritage antique à l'adoption de modèles sassanides', in *La Persia e l'Asia Centrale da Alessandro al X secolo*, Roma, 1996, pp. 367–90.

Grenet, Frantz and Nicholas Sims-Williams, 'The Historical Context of the Sogdian Ancient Letters', in *Transition Periods in Iranian History, Studia Iranica, cahier 5*, Leuven, 1987, pp. 101–22.

Gross, Jo-Ann and Asom Urunbaev, *The Letters of Khwāja 'Ubayd Allāh Aḥrār and His Associates*, Leiden, 2002.

Hansen, Valerie, *The Silk Road: A New History*, New York, 2012.

Harris, Colette, *Control and Subversion: Gender Relations in Tajikistan*, London, 2004.

Haugen, Arne, *The Establishment of National Republics in Soviet Central Asia*, London, 2003.

Heathershaw, John, 'Why Is There So Much Construction in Central Asia's Capitals?', *Exeter Central Asian Studies Network*, Exeter, 2013, https://excas.net/2013/07/why-is-there-so-much-construction-in-central-asias-capitals.

Heathershaw, John, *Post-Conflict Tajikistan: The Politics of Peacebuilding and the Emergence of Legitimate Order*, London, 2011.

Heathershaw, John, 'Tajikistan Amidst Globalization: State Failure or State Transformation?' *Central Asian Survey* 30/1 (2011): pp. 147–68.

Heathershaw, John and Edmund Herzig, (eds), *The Transformation of Tajikistan: The Sources of Statehood*, London, 2013.

Heathershaw, John and Kirill Nourzhanov, 'Nation Building in Tajikistan: Soviet Legacy, Civil War and Authoritarian Politics', unpublished typescript.

Helsinki Watch, *Tajik Presidential Election Conducted in a Climate of Fear and Fraud*, Helsinki, 1994.

Herodotus, *The Histories: The Complete Translation, Backgrounds, Commentaries*, Walter Blanco, (tr), New York, 2013.

Horák, Slavomír, 'In Search of the History of Tajikistan: What Are Tajik and Uzbek Historians Arguing About?' *Russian Politics and Law* 48/5 (2010): pp. 65–77.

Hultgård, Anders, 'Zoroastrian Influence on Judaism, Christianity, and Islam', in Michael Stausberg (ed), *Zarathustra and Zoroastrianism*, London, 2008, pp. 101–12.

Ibn Arabshah, Ahmad, *Ajā'ib al-maqdūr fī nawā'ib al-Taymūr* (*Tamerlane: The Life of the Great Amir*), London, 2017.

Ibn Battuta, *The Travels of Ibn Baṭṭūṭa, A.D. 1325–1354*, H.A.R. Gibb, (tr), 5 vols., Cambridge, 1958–2000.

Ibn Ḥawqal, *Kitāb Ṣūrat al-arḍ*, J.H. Kramers and G. Wiet, (tr), *Ibn Hauqal, Configuration de la Terre*, Paris, 2001 [1965].

Ibragimova, Kamila, 'Tajikistan press-gangs an army to defend long Afghan border,' *Eurasianet*, 2 December 2021.

Ibragimova, Kamila, 'President's son adopts growing role on center stage,' *Eurasianet*, 17 February 2022.

Ibragimova, Kamila, 'Tidal wave of austerity crashing against Tajikistan as Russian economy nears precipice,' *Eurasianet*, 14 March 2022.

Imomov, Ashurbai, 'Territorial and Land-Water Conflicts in Central Asia: A View from Tajikistan', *Central Asia and the Caucasus* 14/2 (2013): pp. 111–25.

International Crisis Group, 'Central Asia: Islam and the State', *Asia Report* no. 59, Brussels, 2003.

'Interview with Davlat Khudonazarov', *Igrunov* (16 April 2012).

Istakhrī, Abū Isḥāq Ibrahīm ibn Muḥammad al-Fārisī, *Kitāb al-Masālik wa'l-Mamālik*, in M.J. de Goeje (ed), *Bibliotheca Geographorum Arabicorum*, Leiden, vol. 1, 1870.

'Izz al-din ibn Athir, *Chronicon quod perfectissimum inscribitur* (*Al-Kāmil fī al-tārīkh)*, C.J. Tornberg, (ed), 14 vols., Leiden, 1853–1867.

Jonson, Lena, *Tajikistan in the New Central Asia: Geopolitics, Great Power Rivalry and Radical Islam*, London, 2006.

Kashgari, Mahmud, *Compendium of the Turkic Dialects* (*Dīwān lughāt al-turk)*, R. Dankoff and J. Kelly, (trs), 2 vols., Cambridge, MA, 1982–1985.

Kassymbekova, Botakoz, *Despite Cultures: Early Soviet Rule in Tajikistan*, Pittsburgh, 2016.

Kasturi, Charu Sudan, 'The Russia-Ukraine Crisis is Squeezing Central Asian Economies,' *Al Jazeera*, 16 February 2022.

Kellar, Anna, 'The Apples of Garm: Problems of Land Reform in Tajikistan', *Asian Affairs* 46/1 (2015): pp. 118–22.

Kellens, Jean, 'Considérations sur l'histoire de l'Avesta', *Journal Asiatique* 286/2 (1998): pp. 451–519.

Keyser, Christine et al., 'Ancient DNA Provides New Insights into the History of South Siberian Kurgan People', *Human Genetics* 126 (2009): pp. 395–410.

Khalid, Adeeb, *Making Uzbekistan: Nation, Empire, and Revolution in the Early USSR*, Ithaca, 2015.

Khalid, Adeeb, *Islam after Communism: Religion and Politics in Central Asia*, 2nd ed., Berkeley, 2014.

Khalid, Adeeb, *The Politics of Muslim Cultural Reform: Jadidism in Central Asia*, Berkeley, 1999.

Kucera, Joshua, 'The Narcostate', *Politico* online (March/April 2014).

Kuz'mina, Elena E., *The Prehistory of the Silk Road*, Philadelphia, 2008.

Kuz'mina, Elena E., *The Origin of the Indo-Iranians*, Leiden, 2007.

Laruelle, Marlene, (ed), *Tajikistan on the Move: Statebuilding and Societal Transformations*, Lanham, 2018.

Lazard, Gilbert, 'Darī', *Encyclopaedia Iranica* online, 2011.

Lazard, Gilbert, *Les premiers poètes persans (ix – xe siècles): Fragments rassemblés*, 2 vols., Paris, 1964.

Lemon, Edward, 'Tajikistan Country Profile', *Nations in Transit*, 2018, https://freedomhouse.org/report/nations-transit/2018/tajikistan.

Lerner, Judith, 'Some So-called Achaemenid Objects from Pazyryk', *Source: Notes in the History of Art* 10/4 (1991): pp. 8–15.

Levi, Scott C., *The Rise and Fall of Khoqand, 1709–1876: Central Asia in the Global Age*, Pittsburgh, 2017.

Levi, Scott C., *The Indian Diaspora in Central Asia and Its Trade, 1550–1900*, Leiden, 2002.

Litvinskii, B.A. and V.A. Ranov, (eds), *Istoriia tadhziksogo naroda*, vols. 1 & 2, Dushanbe, 1998.

Livshits, Vladimir A., *Sogdian Epigraphy of Central Asia and Semirech'e*, Corpus Inscriptionum Iranicarum Part II, vol. III, London, 2015.

Loy, Thomas, *Bukharan Jews in the Soviet Union: Autobiographical Narrations of Mobility, Continuity and Change*, Wiesbaden, 2016.

Lyonnet, Bertille, 'Another Possible Interpretation of the Bactro-Margiana Culture (BMAC) of Central Asia: The Tin Trade', in Catherine Jarrig and Vincent Lefèvre (eds), *South Asian Archaeology 2001, Vol. 1: Prehistory*, Paris, 2005, pp. 191–200.

Mairs, Rachel, *The Hellenistic Far East: Archaeology, Language, and Identity in Greek Central Asia*, Berkeley, 2014.

Mallory, J.P. and D.Q. Adams, *The Oxford Introduction to Proto-Indo-European and the Proto-Indo-European World*, Oxford, 2006.

Marshak, Boris I., *Legends, Tales, and Fables in the Art of Sogdiana*, New York: Bibliotheca Persica, 2002.

Martínez-Cruz, B. et al., 'In the Heartland of Eurasia: The Multilocus Genetic Landscape of Central Asian Populations', *European Journal of Human Genetics* 19/2 (2011): pp. 216–23.

Masov, Rahim, (ed), *Istoriia tadhziksogo naroda* (History of the Tajik People), vols. 3 & 6, Dushanbe, 2013.

Masov, Rahim, *Istoriia topornogo razdeleniia* ("History of an Axe-Like Dividing"), Dushanbe: Irfon, 1991.

Mastibekov, Otambek, *Leadership and Authority in Central Asia: The Ismaili Community in Tajikistan*, London, 2014.

McChesney, Robert D., *Waqf in Central Asia: Four Hundred Years in the History of a Muslim Shrine, 1480–1889*, Princeton, 1991.

Menga, Filippo, 'Building a Nation Through a Dam: The case of Rogun in Tajikistan', *Nationalities Papers* 43/3 (2015): pp. 479–94.

Mīrsanjarī, Mīr Mehrdād, 'Negāh-e Tāškand be mellīgarī-ye Tājīkī dar Ozbakistān' (Tashkent's View of Tajik Nationalism in Uzbekistan), International Peace Studies Centre, 10 Mordād 1395 [31 July 2016].

Mirzoyev, Abdul-Ghani, *Mas'alahoi rūzgor va osori Abūabdullohi Rūdakī: majmūai risolavu maqolaho* (The Life and Works of Abu Abdullah Rudaki: A Collection of Treatises and Articles), Dushanbe, 2014.

Mirzoyev, Abdul-Ghani, *Saĭido Nasafi i ego mesto v istorii tadzhikskoĭ literatury* (Sayido Nasafi and His Place in Tajik Literature), Stalinabad, 1954.

Morrison, Alexander, *Russian Rule in Samarkand 1810 – 1968: A Comparison with British India*, Oxford, 2008.

Mutribi Samarqandi, *Conversations with Emperor Jahangir*, Richard Foltz, (tr), Costa Mesa, 1998.

Nafīsī, Sa'īd, *Moḥīṭ-e zendagī va aḥvāl o aš'ār-e Rūdakī* (The Life and Times and Works of Rudaki), 3rd ed., Tehran, 2357 [1978].

Najibullah, Farangis, "SMS Divorces" Cut Tajik Migrants' Matrimonial Ties to Home', *Radio Free Europe/Radio Liberty* (6 December 2009).

Najibullah, Farangis, 'Doctor Drain: 'Exodus' Of Tajiks To Russia Seen As Migration Laws Eased,' *Radio Free Europe/Radio Liberty*, 12 February 2022.

Najibullah, Farangis and Ganjinai Ganj, 'The Skype Ceremony – The Young Tajiks Getting Married Online', *Radio Free Europe/Radio Liberty* (23 July 2015).

Narshakhi, Abu Bakr Muhammad ibn Ja'far, *The History of Bukhara*, Richard N. Frye, (tr), Cambridge, MA, 1954.

Nourzhanov, Kirill, 'Nation-Building and Political Islam in Post-Soviet Tajikistan', in Mariya Y. Omelicheva (ed), *Nationalism and Identity Construction in Central Asia Dimensions, Dynamics, and Directions*, Lanham, MD, 2015, pp. 71–90.

Nourzhanov, Kirill and Christian Bleuer, *Tajikistan: A Political and Social History*, Canberra, 2013.

Olcott, Martha Brill, 'Nation Building and Ethnicity in the Foreign Policies of the New Central Asian States', in Roman Szporluk (ed), *National Identity and Ethnicity in Russia and the New States of Eurasia*, Armonk, NY, 1994, pp. 209–29.

Panaino, Antonio, 'The Yaghnobis and Their Valley: Towards a New Historical Perspective', in Antonio Panaino, Andrea Gariboldi and Paolo Ognibene (eds), *Yaghnobi Studies I: Papers from the Italian Missions in Tajikistan*, Milano, 2013, pp. 13–30.

Pannier, Bruce, 'Kyrgyzstan, Tajikistan Withdraw Military Units From Border After Deadly Armed Clashes,' *Radio Free Europe/Radio Liberty*, 3 May 2021.

Parham, Steven, 'The Bridge That Divides: Local Perceptions of the Connected State in the Kyrgyzstan–Tajikistan–China Borderlands', *Central Asian Survey* 35/3 (2016): pp. 351–68.

Paymon [Tūkhtamysh Tūkhtayev], *Az Samarqandī čō qand*, Tehran, 1384 [2005].

Paymon [Tūkhtamysh Tūkhtayev], *Dānešnāme-ye zabān va adabiyāt-e fārsī-ye Ozbakestān*, Tehran, 1385 [2005].

Paymon [Tūkhtamysh Tūkhtayev], *Fārsīsarāyān-e Ozbakestān*, Tehran, 2010.

Perry, John R., 'Tajik', *Encyclopaedia Iranica*, online, 2009.

Rahmonov, Emomali, *Tojikon dar oina-i ta'rikh* (The Tajiks in the Mirror of History), 2 vols., Dushanbe, 1997.

Rajabīān, Dārīūsh, 'Goftogū bā Ṣafar 'Abdollah, dāneshmand-e Tājīk', *BBC Persian Service* (6 September 2014).

Rajabov, Askarali, 'Historical Traditions of the Time of Rudaki', in Iraj Bashiri (tr and ed), *From the Hymns of Zarathustra to the Songs of Borbad*, Dushanbe, 2003, pp. 152–59.

Reeves, Madeleine, *Border Work: Spatial Lives of the State in Rural Central Asia*, Ithaca, 2014.

Rotar, Igor, 'Xinjiang's Ismailis Cut Off from International Ismaili Community', *Forum 18 News Service* (23 September 2003).

Rowe, William C., 'Agrarian Adaptations in Tajikistan: Land Reform, Water and Law', *Central Asian Survey* 29/2 (2010): pp. 189–204.

Roy, Olivier, *The New Central Asia: Geopolitics and the Birth of Nations*, rev. ed., New York, 2007.

Rubin, Barnett, 'Russian Hegemony and State Breakdown in the Periphery', in B.R. Rubin and J. Snyder (eds), *Post-Soviet Political Order: Conflict and State Building*, New York, 1998, pp. 128–61.

Rustam, Qodiri, 'Tojikon va Zaboni Forsī', *Ozodagon* 13/517 (28 March 2018): pp. 8–9, 15.

Saadi-Nejad, Manya, 'Arəduuī Sūrā Anāhitā: An Indo-European River Goddess', *Analytica Iranica* 4–5 (2013): pp. 253–74.

Sarianidi, V[iktor], 'Excavations at Southern Gonur', *Iran* 31 (1993): pp. 25–37.

Sarkhatzoda, A. 'Durdonai šarq: majallai adabī, ilmī va farhangii Tojikoni Uzbekiston' (The Faraway East: A literary, scientific and cultural journal of the Tajiks of Uzbekistan), *Ovozi Tojik*, 4 March 2022.

Scarborough, Isaac, '(Over)determining Social Disorder: Tajikistan and the Economic Collapse of Perestroika', *Central Asian Survey* 35/3 (2016): pp. 439–63.

Schottenfeld, Joe, 'The Labour Train – Following the Migrant Workers of Tajikistan', *The Guardian* (10 July 2016).

Shafiev, Abdulfattoh, 'Tajik Authorities Hunt the Hijab and Battle the Beard', *Global Voices* online (15 April 2015).

Shafi'i-Kadkani, Mohammad Reza, 'Borbad's *Khusravani*s – First Iranian Songs', in Iraj Bashiri (tr and ed), *From the Hymns of Zarathustra to the Songs of Borbad*, Dushanbe, 2003, pp. 133–41.

Shakurī, Muhammadjon, *The Imperialist Revolution in Bukhara*, Anvar Shukurov and Bahriddin Alizoda, (tr), Dushanbe, 2013.

Shakurī, Muhammadjon, *Khuroson ast in jo: ma'naviyat, zabon va ihyoi millii Tojikon*, 2nd ed., Dushanbe, 2005.

Sharifzadeh, A. 'The Persian Vernacular of Samarkand and Bukhara: A Primer,' 24 May 2019, <https://borderlessblogger.wordpress.com/2019/05/24/on-the-persian-vernacular-of-samarkand-and-bukhara>.

Sima Qian, *Records of the Grand Historian*, Burton Watson, (tr), rev. ed., New York, 1993.

Sims-Williams, Nicholas, *Sogdian and Other Iranian Inscriptions of the Upper Indus*, 2 vols., London, 1989 and 1992.

Sims-Williams, Nicholas, Frantz Grenet, and Aleksandr Podushkin, 'Les plus anciens monuments de la langue sogdienne: Les inscriptions de Kultobe au Kazakhstan', *Comptes rendus des séances de l'Académie des Inscriptions et Belles-Lettres*, Paris, 2007, pp. 1005–34.

Stalin, Joseph, 'Marxism and the National Question', in Bruce Franklin (ed), *The Essential Stalin: Major Theoretical Writings, 1905–1952*, London, 1973.

Staviskij, B.Ja., *La Bactriane Sous les Kushans: Problèmes d'histoire et de culture*, Paris, 1986.

Stern, S.M., 'Ya'qub the Coppersmith and Persian National Sentiment', in C.E. Bosworth (ed), *Iran and Islam: In Memory of the Late Vladimir Minorsky*, Edinburgh, 1971, pp. 535–56.

Strabo, *Geography*, Horace Leonard Jones, (tr), Cambridge, MA, 2014.

Subtelny, Maria, *Timurids in Transition: Turko-Persian Politics and Acculturation in Medieval Iran*, Leiden, 2007.

Subtelny, Maria, 'The Symbiosis of Turk and Tajik', in Beatrice Forbes Manz (ed), *Central Asia in Historical Perspective*, Boulder, 1994, pp. 45–61.

Ṭabarī, Abū Ja'far Muḥammad, *Tarjome-ye tafsīr-e Ṭabarī*, Ḥabīb Yāğmā'ī, (ed), 7 vols., Tehran, 1339–44 [1960–65].

Tahir, Muhammad and Bruce Pannier, 'What's Happening In Tajikistan's Gorno-Badakhshan?' *Radio Free Europe/Radio Liberty* podcast, 13 February 2022.

'Tajikistan: Chinese Company Gets Gold Mine in Return for Power Plant', *Eurasianet* online (11 April 2018).

'Tajikistan Human Rights Fears as Banned Party's Ex-Leaders Jailed for Life', *The Guardian* (2 June 2016).

'Teflon Rahmon: Tajik President Getting "Leader" Title, Lifelong Immunity', *Radio Free Europe/Radio Liberty Tajik Service* (10 December 2015).

Termizī, Ja'far Muhammad [Ja'far Kholmu'minov], *Hanūz ešgh* (Still Love), Tehran, 1390 [2011].

Tolipov, Farkhod, 'Border Problems in Central Asia: Dividing Incidents, Uniting Solution,' *The Central Asia-Caucasus Analyst*, 16 July 2020.

Tondo, Lorenzo, 'Twenty-five Ethnic Pamiris Killed by Security Forces in Tajikistan Protests,' *The Guardian*, 19 May 2022.

Tor, D.G., 'The Islamization of Central Asia in the Sāmānid Era and the Reshaping of the Muslim World', *Bulletin of the School of Oriental and African Studies* 72/2 (2009): pp. 279–99.

Treadwell, Luke, 'The Samanids: The First Islamic Dynasty of Central Asia', in *Early Islamic Iran, The Idea of Iran, vol. 5*, Edmund Herzig and Sarah Stewart, (eds), London, 2011, pp. 3–15.

Trilling, David, 'Tajikistan: Migrant Remittances Now Exceed Half of GDP', *Eurasianet* online (15 April 2014).

Van Atta, Don, '"White Gold" or Fool's Gold? The Political Economy of Cotton in Tajikistan', *Problems of Post-Communism* 56/2 (2009): pp. 17–35.

Webber, Lucas, 'Islamic State uses Tajikistan's Dictator in Recruitment Drive,' *Eurasianet*, 2 June 2022.

Webber, Lucas and Riccardo Valle, 'Islamic State in Afghanistan Seeks to Recruit Uzbeks, Tajiks, Kyrgyz,' *Eurasianet*, 17 March 2022.

Whitlock, Monica, *Land beyond the River: The Untold Story of Central Asia*, New York, 2003.

Witzel, Michael, 'Linguistic Evidence for Cultural Exchange in Prehistoric Western Central Asia', *Sino-Platonic Papers* 129 (2003): pp. 1–70.

Xuanzang, *The Great Tang Dynasty Record of the Western Regions*, Li Rongxi, (tr), Berkeley, 1996.

Yaqubshah, Yusufshah, 'The Image of Funerary Dances on Sughdian Ossuaries', in Iraj Bashiri (tr and ed), *From the Hymns of Zarathustra to the Songs of Borbad*, Dushanbe, 2003, pp. 174–83.

Yarshater, Ehsan, (ed), *Encyclopaedia Iranica*. London, 1982–9 and New York, 1992–present.

Yuldoshev, Avaz, 'The Majority of Tajiks Fighting for ISIL in Iraq and Syria Salafists, Says Tajik Chief Prosecutor', *Asia-Plus* online (3 March 2016).

Zheleznyakov, B[oris] A., *Tamgaly: The Rock Art Site, Nature, Vicinities, Reserve-Museum*, Almaty, 2016.

'Zoroastrian Cemetery found in Xinjiang, Tashkurgan Tajik Autonomous County', *Chinese Archaeology* (26 October 2013).

Index